*W*OMEN ALONE

by *ISABELLA TAVES*

FUNK & WAGNALLS
NEW YORK

CONTENTS

For

Adelaide, Audrey, Bam, Belle,
Bernice, Betty, Betsy, Beth,
Cathy, Clara,
Doria, Doris, Dottie, Elba, Fanny, Freda,
Helen,
Hope,
Janet, Jean, Jo, Joy, Julie, Kay,
Libby, Lisel, Laura, Lemmy, Lorraine, Madeleine,
Mary, Maryjane, Martha,
Merrill, Myra,
Nancy, Niecy, Pat, Reg, Rose, Sally,
Sylvia, Syble, Toni,
Vera, Wendy,
Zimi,
my darling Aunt Flora

And all the other gracious ladies who helped me research
and write this book

PROLOGUE:
THE QUESTIONNAIRE

O_{NE} midnight in a restaurant on Chicago's Michigan Avenue that welcomes unescorted women, I sat drinking coffee with a group of widows and divorcees. We had gone all the way from how to manage back zippers and alimony payments to what to do when your best friend's husband makes a pass. Suddenly a young woman asked, "Why are you writing this book?"

It was, as we like to say when we don't want to answer, a good question. But they had been honest with me, sometimes painfully honest. I said, "I've been a widow seven months. I don't know the answers to living alone, and I want to."

Before I had started out on a research trip around the country, I had armed myself with a list of questions and problems, all relating to the woman alone. A number of the questions came out of my own personal curiosity about what direction to take. Others were contributed, or amplified, by divorcees, widows, and single women whom I had interviewed in New York. The problems were real case histories, from women who asked what I would do if I were in their shoes.

Some of the questions seem easily solved to me—now; but when I started out, I was pretty much in the dark. Other questions are still unanswered in my mind; on some subjects, particularly sex and children, there was wide diversity in the answers. And as I went along, the questionnaire grew and changed; I dropped some questions, added others. The problem of a woman in Larchmont, New York, was so similar to that of a woman in San Francisco that I combined them. I had started with a dozen case-history problems; when I came home I had eighteen.

Hundreds of women helped me. Some were old friends from school days. Others were casual acquaintances whose problems I never suspected before. Others were strangers who wanted to tell me things about themselves that they had hesitated to discuss with relatives or friends. Once in a while an item in the newspaper—in Detroit my appearance at a luncheon of twenty-four women alone was mentioned in the society column of the *Free*

Press—brought calls from widowed and divorced friends I had not seen for years, and from strangers who had things to say to me. A national singles organization, Parents Without Partners, allowed me to come to meetings and to interview individual members. I also went to meetings of other singles groups, notably one in New York where the membership requirement is a college degree or the equivalent.

Wherever I went there was so much curiosity about my questionnaire that I have included it. It might be interesting to read it over, then check back later to see if your opinions have changed. I confess that even as I was working, researching, mine did.

THE QUESTIONNAIRE

1. Do you think the best place for a woman alone is in a big city, the suburbs, or a small town?

2. Is it better for her to live by herself or with another woman —a relative, friend or roommate? Does age make any difference in her decision?

3. Have you any suggestions about living arrangements—a house versus an apartment, a place in the country, etc.

4. When you are left alone, either by divorce or death, is it better to live in the same place or tear up roots and make other arrangements?

5. Would it make a difference in your decision if children were involved?

6. Do you feel lonely sometimes? What do you do about it?

7. What are your major interests? Have they changed since you have been alone?

8. Are some times worse than others?

9. What do you do about weekends and holidays?

10. What do you miss most about not being married?

11. Have you met new friends since you have been alone? Men or women? How did you meet them?

12. Do you think being financially secure is a blessing—or is it better to have to earn a living?

13. How about volunteer work versus a paying job?

14. Do you go out with groups of other women who are alone? How often?

15. Do you still see people whom you knew when you were married? Who makes the effort to keep up these contacts—you or they?

16. Do you feel uncomfortable in a restaurant without a male escort? At the movies or theater?

17. Would you go to Europe alone? Would you go on a cruise alone?

18. How many unattached men do you know?

19. How do you pay back social obligations?

20. How do you return hospitality when you do not think the couple would enjoy the entertaining that is possible for you to do?

21. Would you go to a party alone?

22. Would you go home alone?

23. Do you think the pressures of holding a job are worse if a woman is alone?

24. Is an unattached woman in an office subject to unfair passes? How does she handle this?

25. Should she quit if her boss falls in love with her?

26. Do you feel that in your daily life, your contacts with tradespeople, plumbers, etc., you are discriminated against because you are alone?

27. Have you had any unpleasant experiences with service- or repairmen who work for you?

28. Is your job more important to you because you don't have a husband?

29. Who repairs the little things around the house now?

30. Do you feel free to call on the husband of a neighbor—or a friend's husband—when you need things done which require heavy lifting, etc.?

31. How do you meet unattached men?

32. Have you become more aggressive about meeting men than you were before?

33. Would you date a man you met at a bar?

34. Can you ask friends to look about for eligible men?

35. Do you think your chance of remarriage would be improved if you moved to a community where people didn't know your husband?

36. Would you sign up for a computer program to help you meet men?

37. Would you remarry? Or do you just want an escort? Would you settle for an escort who is homosexual? Married?

38. Would you date a married man regularly if he says his wife has no objection?

39. Do you feel safer with a married man who says he loves his wife than with one who indicates there is trouble at home?

40. What would you do if the husband of a neighbor or a good friend made a pass at you?

41. Would you go out with a man who is much younger if he asked you?

42. Would you enter into an intimate relation with him?

43. In whom do you confide if you have problems? To whom do you go in a crisis?

44. Do your children object to your going out on dates?

45. Is there more jealousy from a boy than a girl?

46. Are you timid about living alone? What precautions do you take?

47. Do children of divorced or widowed parents suffer more than ordinary children? Do you find discrimination against them by other parents or children?

48. Are women alone resented by wives? Do you feel you are deliberately excluded from parties because you are alone?

49. How do you define promiscuity?

PROBLEMS

1. An attractive divorcee with young children did everything possible to get her husband to return to them after a trial separation because of his infidelity—even to agreeing to allow him to have mistresses. He loves the children, and wants to see them, but

thinks he must be free. Often he takes them on weekends with his various girls. Should she allow this?

2. A divorcee with young children feels her disposition and serenity are suffering because she has no sex life. The only prospects she has are two married men whose wives she has not met. One says he is madly in love with her and wants to divorce his wife. The second says he finds his home life and wife satisfactory but is attracted to her physically and would like an affair. Which should she pick?

3. A widow with teenage children is courted by a bachelor who resents any mention she makes of her late husband. He is pleasant with the children but does not warm toward them. Should she give him up or try to fit him into the family?

4. While a woman neighbor is away, her husband escorts you to local parties. One night he makes a pass, promising you it will only be this once—he will tell no one. You are secretly a little in love with him. Should you weaken?

5. A woman who has never been married but has achieved success in a job has a client who wants to divorce his wife and marry her, but insists she quit her job. She likes him and wants to get married but feels she is not domestic. What would be your advice?

6. You meet a man to whom you are immediately attracted and begin an affair with him at his apartment on your second date. Afterward, instead of dressing and taking you home, he gives you $5 for a taxi. Do you see him again when he calls you?

7. You meet a man at a cocktail party given by mutual friends. He asks for your telephone number but does not call you. Do you call him if you are giving a party?

8. At the suggestion of a mutual friend, a man invites you to dinner and escorts you to a party at her house. Do you wait for him to call or do you invite him to dinner next?

9. Your eighteen-year-old daughter is violently opposed to your marrying a nice widower. To show you how unsuitable he is, she makes a pass at him herself (or says she has) and tells you that he was interested. What do you do?

10. You are a divorcee with a young daughter. You meet an attractive man, also divorced, who has weekend custody of his two boys. You go to his house with your child on weekends and cook for the group and treat them like family. The boys become fond of you, so he goes out sailing and playing golf and leaves you alone with them more and more often. Do you tell him off? Or do you continue, hoping that this will become a pattern and he will marry you?

11. You are having an affair with a divorced man. He tells you how much he hates his ex-wife, but is over there a great deal. He explains this is for the sake of his children. But when you try to get him to settle down and pick a date for marriage, he says he is afraid his ex-wife will turn the children against him if he remarries. Should you give him up?

12. You are a recent widow. A woman in the neighborhood, a divorcee, has been very good to you. Gradually you begin to wonder if she is a little too fond of you and might have homosexual tendencies. You are not sure and you dread any direct confrontation. What do you do?

13. You meet a widower to whom you, a divorcee, are much attracted. He seems to like your teenage son. But you are disturbed by the fact that he lives with his twenty-eight-year-old daughter who is also his assistant in his law office. You have never met her, but the mutual friend who introduced you tells you that he has kept his dates with you a secret and that his daughter resents any woman in whom he shows any interest. Do you give him up—or do you ask to meet his daughter and try to make friends?

14. Your husband left you for another woman after twenty years of marriage. You can't believe it is anything more than a temporary attraction, for the girl is stupid and silly, although she is physically beautiful. What do you do? Your children want you to refuse to divorce him. But you resent him so much you don't think you could ever live with him again.

15. You have been a widow for four years, and have made what your friends call a "good" adjustment, which includes friends, mostly women or married couples, and a pleasant job teaching

bridge. One of your pupils, a man slightly younger than you, proposes. He has never married, and, up until two years ago when his mother died, lived with her. Your friends say he is looking for another mother, or is marrying you for your money. What do you do?

16. A woman friend with whom you have been playing bridge introduces you to her "beau"—a widower. The next day he calls and asks you to go out to dinner with him. Do you ask her advice about going? Or do you go without telling her? Or say no?

17. You are a widow. A man some years your senior, a widower, has been taking you to dinner occasionally. On your birthday, he gives you a pair of pretty earrings. You are delighted, thinking they are costume jewelry. Your daughter tells you they are real and worth quite a sum. What do you do?

18. An old friend-of-the-family, who has never married, suggests that you and he travel together. You will have separate rooms, etc. What do you do?

The answers I collected are discussed at length in the various chapters of this book. But if you would like a quick preview of the author's personal reactions after a year of research, see The Questionnaire Revisited, p. 289.

1 WHAT KIND OF WOMAN ARE YOU?

Living alone in a Midwestern town, I've almost forgotten there are two sexes.

IOWA WIDOW

The happiest period of my life was after my divorce, before I remarried. People sent me flowers—something which hadn't happened since I was a young girl. I never knew what was around the corner, what it meant when the telephone rang. I'm not sorry I remarried, I wanted security for my children. But I wish I had some of my old freedom back.

REMARRIED NEW YORK DIVORCEE

I can think of two advantages of being alone. You don't have to share your bathroom and you don't have to wonder what you're going to have for dinner every night. Maybe these aren't the most important things in life, but they help.

MINNESOTA DIVORCEE

Do you know what I had for dinner last night? Two martinis and a peanut butter sandwich.

MANHATTAN DIVORCEE

Life alone is not bad at all if one has the proper memories.

TOKYO WIDOW

W HEN I was newly alone and hardly realized what I was saying, I blurted out, "I'm not going to spend the rest of my life with other women."

A charming older woman who had been a widow a number of years looked at me with some amusement. "My dear, you won't have much choice. Besides, it isn't that bad."

Actually, once you have found out that women aren't just women, they are people, it isn't that bad. And you don't necessarily need to lead an all-woman life even if you don't date or remarry. But in the beginning, when it takes all the courage you possess to identify yourself as a divorcee, or a widow, you feel part of a second-class mob scene . . . which, if you look only at statistics, you are. There are roughly fourteen million women in the United States who can be classified as women without husbands. Nine million are widows, over two million are divorcees or are separated from husbands, and three million are women over thirty who have never been married.

Women alone come in all shapes, sizes, ages, and temperaments. Some of them need men more than others. Children are vital to the lives of many women who do not really need husbands, once the men have fulfilled their function. Other women's need to dominate is so intense that they actually destroy the men they pretend to love.

We all know the divorcee who should never have been married in the first place but keeps trying, repeating past mistakes, until she is desperate. Other divorcees have had bad breaks, have married the wrong man; but, as a divorced gentleman reminded me gently, "Don't forget I married the wrong woman, too."

Some widows cannot contemplate going it alone; just the idea is humiliating. After a few preliminary struggles, they discover the joys of being independent and not sharing a bathroom. And the ones who swear they are too grieved to marry again, ever, are often those who remarry fastest; they need to be needed, and often their standards are not so high as those of the woman who is basically independent and self-sufficient.

Many unmarried women over thirty are married to their careers. Even if they pretend to hope for husbands, they are fooling themselves. They have refused to become involved emotionally with any male except that Impossible One who is too old or too young or too married to someone else. Or they have never found anyone who happened to be at the right spot at the right time. I frankly do not believe the successful career woman who says wistfully that she would give it all up, anytime, for a husband. Her standards are usually so impossibly high I am sure she is not really looking.

It can happen. I have known some women in their middle years, or older, who have married or remarried and found everything they have dreamed of—romance, pink clouds, and rubies. But I suspect that, after a while, the pink clouds disappear and the woman who sacrificed her career begins to wonder if it was worth it. The important basic—and difficult—discovery every woman alone must make is what kind of woman she really is, and what she really wants.

Meanwhile, there is the day-by-day battle to fight, in a strange new world, populated by far too many other women alone.

For those of us who have lost husbands either through divorce or death, the identification with the world of women without men comes hard. An Evanston, Illinois, woman told me, "It's easy to be wonderful at the time of death. You are the center of a drama, a tragic drama. You are also numb. The bad time comes when everyone else returns to normal life and you are expected to do the same. The daily grind of survival has to go on and on."

We ex-wives are so used to being half of a pair, even if we used to complain about our loss of identity and lack of appreciation, that it is almost impossible to realize that from now on we are alone and have to function alone . . . as millions of other women have done before us. A Minnesota divorcee put it this way. "Just to say 'divorcee' made me feel tainted. Yet even before the divorce came through, I found other people describing me this way quite casually, taking this new state of mine for granted.

I was a member of the new class in society called the Fifth Wheel, and there was nothing I could do about it."

The woman alone, the new member of the Fifth Wheel society, is lucky if she has a variety of friends, if she has maintained contacts during her married life that had nothing to do with her husband. Most women do not. And they discover, with a rude shock, that they are facing the loss not only of a husband but also of a way of life.

Even the busiest and brightest and richest and youngest woman alone has her bleak moments, days when she wonders why she should go on living. We all have areas where we feel cheated, and desperate moments when we wonder why we have been singled out for unhappiness, depression, rejection. But whether I stayed home talking to women alone, or encountered them traveling—solo, in duets, or in packs—I found certain patterns emerging, certain routes that offer more hope than others, and certain common traps.

One woman told me, "For fifteen years, all the time my children were growing up, I kept saying how happy I would be if I only had a man. Yet when my friends would find widowers or divorcees for me, I always found them boring, impossible. I had one love affair, yes, but the man was far more deeply attached to his mother than to me. When he died, I felt sad, but a sense of release, too. Now I realize that, although I'm a completely female woman so far as sex and having babies are concerned, I wanted to bring up my children alone, without anybody else telling me what to do. They've turned out fine and now that I'm completely alone, I am too comfortable, too set in my little ways, to want anything except my job, my new friends, and my cat."

Another, a beautiful woman who refused to say how many proposals she had turned down, said, "At first I thought I couldn't bear being alone. I had to have a man. I put up with a lot of them who didn't interest me a bit. Now I've come out of that phase. Perhaps if I were younger I might feel marriage was important. Now I want to be myself, even if I am lonely sometimes."

A pediatrician from New Jersey told me "I think I fell into the trap common to many women. I divorced my husband because he was an alcoholic dangerous to the children. I wanted to remarry very much. But I didn't like any of the men who were willing to date me. Now I know what I was looking for was *a man just like my husband but without his faults*. Some of the widows I know are doing the same thing—looking for a duplicate of that precious husband, without the faults they have forgotten."

A fourth woman, who has never married and is one of those rare and lucky persons who has created a full and interesting life for herself, said, "I realized when I was in my late teens that I wasn't pretty and I would never have the kind of figure men whistle at, so I devoted my life to studying things which interest me. Now I don't have time for all of them—or for all of the people I want to see. Today, at sixty-three, I think I am busier and happier than most of the married women of my acquaintance."

There is nothing more appealing in this artificial world than someone who is frankly herself. Perhaps this is why this last-mentioned lady has more friends of all ages than anyone I know. Meanwhile, from her and from all the other women alone with less security who talked with me about their problems and the general difficulty of trying to fly solo in a couple society, one important fact emerged: the resiliency and courage of most of these women. We are in a situation we do not like. But we are alive, we can find comfort and reassurance in the true friendship of other women in the same position and, for the first time in our lives—if we can only take advantage of the opportunity—we can be ourselves.

It may take a little time to discover our real selves, under the thick façade we have built up of wife-mistress-housekeeper-mother-hostess et al. But it is worth the time. Because, once you discover yourself, you can be free as never before in your life. Maybe you will decide you do not want to marry—it's not for you. Maybe you will decide in favor of remarriage; knowing exactly what you are like, and what you want, will simplify your quest. When you see a man you want you can go after him without embarrassment or desperation. Maybe you will decide the life you have led all these years has been contrary to everything you should be doing; now is your chance to change.

You may not think you are free, but you are. The strings that tie you to possessions and responsibilities can be cut more easily than you suspect. Parents should not be thought of as burdens. For you to feel free, unhampered by their problems, is a joy and a reassurance to them. Children are given to you for a short time. You can do your best by them by not making them your reason for living, and by not "sacrificing" yourself for them. They will be gone soon enough and you, as a parent, do not want to hang heavy around their necks. Yet, by the same token, you are free to help other people as never before, and to keep alive and green your sense of participation and identity with the rest of the world.

A New York divorcee told me early in my research that every woman alone should have a motto on her bathroom mirror: "You don't have to do anything you don't want to do."

Think about that. It will help you discover what kind of a woman you really are.

2 THE FEMALE EGO

It was like the building was on fire and I had to rush out and grab the first man ... that if I didn't remarry within a year, I would die.

NEBRASKA DIVORCEE

I try to think of myself as a survivor on a desert island.

COLORADO WIDOW

The son-of-a-bitch smoked himself to death, and here I am with five children.

CHICAGO WIDOW

Marriage is supposed to build up a woman's ego. In most cases, it does just the opposite. When I was left alone, I felt absolutely worthless, like I should apologize for being alive. Even when people invited me to dinner, I didn't think they wanted me, they just did it for Joe's memory.

WISCONSIN WIDOW

Men are what they do, women are what they are.

RANDALL JARRELL

Aɴ attractive divorcee in her early forties said impatiently: "Why should I be so ashamed when I have to go to a party alone? What's so humiliating about not having a husband to take me— or an escort? And why do I cringe when friends, goodhearted friends, say playfully, 'When am I going to see a ring on that engagement finger?' My God, it's nonsense for me to be so frantic and I'm going to stop it."

The next time I saw her was at a cocktail party. She had come alone and was looking pretty frantic, hopping all over the room, making contacts. She drew me aside. "My God, I had a date all lined up. Then his company sent him to Africa at the last minute. It was too late to get somebody else. So I came alone. And I'm having a terrible time, I have to admit it. I feel like a wallflower at her first dance. What's wrong with me?"

What ails her, and the rest of us who are alone, is that old devil, the female ego. Women of all ages have been conditioned to feel inferior. They have been made to feel as inadequate as do Negroes, perhaps more inadequate. I mentioned this the other night at a fund-raising dinner for the college I'd attended. Two men at the table looked at me as though I had let loose a string of four-letter words. The wife of one of them dropped her head, saying, "You're right." The third man, a doctor practicing in New York City, said, "Of course you're right. But don't blame men entirely. Women have done their share of downgrading themselves. Back to your comparison with Negroes—I have seen many qualified Negro doctors but other Negroes will not go to them as patients. The patients they have are white. I have the feeling that women are the same way. They certainly don't like to go to women doctors. I suspect they don't like themselves, so they don't trust or like each other."

It isn't quite that bad. Women do like each other, perhaps more than men do. With certain reservations, mostly concerning men, women trust each other. But the good doctor is right when he says we feel inferior, and so we underrate the female sex. Consequently, when we are seen alone at social functions, or in the company of other women alone in restaurants, we are ashamed. I remember one hot night when a divorcee friend of mine and I were about to sit down for dinner at a sidewalk cafe on Third Avenue. Suddenly, she dragged me inside. "We can't do that. If anyone saw us eating alone, it would destroy our image."

Men are the prizes in the Cracker Jack box. God is a male. Ditto Jesus, Buddha, and Mohammed. A man wrote, "A major difference between the sexes is that man must choose and shape his own destiny from the beginning. A woman can wait and decide between a dozen futures via marriage. Men create their own status levels. Women can hitch onto wealth or talent or day-to-day security."

What he is saying is, "Man's ego lies in his work, in the money he has, in the power he wields. A woman's lies in her husband."

From the cradle up, women are taught they must marry, and marry "well." Marriage is the ultimate goal held out to them. (Motherhood comes in a very poor second and is described in this market as "giving him children.") That is why there is still so little enthusiasm about training women for careers in the professions; men and women bosses know that a woman, if she is a proper woman, will give up her career any day for the right man. And, they add piously, that's the way it should be; a woman who does not make her husband feel he is the boss, castrates him in business and in every other way.

Women alone, particularly women who have never married, feel scorn for the wife who pushes her husband around. An executive in a large public relations firm who deals almost entirely with men—married men, of course—said firmly, "If I ever marry, the man will wear the pants, believe me." A widow who has a seemingly endless variety of fur coats said, "The women who let their husbands be the boss are the ones who wear sable."

The idea of female inferiority has been planted by the male. In the lower order of work, such as the domestic area, women can always get jobs and men cannot, hence matriarchy and trouble. Negroes have accused the white man of downgrading the black male. But it is not quite that simple. In all lower income groups, where women are economic necessities and therefore important, they have the final say on all important decisions and purchases. The children belong to her, they are her responsibility. Often the father is not married to her; he is just one of many men, passing through her life. And, whether or not she works to contribute to the family income, there is no problem about her obtaining a job; often she earns more than her husband—even when he works.

But as incomes increase, in the middle and upper brackets, the husbands more and more have some kind of authority in their work. And the executive in the home tends to have the final say (or thinks he does) on all big issues, such as holidays, children's school, and on large purchases, such as houses, cars, and his wife's furs and jewels.

Sometimes the home becomes an adjunct of the office, run for his convenience, with the wife as a kind of super-secretary. Up to a point, this can be satisfying. The wife feels a sense of importance at being in on the secrets of his business; I have seen such a woman derive her ego-fun by making cryptic remarks to her husband's underlings at social functions. She also is cast again in the role of little girl, doing everything she can to please a father figure and receiving tangible awards in the form of jewels and furs. But she is so conditioned that her rebellions represent the tyranny of the weak—she fights her master with tears, sickness, withdrawal of sex, the so-called "women's weapons."

This in itself is demeaning, without dignity. I heard of one wife of a Midwestern executive whose fury and resentment against him and his authoritarian methods of running the home built up until she reached the breaking point, usually after one or two drinks at a party. Instead of turning against him, she took a far more effective revenge by insulting other people, invariably customers important to him. Any complaints he made afterward were answered by hysterics. One night, in frustration, he hit her. Long after the black eye had healed, she went around in dark glasses, a not-so-subtle reminder to him of his brutality.

Yet when he died, suddenly, she was left so entirely without inner resources that she tried to kill herself three times.

No matter how much she is supposed to be suffering, such a

woman rarely leaves her tormentor, unless there is another, presumably kinder, father figure waiting in the wings. More often, she turns to psychiatry, and invariably the psychiatrist is a man. An analyst friend used to describe the difference between male and female tactics this way, "Two men are on a desert island. The one that arrived first has the water supply. The second male fights him for it. But let's say the second arrival is a woman. She doesn't fight. She goes over and lures the man into sharing the water supply with her." You can call this low female cunning, or just using your head. But it is the method most of us have been taught by our mothers.

A gentleman whose major interest is primitive tribes told me recently, "Western civilizations are the only ones which don't give unmarried women and widows their own status and responsibilities. That is because women in other civilizations are more valuable."

The gentleman in question is also a scholar. Thus he pinpointed another reason why women alone tend to be more than a little frantic, no matter how loudly we insist that it is all nonsense, we are the equals of men, perhaps their superiors. After all these years of conditioning, we have no inner feeling of worth, of security without men. We are "extra" women. We have no husbands to complain about, to cook for, to push up the ladder of success. We are not invited to company dinners, to business cocktail parties where husbands must make command appearances; nor are we included in the committees of wives who are lined up by corporations to support their male activities. Even on a social level, we are redundant. We may be charming, bright, witty, and lovable, but at a sitdown dinner, when the couples come in two by two, we are problems. Unless somebody's wife is having a baby, or there is a spare bachelor with a free night, we just cannot be invited. And the wives make it up to us by asking us to family dinners, all-female lunches, or those lady bridge parties.

We don't complain—out loud. We take our seats with the aged aunties and grandmas and other females alone at family functions. We are younger, a bit. We are the new generation of surviving females. But we are all lumped together in the same pasture. Is it any wonder we get a bit frantic and chase after eligible men, turning their heads out of all proportion to their worth? For, in order to feel accepted we need some kind of an escort, and, heaven help us, we are not quite ready yet to become permanent members of the sidelines brigade.

A psychiatrist friend tells me it is necessary for inferior people to have others they can look down on, hence man's relegation of the female to second sex. But we women have gone along. A mother has perennially had one aim for her son, that he be successful in business or a profession; if he marries "some nice girl" who devotes herself to his career and his children, that is also good. But unmarried daughters, no matter how successful in careers, reflect small credit on their mothers. I know one mother who made life miserable for her older daughter, although the girl was a prominent scientist, because she had never married. When, at forty, the girl finally became engaged, Mama was overjoyed—even though the man in question was already married and had to go through a rather messy public divorce in order to become free.

The nicest compliment that can be paid a woman by either sex is that "She's a man's woman." Or if she is bright and successful in business, "She thinks like a man." I am not being a gnawing feminist. I am simply repeating things that every woman knows and seldom remarks on because it gets her nowhere. The women I know are getting tired of reading books about the Second Sex; they would much rather spend the evening with a nice man. It is more fun and can be, finally, more rewarding.

Even among the very young, something happens when a man's superiority is threatened. For example, if a wife is working to put her husband through college, there arises a strange and not happy reversal of roles. Because she makes the money, she feels she should also make the decisions on how it is spent—and the marriage can break up because both of them resent this.

In another two decades, by the time their babies are grown up and ready to marry, everything may have changed. We may have temporary marriages, as Margaret Mead suggests, and permanent ones into which children are born. But right now, middle-class American women, the most marriage-prone women in the world, occupy an inferior position in our society. Some of them like it. Some of them mew and scratch at their husbands without really trying to change the basic situation. Others hold down good jobs while their husbands drift from one position to another or (as in one case I encountered where the wife finally left home with the children) sleep all day; instead of recognizing that their choice of husbands was dictated by what is falsely regarded as an unwomanly power drive, they angrily call on men to assert themselves and their masculinity.

The last type of woman, who is essentially dominant, suffers least if and when her marriage collapses. She may miss a sexual relation. But, even if she is able to arrange to have that with one man, or a series of men, she wants to marry again because society requires it of her, as a status symbol. The fact that she invariably chooses another weak man—who performs sexually if not in the marts of trade—is not surprising. Second or third time around, she usually is smart enough to see the pattern herself, and accept her husband for what he is.

As for the women who have been turned out in the cookie-cutter mold of femininity by mothers, they get along fine so long as they have their husbands. But when they lose them, they don't know where to turn.

Women alone who have been married tend to envy the women who have never had husbands and have followed careers and worked out their lives themselves. Seen casually, these women appear to be perfectly in control. They have attractive homes, a collection of escorts to take them out, and are invariably present at all the important events in the community.

However, when you talk to these career women without the trappings of an opening or a party, you discover they feel just as maimed as the rest of us, perhaps more so. They mention their unmarried state a bit apologetically. Then (after about the second drink) they begin talking of the men they almost married, or of that ubiquitous Great Man with whom they had the big affair.

Usually these women are strangers to me. Their close friends, who obtained the introductions, are surprised when I come back from interviews with full details of love lives that have only been whispered about in the community or neighborhood.

But it is not really so surprising. The woman has not married, which tends to be a black mark against her in society, and she wanted to let me know that it was not from lack of opportunity, or sexual undesirability. In the same way, the divorced or widowed woman, once her first shock is over, hints of suitors to her married friends. She may joke about them, she may tell amusing stories of fighting off advances (or, to women, of not fighting very hard) but she does not want people to pity her because she has no man, and cannot get one. (It is, I have found, a very different story when women alone get together. Then you get the truth, and it is not very glamorous, as a rule.)

If the husband has asked for the divorce, the rejected wife is more vulnerable than the widow or the woman who has instigated the divorce. Out of *noblesse oblige* he may let her sue, and out of guilt he may give her a nice fat settlement of money. But other single women look down on her because she has not been able to hold her man, her symbol of power and prosperity. Among the various singles clubs, there is a great deal of snootiness on the part of widows toward divorcees. The theory seems to be that when a man leaves involuntarily, by death, the woman is a shade higher in the pecking order.

Even when a situation is so untenable that his relatives as well as hers encourage the wife to divorce him (alcoholism, excessive gambling, mental disease, nonsupport, or a combination of these), she still suffers more than the widow. She does not even have the satisfaction she earned when she "put up with the bastard." If he marries again, which he is often apt to do, she is hurt and bitter. She can be a bit jealous, wondering what the other woman has that she can control him, or at least be happy with him. One woman told me that she went through agony after divorcing an alcoholic husband because her children would return from visiting him and his new wife and report "how happy Daddy seemed." (Actually, it turned out, he was putting up a front for his youngsters; it wasn't long before the second wife was calling the first, asking how to handle him in his cups.)

It takes a great deal of maturity to accept blame. Few divorcees are willing, particularly when they are first alone, to admit they were in the least responsible for the failure of the marriage. Their anger at finding themselves alone, fifth wheels, becomes a way of life. I have met divorcees who make a career out of hating ex-husbands, and annoying their current wives, instead of trying to rebuild their own lives. In a curious way, I suppose this is a way of hanging onto the past, a struggle to keep at least a toehold in the couple society. Of course it doesn't work. Once the trauma and excitement of the divorce are over, the couples who stood by and listened avidly for developments usually take to their heels and disappear in search of fresh excitement.

At first I was shocked to hear widows sounding like divorcees when they talked of their late husbands. A woman in Massachusetts, who had to go to work after her husband died, blamed him for having a heart attack at forty-four—"He was too damned ambitious, he burned himself up. And what am I left with? A house I can't afford to keep up, a mortgage, three children." A Chicago woman said, "The son-of-a-bitch smoked himself to death and here I am with five children." A New Yorker whose husband had been in the garment business told me how desperately she had economized during her married life: "Sometimes I walked twenty blocks to save a few cents on a chicken. Then when he died, we found fifty thousand dollars in his safety deposit box. Believe me, I'm spending it on myself now."

Yet it is all part of the pattern. Because she has lost security and status, a woman feels she has to place the blame on someone. And, floundering in her feeling of loss, she deposits it on the man himself, accusing him of lack of consideration because he died and left her to cope.

This may sound brutal and unsentimental, but many a woman misses the prestige she had as a wife more than she misses the man who died. A widow of four years told me, not without some self-pity, "I used to be the doctor's wife. People made a point of fussing over me. Even if he couldn't get to a party, I was always taken care of, because I was important. After he died, I turned into *nothing*. People even were nasty about paying money they owed us. It's the wife of the new doctor who gets all the attention."

A prominent rabbi told me, "Often the wives of important men have a far harder time adjusting than widows in humbler surroundings. They have been so used to accepting attention because of his position that they cannot adjust. Rather than try to establish themselves as individuals, they keep on malingering in his shadow."

Personally, I hardly think it is fair that a woman, either because of beauty, money, or luck, who happened to marry a greatly admired man, should have basked in reflected glory in the first place. But it is the way we live. And a wife who shares in the excitement and privileges accorded her husband cannot be faulted too cruelly for taking some time to get used to her reduced status. For even if she has no money worries, she is catapulted back into the world of reality after enjoying vicarious importance.

The widow of one of America's great industrialists told me, "I'm not lonesome. I entertain, and people ask me back. But it's a far cry from the days when we flew all over the world at a moment's notice and had access to heads of state. Now I sit back and try to listen politely when wives tell me about their great adventures going to California with their husbands. And when I travel, even though I go first class, it's like a demotion. We used to have flunkies buzzing around us, spreading the red carpet. It's insolent of me to mind, but I'd be less than honest if I said I didn't."

Another widow, who was used to pampering as the wife of a well-known musician, still creates a stir when she chooses to frequent the world of music, where her late husband continues to be greatly admired. In her case, she is reluctant to accept kudos which she does not think belong to her. She told me, "I don't go out very much. Old friends complain about that. They think I'm getting queer in the head. Actually, what I am afraid of is that I'll turn into one of those dreadful old dodos you see around, hanging on to the coat-tails of anyone who says a kind word to them, living in the past."

Occasionally, we hear of the woman who blooms after a divorce or the death of her husband, who revels in her freedom and her right to live and spend money as she chooses. I think the cue here is the word "money"—a wife can feel liberated when the tight-fisted husband vanishes. However, money is not enough. A rich woman alone can buy dancing partners, companions on cruises, lovers, even a husband. She can keep relatives on a taut string if the sum of money she controls is large enough. But, deep in her heart, her ego suffers. We all want to be loved for ourselves.

An articulate and fascinating divorcee in Nebraska with four children told me, "I've had plenty of chances for affairs. I don't want them. A woman is never a complete person until she is married. I've had a career, on and off for twelve years. Now, because I have money problems, it's on. But in many ways, I am drifting, hanging by my fingernails. I want very much to care for some man. I want someone walking in the door at night. I thought after the divorce, 'If I don't get married soon, I won't be accepted.' It was like the building was on fire, I had to rush out and grab the first man. I thought if I didn't remarry within a year, I would die. It's been longer than that, and I'm over the feeling of rush, yet I still am incomplete."

No matter how much money we have, no matter how successful we are "in our own right," we women feel that we need men—if not sexually, just to be part of what goes on. Some years ago, I worked with the widow of a prominent man, a woman who wrote cook books. During our conferences, she would spend what seemed to me an obsessive amount of time on the telephone, trying to line up "escorts" to take her to the various functions she wanted to attend in the line of duty of her profession. Now I understand her motivation.

A widow vacationing in Florida met one of her late husband's colleagues at the race track. He was a vulgar man and in the past had been quite shy with her, aware of her standing as the wife of an important lawyer. He had come to call shortly after her husband's death, but she had not heard from him since, a matter of two years. But at the track, he put his arm around her and said, "Honey, what you need is a man to take you around. I've got a date myself, sort of a regular thing I can't skip, but let me introduce you to some of the fellows who aren't tied up."

"And," the widow told me, "I couldn't be outraged. The poor man was just trying his best to be kind to a lonely widow."

Recently, in a column written by Miss Amy Vanderbilt, I read a letter from a widow of fifty who said she was in good health and still liked to go out socially, and what should she do? Miss Vanderbilt replied that she must cultivate a "group of escorts."

I do not know how the widow in question reacted to this advice, but a lot of women alone that I know wanted to laugh and cry, at the same time. Escorts aren't a dime a dozen. I met a man close to eighty who bragged happily about the women alone who try to pick him up when he has his usual noon martini on Sunday at Schrafft's. What's more, I believe him. Any unmarried man who is even half presentable is spoiled. He is sought after by hostesses and cushioned financially by rich women alone. He feels he can get away with murder; and sometimes, of course, he can. I have an occasional escort who told me quite blandly, "I call for you when we're going out because you live around the corner. I meet the other girls I date at the restaurant or the movie." I presume he also allows them to go home alone; frankly, I did not want to ask.

A divorcee friend of mine, who was escorted to a party by a blind date arranged by the hostess, said her date spent the evening telling her how popular he was, how women called him constantly. He did not want to leave as early as she did, so she got a ride home with a young couple she knew and said goodnight to her erstwhile date in this fashion: "Thanks for spending your valuable time on me." She reports that he did not even blink.

Yet what are we to do?

Some restaurants will not seat women alone, or even in pairs. Others give such poor service that you never want to go back. In certain areas—and here I include small towns as well as big cities —for a woman to go alone to a movie even in the afternoon is to invite unpleasant advances. A friend who has been in the theater often goes to Broadway shows alone when she feels low but says,

"I wait until the last minute before the curtain goes up. Then I scurry in so no one will see me. Between the acts, I go out, moving around purposefully so people will think I am joining friends. Yet when my husband was alive and didn't want to see a certain play, I thought nothing of going alone. It's a state of mind—but I'm stuck with it."

A divorcee who travels a great deal said, "I have to eat alone in restaurants a great deal. But it's no fun to look up and see people staring at you. I don't want pity, nor do I want them to think I'm on the make. So I take a book. Even when the light is very bad, I pretend I am reading. And often I hurry so much I end up with indigestion."

The single woman is fully aware that well-meaning friends hope a man will come along and solve her problems—and their responsibility for her. Safely back in the fold, she will be easier to entertain, talk to. But one of the things a woman learns the hard, slow way is that she cannot count on a quick replacement for a lost husband. Even if she gets one in record time, she runs the risk of making a move of desperation, ending far unhappier than she was alone.

The only possible answer for us is to stop thinking we are incomplete because we are alone, and start force-feeding our battered egos.

The poet Randall Jarrell wrote, "Men are what they do, women are what they are."

This has been one of our difficulties.

Ask a man what he is and the answer comes automatically. I am a stock broker, lawyer, doctor, etc. Ask a woman what she is, and she answers she is so-and-so's wife and leaves it at that—unless some kind feminist inserts the statement that, "Mrs. X. is also a career women [or a doctor or a lawyer] *in her own right.*" With the woman alone, the going is even rougher in a social situation. Wives resent the woman who works. So we wander faceless, without name tags. One widow I know who has some prominence as a writer under her pen name was introduced recently at a party in London as: "This is Mrs. J. She's—she's an American."

The problem is, of course, that women are by no means inferior. Scientists and anthropologists have long pointed out that they are the surviving sex. Women are both biologically and numerically a superior group and survive all sorts of devitalizing experiences better than men: birth, starvation, shock, illness. (They also, in their quiet way, survive being alone better than men do.) And anthropologist Ashley Montagu adds, "the one thing we may be certain women will never do is lord it over men as men have so long lorded it over them. The truly superior person doesn't need to lord it over anyone; it is only the inferior person who, in order to feel he is superior, must have someone to look down on. The genuinely superior person neither looks up or down—he looks straight at you."

A woman I met on the North Shore of Chicago said, "Women marry for sex, security, and companionship. I'm not interested in sex any more, my job gives me security and companionship. Why should I remarry?" She was not boasting, she was not looking down at men, she was merely asking a question which she has already answered for herself. But it takes time, and soul-searching, to be able to look at the world around you with a calm and unfrantic eye—and to shrug when those married friends ask you that inevitable, "When are you going to get married?"

Even those of us who were happy in our marriages realize secretly that as wives our identities had to be smothered to some degree. We all have sacrificed, some more than others. Some women have given up abilities and careers for the sake of a male ego, and without qualms. Perhaps that is one of the reasons for female superiority.

Any female living in a household, whether she is with a husband or parents or relatives, has to submerge herself to some extent, for the sake of harmony. A man may say of his wife, "We're a team." What he really means is that he runs the team and she is his assistant, his trusted second mate who carries out his orders. A widow in California told me she gave up an acting career—just at a time when she was getting good billing—to nurse her dying husband for two years. She was not asking for kudos, she was simply reporting. Yet would we expect a man to do the same? Of course not. We would criticize him, perhaps, for weakness.

A prominent woman scientist told me that if one of her daughters happens to be taken ill at school, she is always summoned from the hospital. The nurse in charge never dreams of calling the husband, who could much more easily spare the time from his job of fund-raising for the same hospital. And the school nurse invariably gives the woman doctor a hard time because she feels she should be home taking care of her children, instead of working. Another woman, a widow, told me that all the time her husband was alive, she never asked him to do anything around the home, even something as simple as buying a loaf of bread, because she felt guilty about having a job she enjoyed.

When such a woman finds herself alone, her first reaction from that poor battered ego is more guilt. And even the woman who sacrificed her career told me, "At first when I was left alone, nothing seemed to matter. I didn't have the heart to go back and start the foolish business of face-making again. Only gradually did I realize that having something to do was my redemption—and that really, for the first time, I could devote as much time and energy to my work as the men around me did."

Work can be good for the self-confidence of a woman alone. Merited plaudits build her up and make her a more understanding and generous person. But a job is not the answer for every woman alone, and the search for importance in a career can depress as much as it can exhilarate. However, some form of activity must be found to take the place of the full-time job of a wife. If a woman is lucky enough to find a consuming interest—whether it is a cause or a fascinating hobby—she soon discovers that she no longer feels that the house is on fire, or that she will die if she does not find a replacement for the lost husband.

Meanwhile, we must clean house emotionally, ridding ourselves of habits that no longer have any meaning. A divorcee in Boston told me that, to her disgust, she found herself still overcooking meat, something which she deplored but which her husband had insisted on, a year after their separation. And do you remember the heroine in Marquand's book, *B. F.'s Daughter?* During a discussion about divorcing her husband, she dropped her cigarette in her coffee cup to extinguish it—one of the loathed habits of her husband, which she had picked up against her will.

Everything takes time. The growing process, like any new experience, may be uncomfortable, as any transition can be painful. As Mr. Marquand, who probed so deftly into his character's motivations, puts it after his heroine has ceded her husband to his mistress:

> You could clear away dishes and empty ash trays, but you could not clear away years of living with a man. You could not close off those years as if with a closet door because parts of the years, in shreds and tatters, would always be drifting through the cracks. There was bound to be reaction, and she was facing it already. The best thing to do was to put it off as long as possible. All that she was sure of was that she was quite alone and that she had arrived on some new plane.

We can try to postpone facing facts. We can hide and compromise and lie to ourselves. But we cannot go back any more than we can make time stand still. Life goes on, and we either move with it, or go under. And each woman has to do this alone. No matter how much money she has, or how much talent or good looks, or how many friends and relatives, the only way she can build her own life is to stand alone, on her two feet. Nice things may happen to her along the way, unexpected helping hands extended; those are pleasant interludes, but unimportant. The experiences that build and broaden are the difficult ones.

About a year after I had started to write this book, two women I had interviewed at the beginning came back to see me, one a widow, the other a divorcee. I asked the usual question, which is a cliché in our society: "How is it going?"

The widow said, "Surprisingly well, most of the time. Of course you have to learn to be an entirely different person."

The divorcee, whose husband of twenty years had left her to marry a young girl, corrected her friend, "No. You have to learn to be more yourself."

I had women tell me, "My life is over. I'm too old to try any-

thing on my own. I'll be better off dead." One of the women who
said this was forty-six. It is true she had few resources and she was
losing friends and the sympathy of her children because she was
unable to talk about anything except her own unhappiness. Yet
she had money and health; the possibilities of helping others in
need were limitless, although she could not see them.

A few days before, I had lunched with a widow of seventy-eight
who was cheerfully going off on a trip to India alone, with indefinite reservations so she could move on if she was not having a
good time. Age has little to do with the desire to live. In fact,
sometimes I think that those with only a few years' expectancy get
the most out of each day. A man of eighty-six who lives in my
apartment building said to me not long ago, "I find each day a
glorious experience. Don't you?" (I am ashamed to say I don't,
but I try to think of him when I am having one of my bouts of
feeling sorry for myself.) None of us knows how many productive
years are left to us, so why should we waste even one day?

A woman whom I call My Romantic Friend, although she has a
brain like a steel trap, has embarked on a five-year plan of travel.
Despite her slender loveliness and long honey-colored hair, she
approached her problem with scientific cool. She computed her
life expectancy on the basis of actuarial tables and decided she
has five good years in which to go every place she has ever
dreamed of, to see all the things she has heard about. After that,
she will sit down and determine how to arrange the unpredictable rest of her life. A dark-eyed Minnesota divorcee, whose looks
also belie her brains, explained that the next ten years of her life
belong to her two sons. As soon as they are graduated from college, she stops being a housewife and a member of the PTA and
takes off—perhaps for the Peace Corps, perhaps for work with
Catholic missions. Meanwhile, her preparation for freedom is a
course in stenography and typing, which she expects (with considerable reason) will be her passport to a job anyplace.

Age is not entirely a state of mind, despite the clichés. Health
imposes restrictions upon our actions, and there is hardly a
woman alone who does not worry about becoming a burden. But
there is small satisfaction in postponing things you want to do,

which will enrich you, for the indefinite and decidedly unglamorous future.

A woman of forty-five, who married early and had babies right away, had wanted during her girlhood to be a model. When her husband died, she took her first earnings and enrolled in a modeling course. She does not pretend to work at modeling, but the experience and discipline have helped her in her present job in the Chamber of Commerce in her area.

Another woman, who cheerfully admits to seventy, says that only in the last five years of her life has she become a whole person. She was divorced when her children were young, and waited until they were in college to marry an Englishman with whom she had been in love since she was a girl. She was in the process of selling her house, cutting her ties with America, when he was killed in an airplane crash. She told me, "It took me less time to throw off the shackles which bound me to my second husband because I hadn't lived with him long. But it took me another ten years to be myself, independent of everyone. My ex-husband now comes and stays with me when he is in town and we are great friends. He even asks my advice on how to handle his wife. We go to see our grandchildren together, but I'm definitely not the doting grandma in a bonnet. I ride to hounds and have a house in the country, and I have a carefully pruned number of aging beaus who don't want to marry me any more than I want to get married. Of course, the list gets smaller all the time—a few of them marry and more of them die. But I'm having a lovely time, maybe more fun than when I was young, because it's so unexpected."

Remember: "Men are what they do, women are what they are."

The meaning lies in your interpretation. To me, this means that women are essentially more real (that is, superior to men) because they become more themselves as they grow, and do not have to depend for ego on false identifications like career accomplishments and money earned. So why be ashamed—or embarrassed—when you are doing something you enjoy?

A widow from Alabama, who has a married son in Illinois and friends all over the country, used to travel by car with her husband a great deal, visiting, exploring, "gypsying." She hesitated a long time before she decided to drive alone to Illinois to see her son. On the way out of town, with the car all packed, she stopped at her regular service station for gas and told the attendant, "I think I'm out of my mind. Should I turn around and go home?"

He answered, "Once you get started, it will be all right."

She told me, "Now I always think of that when I want to turn tail and run."

3 THE FIRST YEAR

I went crazy for a little bit, after my husband was killed. People used to look at me laughing it up and say, "Is SHE the widow?" I wouldn't let myself believe this had happened to me, so I guess I was really running away. But you can't escape forever. I lost weight and one day, at the office, I passed out. I woke up in the hospital with a bleeding ulcer. That put an end to me, the go-go girl. I'm engaged now to a young doctor who is so dedicated to his job that he doesn't dance or drink.

NEW JERSEY WIDOW

Of course I'm not happy. I lie awake nights. But at least I don't lie awake wondering what bar he's in, or what whore he's sleeping with. I worry about sensible things, like what I am going to use for money.

DETROIT DIVORCEE

For six months after my husband died, I was "wonderful"— that's what they said. Then the log jam broke and I cracked up. I was in the hospital with all sorts of complaints resulting from tension. But I learned a lot. You can't hold things in. Something's got to give.

NEW YORK WIDOW

A widow, never noted for her tact, came from Florida to New York to attend the funeral of her lawyer and told his widow, "Don't expect it to get easier."

THE most difficult adjustment a woman is ever called on to make is learning to live alone after being married. The security of having another person on whom you can count, with whom you come first, is something most of us appreciate only after we have lost it. Even after a bitter divorce, the woman who is left alone has her poignant memories. A divorcee who told everyone *ad nauseum* how relieved she was to be rid of a philandering husband suddenly found herself unable to zip up a ski jacket he had given her as a surprise. Struggling with it, tears spurting out of her eyes, she blurted out to me, "He was really very sweet at times."

The sense of loss can be numbing. Even when there has been illness—or previous trial separations in the case of a divorce—few women are prepared for the shock of being left alone. For the first few days or weeks, sometimes for as long as several months, nature comes to the rescue. There seems to be a cushion between you and reality, a shock-absorber. You cannot take in all that has happened, and the implications, so your calm and acceptance—"She's being wonderful"—are simply part of the blessed blackout. Then, bit by bit, the cushion wears thin and you see what is ahead of you.

The first year alone, with its poignant responsibilities and its painful anniversaries, is difficult, often incredibly difficult. Some women try to escape through travel, drugs, alcohol, sex, hectic activity, or pretending the past had never happened. It would be nice if you could slumber emotionally during the first year. But part of adjustment is living through it, day by day, week by week, and gradually finding acceptance and some kind of adjustment. For, despite all the difficulties, life does get easier. But you have to cross rugged country before you come to the relative calm of the plateau.

A Denver divorcee who had rushed back to work after the divorce that she had not wanted said, "I could bear the days. My boss had passed the word around that people weren't to mention what had happened. My trouble began after I got home. Even when John and I weren't really getting along, I used to save stories about what had happened during the day to amuse him, and we shared those long after we lost interest in sharing other things." A Texas widow told me, "I went on a weekend with a married man about six months after my husband died. It wasn't so much the sex I needed. It was the idea of being with a man again, sharing experiences and jokes. I didn't mind when the hostess in the dining room gave me a fishy look; later I realized that my so-called lover made a habit of taking women to that hotel."

Sharing is a vital part of marriage. Even quarrels are sharing. Long after a woman has accepted her new status intellectually, she still suffers acutely when something touches her emotions unexpectedly. You never can anticipate what will hurt—a popular song on the radio, the kind words of a stranger, even a remembered phrase which brings him back can start tears. A widow told me six months after her husband's death, "Dammit, the things I miss most are the ones which annoyed me about Bill—the way he used to read in the bathtub and get the magazines all splattered, his messy habits of smoking. Last week I found myself looking at a blanket he'd burned and I cried like a baby."

A divorcee, who lived in a basement apartment on Riverside Drive in New York City, felt she had to move after she was alone because it was too dangerous. One of the reasons she was glad to leave the old place was that she and her husband had been wakened every morning at 4:30 by the janitor starting the furnace. But, "When I got to the new place, I used to wake up automatically at 4:30, and brood over the fact that Fred was no longer in the next twin bed where I could crawl in beside him. The next step was wondering if I hadn't been a fool, pushing him too far, and perhaps he wouldn't have left me."

A woman in New Orleans, married to an insomniac lawyer, told me, "I'd complain he kept me awake, reading all night. Now I have to turn on his light or I can't sleep in the room."

After death or divorce, we all have those private regrets. Mrs. Jacqueline Kennedy, it has been reported, distressed that she had not been of more help to her husband in his political career, has determined, in vindication, to make his memory live. After there has been a long illness, the most devoted wife blames herself for lapses in attention, caused by her own exhaustion. A New York divorcee, going through her first sleepless nights alone, went back over her courtship with her husband and decided she had triggered off his postmarital infidelities by sleeping with him before they were married.

Living alone seems unnatural. Even children cannot begin to fill the gap; sometimes, indeed, they accentuate the loss. Most of us were raised in households centered around the man, paced to his going off to work in the morning and returning at night for dinner. Then, after a brief period of being on our own, surrounded by other young people either at work or at college, we were married, and settled into our own male-dominated worlds. To have the pattern broken after ten years, twenty years, or more, is brutal. There is grief, yes. But it is not the grief felt at the loss of parents or friends or relatives. Evidence of the loss is everywhere, and no matter how much you try to change the ritual of your days, memories trap you.

I met one beautiful Minneapolis woman who moved out of her home directly after her husband's funeral, and ordered her children to sell the house and furnishings. All the clothes she was not wearing were sent away to Thrift Shops along with her husband's. After a trip abroad, she started fresh in a new apartment, with new furnishings, a new wardrobe. Although she still had her friends, when she entertained, she never mentioned her husband, or the days when they were married. Her children were away—one in Switzerland in school, the other in the Army. Old snapshots of them had been thrown away, and only ones taken after their father's death were on display.

Then one morning, when she was making coffee, she found herself putting out two cups, as she had done for so many years, for her husband and herself.

The bad times of being alone vary from person to person. A young widow who was married to an airplane pilot says her pain is worst after the children have gone to school, the time of day when, if her husband was not flying, they used to have to themselves, to drink another cup of coffee and to talk. Sometimes it is weekends, a family time when a woman alone hesitates to intrude on other families, and the presence of children only emphasizes the loss. Even weekday breakfasts, though all they meant was a cup of coffee handed to Father on his way out of the door, give you a lump in the throat. Evenings, when other men are coming home to their families, are worse. One young woman still can remember "those nights at dusk, when the other kids would be called in to wash and brush their hair for Daddy, and my brother and I would sit in front of the television set while Mother tried to keep busy in the kitchen . . . days just didn't have an end any more."

Cooking becomes a monumental chore; many a woman who has always cooked easily discovers she can do no more than scramble a solitary egg for herself when she does not have a man coming home for dinner. Doing for children is not enough; a woman alone is apt to turn them loose on hot dogs and TV dinners. She discovers, to her horror, that if she invites guests, she no longer can get a dinner on the table; pots boil over, roasts burn or are raw, the simplest tasks seem gargantuan. After a few trials, many women just give up trying to entertain. In one Midwestern city, I found a group of women alone who meet for cocktails every night at one house or another—a pale imitation of the parties they used to attend when they had husbands—and then go home to their cans of tuna fish or frozen dinners. The gruesome fact is that, no matter how lavish a table a lady sets when she is married, she tends to be a poor provider when first she is on her own. This divorcee's reminiscence is typical: "When I was married, even though I was just learning to cook, there was always enough for one more if my husband brought a friend home for dinner. There was always something in the refrigerator if we decided to stay home instead of going out. Now it's as bare as Mother Hubbard's cupboard. So are my shelves of canned goods. I eat out a good bit, of course. But the brutal truth is that I can't stand the idea of leftovers any more. They sit around staring at me when I open the refrigerator door until eventually they get rancid and I throw them out. So I buy just enough for one, or two, if I happen to invite one of my friends who is also alone."

Keeping house no longer seems to matter. A Midwestern divorcee with three children finds herself putting clothes in the washing machine compulsively. But she is bored with ironing so her once attractive dining room and living room are filled with rumpled piles of clothes—clean, but spectacularly messy. On the other hand, a Detroit woman told me, "I walk around the house with an ash tray in my hand so I won't dirty more than one. Yet I remember the days when I thought a house was only for people. I had new carpeting put in while my children were away at college, and when they came home at Christmas, I was delighted to see them and their friends tramping all over it, bringing in mud and snow." A Winnetka woman, whose home used to be the neighborhood center of activity, said, "I put the dishes in the dishwasher, and I make an effort at dusting the downstairs. But sometimes I don't make my bed for weeks at a time. Unless my daughter and her husband are coming, I figure nobody will go upstairs."

An odd angle is that you never can count on what your own reaction will be. The habitual lint-picker wonders why she fussed so much all these years. And the ones who lived happily in confusion decide to organize. I have a once-carefree friend who became a compulsive cataloguer. Everything she had ever owned was packed in boxes, labeled, and put away. I finally came across a box marked, "Old blue tennis shoes, ready to throw away."

I suspect that whether you are super-tidy or let things go, the reaction is against the tyranny of possessions. For possessions can be the very devil when you live alone. A widow in Minneapolis, whose husband had died of a heart condition which kept him at home the last two years while she worked, told me that all the things he had fussed over seemed to give way when he died: Venetian blinds, the boat, the car, the dishwasher, even her ironing board. In this case, he had been a tinkerer. In other cases, where certain possessions—say, power mowers or cars—came under male jurisdiction, it is understandable why they should rebel in the hands of a woman who is already absent-minded with grief. But even when a husband was not a do-it-yourself-man, possessions seem to fall apart just to annoy you when you are at low ebb, unable to defend yourself.

What used to be the simple routine of taking broken radios out to be fixed and replacing light bulbs, suddenly may seem beyond you. You don't remember to order replacements, and there is nobody to point out that things are falling apart. After a while you don't notice any more. And, if there are young children in your household, the more rebellious and careless they become, the more permissive you are. Unless, in your anguish, you have turned into a nagger and driven them away into the homes of neighbors—who get tired of taking on your responsibilities after a while.

Decisions made during this period of confusion are seldom based on reality. Like many other women, after my husband died my first instinct was to flee, to move back to the city where I was born, where I would have the comfort of relatives who had known me as a child. I also toyed with the idea of returning to my college town, where I still had friends. Fortunately, I did not have the energy to do anything as drastic as moving.

I lived on the periphery of my mind and my apartment. The only part of the place I felt soothed was in bed, where I read and watched television, endlessly. I went through the motions of living. I pretended to read advertisements for apartments in New York, toyed with the idea of a transplant in the city. During long hot weekends, I wandered around New York in shorts with my Dalmatian dog, looking at places for rent. It is no surprise that nobody wanted us as tenants.

Now I know that I did not want to move; the idea of packing and unpacking was beyond me. I did not have the energy to keep my apartment clean. A part-time cleaning woman, unsupervised, made passes at it; everything grew dirtier, increasingly shabby, more difficult to keep presentable. I never went into the living room unless I had a visitor. Pictures fell off the wall and I left them there. I worked, and I went back to bed.

On my travels for this book, I found a lithograph which appealed to me in a shop connected with a Midwestern museum. After it was framed, I borrowed a hammer from a widow who had made her dead husband's fishing tackle box into a tool kit, and prepared to hang it on the wall where an old mirror, a wedding gift, had developed old-age liver spots. Perched on top of a chest, I discovered the mirror was hung in such a way that the wall would have to be plastered and repainted if I took it down. Suddenly, I said to myself, "Why not?"

So I had my apartment painted and, suddenly, found myself forced into the second phase of living alone. I realized that nobody was there to hang pictures or nag me into hanging them, so it was up to me to sweep out the plaster dust and get going. I did not go so far as to clean the spots of dribbled paint off the bathtub and sinks—they are still there, wearing themselves away with the erosion of time—but I did buy my own hammer, ladies' size. I might say I am very fond of it. It gives me a sense of power and accomplishment to switch pictures around the house.

A number of women alone I talked with have become so enamored of fixing things that they can do fairly complicated jobs. One Long Island woman went to night school and took a course in carpentry: "More useful than taking bridge lessons, and I was surrounded by men . . . all married, of course, but at least I talked with them and sometimes got invited out for coffee after class." The utterly helpless female is, I am convinced, either a throwback or an impostor.

Of course there are certain jobs that take experience or strength, such as lifting furniture. The day my rugs came back from the cleaner, the handyman was not available. In my new do-it-yourself enthusiasm I shifted heavy furniture and got the rugs installed. My next caller was a lady who reported she had had a bad back for several years after such an orgy. I decided to be less impetuous next time. Climbing on stepladders also can be foolish if you live alone; teetering precariously on one of them, clutching my trusty hammer, I realized that if I fell and broke a leg it might be a couple of days before anybody discovered me.

However, I have met women who would not dream of opening a can alone. These ladies, from the first week of aloneness, are potential husband-snatchers. Husbands don't mind. If they are good with their hands, they get a special kick out of fixing things for the poor little thing who cannot do it herself, and does not have a husband . . . particularly if she also happens to be terribly appreciative. It is always more fun to perform in a strange house, and get praised instead of scolded for procrastinating.

In the Midwest, I talked with a television actress whose divorce entailed her moving into a new house, so the producer for whom she worked offered to help her. One night when he was in the midst of repairing a socket in the kitchen, his wife banged on the front door. When the socket was fixed and lights were blazing all over the house, the wife sat primly on the edge of a kitchen chair, reciting a list of the things that were falling apart at home and needed fixing.

Other ladies alone are more discreet. They wait until wives are out of town before they ask for help from husbands. A slim, seductive divorcee who works in the registrar's office of a southern university confessed that this summer, while the wives of the summer school professors were at a nearby lake with the children, she had a team of willing men tearing down a wall in her house. All she had to do was act grateful and provide beer.

There are certain ground rules that, unless you are prepared to be a bit furtive, are generally accepted. No woman alone appeals too frequently to the husband of a neighbor for help—unless she is prepared to lose the friendship of the wife. Your cue is to call a handyman, or do it yourself. In an emergency, you can appeal. But don't make a practice of emergencies, even when you are calling on your own married son. Wives don't like it. A divorcee in Nebraska said that when she was first alone, the retired husband of a good friend insisted on coming in and building bookshelves for her. He refused to accept even the price of the wood from her, insisting he enjoyed keeping busy. His wife took a different attitude. When the shelves were half-finished, she yanked her husband home and gave the divorcee the telephone number of an available carpenter. As the divorcee in question had not really needed the shelves in the first place, and was in no financial position to pay a carpenter for something that was not a necessity, she and her sons had to take down the shelves themselves, on weekends.

This woman is understandably a bit bitter. I encountered other once-burned ladies who have a horror of being obligated even to male relatives. A New Jersey widow told me she pays her superintendent to hire workmen to come in and lay rugs and move heavy furniture; she will not ask either of her married sons to lift a finger in her house, or to do chores that were routine when they lived at home. Another divorcee, in Minneapolis, gets up before dawn when it snows to shovel out her driveway so the neighbors will not think they have to help her.

I feel it is wiser to be too independent than otherwise. I met several women who told me that they were discriminated against by repairmen because they are alone. Perhaps this is true in isolated cases. Sometimes I suspect the women are themselves to blame. I was interviewing one widow in a small town who had just had her electric stove repaired. The workman had to come from an adjoining village and she had been told there would be an extra service fee. On the same trip, however, he had been hailed by a neighbor whose furnace was out of order, and he had stopped to fix that. My lady was in a state, wondering whether the neighbor had also been charged the extra service fee, or had got a free ride. She was on the point of calling the company to ask when I suggested that the repairman might be grateful if she kept quiet.

I also talked with women who told me they were afraid to hire men. A Detroit widow, a frail little southern woman, said a painter whom she had brought in to make an estimate tried to rape her. (But she also told of a similar experience in a public park where she was sunning in shorts.) A fifty-year-old Nebraska widow had an unpleasant experience with her paper boy; after she rebuffed him, she found footprints in the flower bed outside her bedroom window. Unwilling to accuse him, she simply canceled the newspaper. A woman in Chicago told me that a neighbor's son she hired as a baby-sitter for her two boys cornered her in the bathroom and tried to rape her. Only when she promised him she would not complain to his mother did he leave her alone.

Incidents like this could happen any place, any time, whether a woman is alone or not. But being alone—and attractive—makes a woman a little more vulnerable. A thirty-one-year-old divorcee with three children, who lives in a small village on Long Island, discussed this with me at some length. She said, "I was brought up very properly. For example, even now when a truck driver whistles at me, I have a tendency to pretend I haven't heard, as though I were inviting rape if I smiled. But I've had some difficult experiences in the community, which is so small that everyone knows me, and knows I am alone. One night I had a call from a man who said he was at the local bar, a bar I used to go to with my husband. The man said, 'My name is Chuck Turner. I used to know you people. How about a date?' I said, 'No,' politely. But when he called the next night, I wasn't so polite. The third time, I hung up.

"I really didn't think about it much, until the garbage truck came for its regular Friday pickup, and the driver said to me, 'I'm Chuck Turner.' And he called again that same night. I told him I wasn't interested in talking to him again. I can't use any other garbage pickup—there isn't one—so I just make a point of not being around when he comes, and he hasn't bothered me again.

"My mother and father came from England to visit me and were terribly upset when they heard the local gas station boys call me Judy. That's another difficult thing. When Harry was here, I used to think the idea of the townspeople calling me by my first name had a nice earthy friendly quality. Now that I am alone, it seems flirty. I now try to correct them and say, 'I'm Mrs. Cooper.'

"I don't want to be a snob, and yet the assumption seems to be that because I am a divorcee, I'll go out with anyone, I'm so desperate. There were some young workmen who came to help me when I first was alone—they gave my name to an army buddy, who asked me for a date on the telephone and was quite obscene when I refused. Next time, when I needed help with my storm windows, I hired a white-haired old man. He made a pass when he found out I was alone in the house with just the baby. I threw him out but then I had to go down to the hardware store and ask for somebody else to finish the storm windows. They acted as if I had invited the pass and were quite difficult about it. What do you do in cases like this? Frankly, I don't know."

Actually, it seems to me that a woman's very instability and helplessness during her first year alone invite these unwelcome attentions, whether she realizes it or not. And her best protection is to hire people whom she knows—or to ask another woman to be in and out of the house while work is being done. As her attitude changes, as she becomes more confident and sure of herself, her fear lessens, and this can be recognized. A California widow who was considering moving to New York told me a story she had heard on television about a young woman who was so terrified after she moved to New York that she never went out on the street. "Finally," the story went, "she married the delivery boy from the grocery store."

Occasionally women alone are bothered by anonymous telephone calls. The telephone company can make arrangements to change your number if this becomes a pattern, and you suspect a crank. Meanwhile, they suggest: "Never answer any queries if you don't know who the caller is."

In previous generations, the single woman and the widow moved in with relations; only the suspect or "wild" widow dared to live alone, unchaperoned. There are still many women today who feel safer when they are not alone. The temptation, for the woman who finds herself suddenly without a husband, is to move in with another woman in the same fix. Even if you are not nervous, the house is so empty and weekends and evenings so intolerable, that the idea of companionship is welcome. And the immediate advantages are obvious.

There is another adult in the house to talk to, to consult, to share household responsibilities. If there are young children, another woman can be a substitute mother, leaving you free to take a job. It also means you can operate as a household, if not quite a family; you can go out for dinner together, take weekend trips, celebrate holidays. You have someone else to take into consideration when you plan meals, a companion if you feel depressed, and—devastatingly important—a human being who will respond to you when you come home with the anecdote or experience you always used to save for your husband.

Living with another woman can also be a help financially, although this is seldom the major reason women enter into this arrangement—and finances often cause the eventual breakup. The push about sharing can come from relatives, especially children who are married and living away from home. Their motives are excellent. But a real estate woman, a widow herself, told me she always discourages women alone from selling their houses, if they can possibly afford the expense, until a full year has elapsed. "Until then," she said, "a woman can't really know what she wants." By the same token, asking another woman to move in and share your home can be a bad mistake, and often a woman who extends a precipitate invitation lives to regret it.

People living together, especially people who are home all day, will have personality conflicts. A retired husband gets on his wife's nerves; I remember a doctor trying to explain to such a man, "How would you feel if Janie had come down to your office and sat there all day long?" But a husband, by priority, has certain rights and higher standing. Another woman in the house, all day long, is something else again.

A California widow told me that when her husband died she invited her cousin, a nurse, to come and live with her. It seemed an ideal situation. The cousin had no problem getting a good job at a nearby hospital, and she was lively and fun to have around—for a while. Then her health suffered and she had to give up her job. Because she had come there originally as a favor, she did not offer to increase the modest sum they had agreed on, for her room and one meal a day. At the same price, she was there all day and ate three big meals. In retaliation, the widow began skimping on food. The cousin accused her of deliberately not giving her enough to eat. Finally the widow pretended that her brother was coming to live with her and she needed the room. The cousin moved into a residence club. After a few months of not speaking to each other, during which time the brother failed to materialize, the two women made up. But many women who have joined forces discover, too late to do anything about it, that the trapdoor has closed and they are doomed, until death releases one of them, to a situation that has become a nightmare.

Two women may like each other very much, but that does not mean they will live happily ever after under the same roof. A charming young divorced Englishwoman, with a big house in London, invited a congenial friend, a TV writer who was away all day, to share it. They enjoyed each other very much, intellectually. They even liked each other's friends. The relation broke down over the fact that the writer liked regular meals, at specified hours, and the owner was used to being far more casual and relaxed about food.

One kitchen is never big enough for two women. Particularly if the two women are mother and daughter, there can be trouble. In this situation, if the move is aimed to help the daughter, she must make the concessions and yield priority. But a daughter should not rush into an arrangement with a widowed mother; there are too many emotional tag-ends involved. A 50-year-old doctor dropped dead suddenly of a heart attack and, almost before the widow realized what was going on, her mother had moved into the bedroom used by the college-age granddaughter. It was the granddaughter, in her young wisdom, who resolved this problem. She hustled her grandmother home, saying, "Gran, you mustn't give up your independence. Mama will insist on waiting on you, taking care of you. She'll make you old before your time. You stay by yourself—cook dinner for her once in a while, but invite her as a guest. Don't make it a regular thing."

Sometimes, however, circumstances make a mother-daughter arrangement necessary. In Nebraska, I had lunch with a vivacious blond advertising woman who was forced to go to work after her divorce, because her husband failed to support her and their three sons. She was faced with the responsibility of making a career for herself and being the head of the family. For her job she had to travel; eventually her company might move her to another state. So that her sons would not suffer, she asked her widowed mother to leave her home in another city and come and live with them. Her request came at a good time for her mother; the company she had worked for as a buyer was changing hands and her mother had decided to retire. Yet it was a sacrifice to give up her own home. Only the fact that her grandsons needed her made her agree.

Mrs. L., the advertising woman, said, "I still feel like a little girl when I go out on a date; my mother and the boys look him over and I know they are watching critically when we go out the door and get into his car." But she is free to date, and to travel, without worrying about hired housekeepers or depending on neighbors to watch the boys. She added, "At first, it used to bother me when I went into the kitchen and found everything rearranged so differently that I couldn't even find a spoon. Now I see it has to be that way. She's in charge. She plans the meals. The boys love it, for she indulges them more in sweets than I ever would. Again, I don't complain. It's bad for their teeth and won't be good for their complexions as they get older, but she has to see these things for herself. I have to keep telling myself how lucky I am to have her, and shut up."

In a large Midwestern city, a regional director of the nationwide organization called Parents Without Partners told me that her household, originally consisting of her and her husband and twin girls, now has five females. The divorce was caused by her husband's alcoholism, and shortly afterward her mother came to the household so Mrs. J. could continue in her career as a special education teacher for hospitalized children. But the mother is now an invalid. Mrs. J.'s sister, a kindergarten teacher who had never married, gave up her job and moved in to manage the household. "In this case, we all realize that we are benefiting. Perhaps my sister least of all, but she is very fond of children and is wonderful for the twins. We get along. Maybe, in a way, it is easier because there are so many females. And we keep in mind that it's a question of expediency. We have to pull together."

Where health is a problem, whether it is your own health or that of a dependent relative, you may have no choice. A woman I met in Chicago, who was married to a man who became mentally ill, developed serious arthritis, which doctors think may be the result of tension. She moved back to Chicago after the divorce, to live near friends. Old schoolmates were very attentive, but gradually it became clear that, during her bad spells, she needed someone with her. An unmarried sister offered to share her very attractive apartment. Although the situation isn't perfect—the sister works and has a place near the Loop, far from Muriel's friends—the apartment is very pleasant and Muriel is much better off than she was before. Her health is improving and she hopes to be able to find work soon. But—and here is the big problem—she is worried that once having moved in with her sister, she may not be able to leave without hurting her feelings, unless it is to get married. And she does not want to get married again, at this moment.

A year can make a great deal of difference in the attitudes of a woman alone . . . and she may find herself doing exactly what she once thought was impossible. A widow in a college town decided, on the death of her professor husband, that she wanted to keep her big house. So she rented rooms to students, including a nephew. It was an ideal setup, she told me. "We each have our own shelves in the refrigerator, cook our own meals, take care of our own rooms. It's like community living, I am not alone, and I have the joy of young people around, which I would have missed." This autumn, passing through New York, she telephoned to tell me she had sold her house and was moving into a small apartment. "I got fed up with all the responsibilities of taking care of a big house, and the kids weren't that dependable. Besides, I missed my privacy."

Another Michigan widow, who had a country home and a Chicago apartment when her husband died, gave up the apartment to live in the deep woods that she loved so much. But after six months, she discovered that the silence and solitude, which had seemed so wonderful when it was shared with her husband, began to bother her. She moved back to Chicago, to a residence hotel, for the winter. But even when summer arrived, she was reluctant to leave. So she put up her house for sale and bought a small cooperative apartment on Michigan Avenue.

She writes: "I am lonesome sometimes here. But there are people in the streets and when I feel blue, I go out and join them, or stop by one of our big cafeterias for dinner. There are always lots of other people eating alone, so I watch them and identify with them. After a little while, I begin to see how much luckier I am than most people. So I go home, quite content."

A prominent New York woman sold her big house after her husband died, and moved into the carriage house on the estate, a small property to which they had planned to retire. But the memories were too bitter, and she found herself resenting the new owners of the large house in which she had been so happy. She left the carriage house and moved back into her girlhood home with her two sisters, one also a widow, another who had never married. The arrangement is not perfect—"We have our little arguments," she told me, smiling, "but it is better than being alone and we do love each other. That becomes more and more important as I get older."

A New York publicity woman, whose husband died suddenly of a heart attack, moved into a suburban house with her widowed sister. "It seemed like a good idea at the time," she told me. But her sister was older, and used to having her own way in the family. She resented the hours Eileen D. kept and attempted to dictate her friends. Finally, Mrs. D. moved into a residence club for women in Gramercy Park. During the winter, she visits her sister on weekends, but this coming summer she plans to take a weekend beach house with two other women who are also alone.

A charming woman in Evanston, Illinois, in her desire not to be a burden to her children, snapped up a vacancy in a residence home a little too fast. The all-woman atmosphere oppresses her now, and she knows that she would have been happier in a small, less luxurious apartment that would demand more of her. Although all meals are included in the residence fee, and are delicious and balanced and attractively served, she sometimes goes across the street to a restaurant because, "I get so tired of the pattern of the club's china!"

Almost any widow can postpone the decision of where and how to live for a year, and she may be a different person after that period of grace, with a different set of new friends. A real estate woman in Connecticut, herself a divorcee, told me, "Women alone shouldn't live in the suburbs. They should get back into the city. It's good therapy getting rid of big houses, old furniture, planning a new setting. But they mustn't move so fast that they feel shunted around, pushed out. Sometimes a divorcee has to get out of her old places, for financial reasons. I hate to have to handle this, because losing the house as well as the husband sometimes seems to be the final straw."

Hard as it is for a woman with children to bring an older relative into her house, the most difficult possible move that any woman can make is into the home of a married son or daughter. At a conference on jobs for mature women held in a New York department store, I sat next to a woman in her middle sixties who confided to me, "My husband died four months ago. The children insisted I sell the wholesale bakery we operated, as they felt I couldn't handle it alone. Now my daughter wants me to give up my apartment and move to upper New York State with her and her family. They don't want me to live alone and they feel I've worked hard enough, I should rest. But if I went, I would be living their lives, not my own. That's why I want to get a job. One of my neighbors heard about this conference and suggested I come. In Brooklyn, I have my church, my own friends, I can be myself. Don't you think I'm right?"

I told her I was sure of it—although her children probably were not grateful for a stranger's unsolicited advice at the time, I hope they are now. No matter what façade a woman newly alone adopts to hide her pain and confusion, the first year is a bridge, a transition, and it must be crossed. A divorcee with young children who moved to Hawaii in order to make definite a painful break with her mentally ill husband told me, "I had to pretend for a while that it wasn't permanent. I moved from one rented house to another, like camping out, always talking about going back to New Orleans. Then a strange thing happened. My husband died. I went out and bought a house I'd been considering in my mind subconsciously, and sent for my furniture. It was like coming out of a fog, saying *fini*."

A widow with two children under five years of age took her teenage brother and her husband's college-age cousin into her home almost immediately. She said afterward, "I had the illusion it would work, the boys would be substitute fathers. Of course they didn't want the responsibility and they resented my trying to be a kind of wife-mother, telling them what to do. First Lou's cousin moved out, because I wouldn't let him have a beer party in the basement. Then one night, when I was criticizing my brother for not taking responsibility, I realized I was the shirker. I sent him back home to our parents and began life on my own, without trying to lean on anyone else."

A widow in Larchmont, New York, with three teenage sons, told me, "My minister must have been worried about me. One night, when Ned had been dead about six months, he insisted I go into New York with another woman, to a meeting of a group called Parents Without Partners. The whole thing sounded like nonsense to me, but he made such an issue about my attending that I went. A psychiatrist was one of the speakers. He looked around the room—and it was a big ballroom in a hotel—and said, 'Everyone here is single.' Do you know it was the first time I had thought of myself as single. It came as a shock. I didn't meet anybody that night. I didn't try. I was too busy thinking. I was single and I darned well had to get used to thinking as one person, before I looked around for a husband. Because what I really expected was some man to come and take care of me."

It takes time to make even a partial recovery, depending on many factors—your age, your variety of outside interests, your own philosophy. One divorcee told me, "It's like growing a new arm after you've lost one."

Perhaps there is no magic in having passed the one-year mark. But I feel, and many other women agreed with me, that once you have survived a whole set of anniversaries, the worst is over. Trying times are still ahead, simply because no life is without its bad moments. But it does help to know that other women have made it; you are not the first, or the last. Each woman has to suffer and learn in her own way.

A Cleveland divorcee: "After you think you are all right, adjusted to being that leprous thing, a divorcee, you will find yourself making ridiculous mistakes, doing things that seem awful.

One night I went to a party and was drinking a glass of tomato juice (I had given up liquor because I was so jittery) and somebody mentioned my ex-husband's name and I spilled the glass of tomato juice all over myself and a strange man. I wanted to die. A nice woman came and wiped us off. She told me later she was a widow and at her first dinner party, after her husband died, she began to cry and had a nosebleed all over her hostess's best lace tablecloth."

A Connecticut widow: "The empty house would seem unbearable. So I rushed out whenever anyone invited me, to dinner, to a movie, for weekends. Yet as soon as I arrived someplace, I would be miserable. Once I went to a bar where they had dancing, with a group I hardly knew. I was so ill at ease, I stiffened up when I tried to dance and stepped all over my partner's feet. I escaped to the ladies' room and said to myself, 'What are you doing here?' But gradually I find it's not so bad spending an evening alone. I only accept the invitations I want."

A Florida divorcee: "I was astonished when other girls alone told me about their trouble sleeping. I had other problems, but the minute I went to bed, I was out like a light. Then, suddenly, I found nights were getting bad. I worried and read and drank hot milk and had to ask my doctor for pills. Finally I figured it out. I stopped sleeping when I faced the fact that my husband wasn't coming back, he was going to stay with his second wife. Before then, I was like a little girl. I felt that if I were good and went right to sleep, everything would be all right in the morning. Now I know it won't. It's harder but I feel I've matured."

A Denver widow: "It is frustrating. Sometimes you make progress. Then everything falls apart, you reach a point where you don't improve and you think you have slipped back to zero. Actually, you haven't. But you don't know that until afterward, because you've lost perspective."

A California divorcee: "The best salve for a wounded ego is self-tolerance, laced with humor."

A widow in Lincoln, Nebraska: "I keep a diary. It's good to look back even a few months and see how far I've come."

A Denver divorcee: "If you can't sleep, get up and do something else. Don't worry about your rest, or start brooding over what's past and done. I knew a dancer who used to get up and practice when she had insomnia. I keep a pad and pencil by my bed. When something is worrying me, I write myself a note about the problem without turning on the light; I've learned to guide my hand in the dark. And don't, above all, keep checking to see what time it is. If necessary, keep clocks out of the bedroom."

A Minnesota divorcee with two boys: "Keep away from the resort-type areas where there are women on the loose, or working on their third or fourth marriages. Go someplace where you can become a stable part of the community. The fast, sophisticated life is far more boring eventually than one with simpler pleasures."

A Minneapolis widow: "There are a lot of silly statements you'll make when you are first alone, things you'll say you will never do. Pretty soon you'll find yourself doing one or two of them. I'd say, don't try to justify your actions. Go ahead and contradict yourself. It's a woman's privilege to change her mind."

And from Dr. Carl Winters, keynote speaker at a Parents Without Partners conference: "It isn't what happens to you that matters. It's what you do about what happens to you."

4 YOUR SOCIAL LIFE

I'm so used to going to parties alone I prefer it. At my age, I also prefer coming home alone. My only problem is those darned back zippers on dresses. So sometimes I drive by the police station and have the young man at the desk unzip me.

MASSACHUSETTS DIVORCEE

My brother-in-law worries about my driving home at night from parties. He gave me a man's hat and insists I put it on. I don't know what good it does, but I wear it.

ILLINOIS NORTH SHORE WIDOW

When I have a party, I ask the husband of a good friend to carve, never the extra man. My friends would resent someone taking my husband's place.

MINNEAPOLIS WIDOW

When my social life gets sluggish, I join things...but deliver me from all-women groups. I won't go to matinees or ladies' luncheons or fashion shows. I see enough of women in the course of ordinary socializing without deliberately inserting myself in an all-woman situation.

NEW YORK DIVORCEE

The trick is to know enough people so if half of them desert you, go off on vacations, or move to Singapore, you aren't at loose ends. It sounds awful, but you must insinuate yourself into different groups, much more than you did when you had a husband.

CALIFORNIA DIVORCEE

On Saturday night I sit home—that's the story of my life as a widow. I am reasonably busy during the week, what with people from out of town and dinner and movies with other women alone. Once in a while somebody even gives a big cocktail party. But weekends are private family times, and Saturdays are for couple dinner parties or for dates. I won't go out with other women on Saturday, it makes it too obvious I can't get a date. So I sit—always.

NEW YORK WIDOW

I think an aggressive woman, divorced or widowed, was probably also aggressive when she had a husband. Some women make fools of themselves going after men.

CHICAGO WIDOW

THE social life of a woman alone is usually a well-guarded secret from the world of couples, not because it is necessarily so interesting, but because it is so unstable. At first, there are loyal friends who make a point of including you, checking up on you, seeing that you are not alone and brooding. But even before the first year is over, you notice a subtle change. The telephone does not ring quite so often. And when you take the initiative—a difficult enough task in itself after you have been pampered—people are not always ready to drop everything and come to see you. Sometimes they are even too busy to talk for more than a few minutes.

Your best friend, who always included you in every party, moves away, or has another woman alone to take care of, one more freshly in need of help. The eligible-bachelor escorts, the perennials who rallied around at first, drop off; sometimes their curiosity is satisfied, sometimes you have not done your expected share of entertaining, sometimes they just get old, or even die. Hostesses in general go back to their couple society. You are invited frankly as an extra, when you are invited, or you are left out, with the wife explaining, "We couldn't find an extra man and we knew you didn't want to come alone."

On your part, if you are invited, you go. (That is, you *should* always say yes, your friends tell you, and mostly you do.) No matter how dull you fear the affair will be, or how inconvenient it is to get there, you, the woman alone, can be counted on. And you can usually find another woman alone to go home with. Wives can afford to turn up their noses at invitations which do not look too promising. You cannot. Otherwise you will turn into the forgotten woman. "After all, you have your memories" . . . "You had a good life" . . . or, as in the case of a divorcee, "It's a shame but she did decide she wanted a divorce and so . . ."

You also have to manufacture your own social life, and the sooner you start, the better. It will not be the kind you had when you were married, or when you were a young girl.

The emphasis will be on other women—but, then, the social

life of a married woman is largely female, too, with the women in one end of the room talking about their husbands, and the men gathered around the TV set watching ball games and talking business. Few of the men will be eligible, at least by your standards, or interested in you. Most of them will be tied up in some way—to wives, to mistresses, to mothers, to other men, or to their own freedom. But at least, when you meet and talk to them at parties, you are, as one New York divorcee put it, "functioning as a female in public again."

Of all these men, the more personable are invariably the ones who are married. While their wives are away, or ill, or maybe just not looking, these men may take you out to dinner. There are many reasons why you should not go out with married men. One divorcee said, "You're wasting time on them you should be spending hunting eligibles." A widow said mildly, "Even your best friend's husband will make a little bit of a pass, just to see how you're reacting these days."

But it is pleasant to have any kind of a date with a man, so you go. And if by chance you become involved emotionally . . . then he is no longer what you can call part of your social life. And many women alone disapprove strongly of affairs with married men not only on moral grounds, or out of consideration for the little women at home, but also because of what falling in love can do to your pursuit of a social life.

For if you want to keep going out, even with temporary lapses to catch your breath and wash your hair and sew buttons on your dresses, you have to work at it, endlessly. As a Texas widow put it, "Women alone have to be reconciled to *always,* without letup, taking the social initiative. Either that or stay alone."

A New York divorcee said, "I give at least one party a week, the salon-type thing, because I'm not much on cooking. But I do think I have skill in mixing people. But you can't just lump together people you owe socially. You have to plan people who will get along, spark each other, who will have enough fun so they will be happy to be invited back. And you can't count invitations, either. Invite the people who will add to the affair, who will make it fun."

A pretty New York executive, unmarried in her middle forties, bought a brownstone house in mid-Manhattan and decorated it as a place for parties. She said, "A woman alone must return hospitality, even if you've been taken out on the expense account. If I'm invited to the theater with a group, I always have them back to my place for a nightcap. My dining room seats eight or twelve comfortably. I do all the cooking, but hire a maid for serving. I give buffets for larger groups. Sometimes I hire a bartender, sometimes I let the men help me—it's rather more intimate. Of course I include married men who are in town without their wives, that's part of my job. But I don't let them get the idea I owe them anything. In fact, I make it a point to entertain their wives when they come to town—make it a friendly affair all around."

A Manhattan divorcee said, "Never invite just one couple for dinner. The man will resent it. If you can't find an extra man whom your friends will find congenial—and be careful about this —invite another couple. And have everything ready in advance. A wife can trot between the kitchen and the living room, but it's a pain in the neck if a woman alone does. It makes guests feel that entertaining is too much of a chore for her."

All this is good sound advice. I recommend it. But unless a woman is a born self-starter, with few inhibitions, starting out from scratch to plan an active social life seems more than she can swallow. As a wife, unless she was the kind who kept pushing her husband up the ladder, she had a certain set of friends who extended invitations more or less regularly. If she got fed up with cooking and wanted company, she could talk her husband into taking them out to a restaurant. She had him by her side as a cohost at a party; if anything went wrong, it wasn't quite so bad with someone to share the blame. On the few occasions where she felt on display and under tension—at company parties, for example—she had her husband. On the way home, they could rip the whole crowd to pieces, or laugh at them, or tell each other how well they did.

The idea of turning aggressive, of promoting herself, sets her teeth on edge. In fact, sound advice on how to behave as a woman alone often so unnerves a woman that she feels it is easier to drop out of sight. Or the alternative, which is even easier—lead an all-woman social life.

My Aunt Flora, who lives in Lincoln, Nebraska, tells a story about her first experience with this type of thing. Another widow invited her to dinner at the country club. When she arrived, she found a table of twenty-five women, all widows, whose husbands she had known. She choked down dinner, but she never went back.

A Dallas country club has a table frankly labeled "The Widow's Table" where divorcees are welcomed, too. There is a tale that one man on his deathbed made his widow promise she would never sit there. Some country clubs offer women alone what they refer to as "bridge memberships." Women start playing early in the morning, stop for lunch, then go on until cocktail time, by which time they are presumably ready to go to their separate houses. Other women alone play golf or tennis or bowl during the daytime, which at least gets them out in the open air. Still others do volunteer charitable work en masse, or go to the ladies' do-good luncheons.

In some areas, including Minneapolis, night clubs welcome long tables of women alone for the dinner show. In Lincoln, Nebraska, I found a group of women alone, some of them with good jobs, who make a point of going together to plays, openings, and the like; when there is nothing interesting going on in town, they entertain each other on Saturday night with gourmet dinners—several have taken *cordon bleu* cooking lessons. A Detroit divorcee who works hard at her Community Chest told me, "Three of my women friends who also have demanding jobs and I often go away for bridge weekends. We take rooms in a hotel and live on room service. We stay in our robes and nightgowns and play bridge all the time. People think we're crazy but it's great fun and a change of pace."

Accepting an all-woman social life fills your date book and takes most of the pressure of making plans off you. You don't need to worry about pushing other women socially. Unless you are breaking into a new community, most of them will be old friends, or friends of friends, and you feel no necessity to put your best foot forward. Even with strangers, intimacy develops fast—you have so much in common to complain about.

That happens to be one of the problems of groups of ladies alone. A group of embittered divorcees in a Midwestern college town cling together tied by a mutual bond of husband-hating. (Of course they hate happily married wives even more.) Whenever they hear a woman is having problems with her marriage, they immediately suck her into the group. In one case where neighbors suspected the trouble might be patched up, they banded together to protect a vulnerable young wife so that she would not be completely brainwashed by what they referred to as the "viper's nest."

In some areas, where women alone outnumber men their own age and couples, this all-woman society is impossible to avoid, and, as a Vermont widow put it, "You make the best of it." But there is danger in depending too much on any group, of spending days as well as nights with the same people. Your individuality and your interests shrink. If the group is protective coloring for someone who is insecure, it also sheds that same dull coloring over the exceptional woman, who would sparkle a bit on her own. You have to be careful not to be absorbed. Even if you have no choice but to spend your life with other women, it is best to be a member of several different groups, not just one.

An Ohio widow said, "When my husband died, I had dozens of letters from women I hardly knew, other widows and divorcees. They wanted me to come and visit, or to travel with them. Older women alone, old enough to be my mother, began filling me in on life without men. They acted as though I was one of them now, there was no hope for me. I felt a little as I had when I was first married and my mother and grandmother began to talk freely about sex in front of me. I heard more about the messy side of being alone than I wanted to know."

From a Moble widow: "In our particular group of what used to be eight couples, six of us are widows. The other two men are sick: one had a stroke and the other has a brain tumor. We sit around together and talk about what used to be. There was talk about the six of us going around the world on a cruise together, then somebody said, 'Shouldn't we wait for Amy and Mary?' It gave me pause. Of course, this is home. But I can't stand it. I'm getting out of town, or taking a job, or something."

From a California widow: "I can't seem to adjust to the lone woman bit. Harry and I used to be fond of a divorcee in the building, she was such a good sport and fun. The minute he died, she attached me. One night she took me to a cocktail bar where the singles gather, a few men and mobs of women. They all were planning a trip to Las Vegas on a bus and wanted me to go. I couldn't—I feel like a sore thumb with them, all trying to act gay and happy. Yet you can't stay home all the time. And with couples I feel like a fifth wheel. Just being out with a man and wife makes me know how much I miss Harry. I go home and weep. At least, with the women, I'm glad to be home alone in my own bed, not listening to their chatter."

Some of these helpful women friends have been acquired during your first year alone, when just being alone seemed enough to have in common as a basis for friendship. But after you have made a partial recovery, you soon learn that you cannot listen, night after night, to the same old stories and recriminations. Unless you find another woman stimulating, unless you share interests above and beyond the basic fact of a life alone, it is better to stop seeing her before your relation becomes, at least in her eyes, permanent.

There is also another hazard: women with homosexual tendencies. A New York divorcee told me, "I never thought one way or another about lesbians when I was married. I was the 'live-and-let-live' type. Since I've been alone, I've had one widow, one divorcee, and one never-married schoolteacher try to become intimate friends. I'm not sure they are queers, either of them. But their approaches were male. They kept sending flowers, bringing presents. The schoolteacher, when she went home after staying until nearly midnight, would always call up to be sure I had double-locked everything—that sort of relation. I got so worried about myself, I went to a psychiatrist. He told me to get rid of them both, and I did—not because I wasn't normal, but because they were smothering me, lesbians or not."

There is another painful truth that should be recognized: no matter how comforting it is to have a full calendar, never a night to brood, it is better to be lonely sometimes than to fall into the habit of going out with a pack of women. A young man I met in the Far East summed it up for me: "Those big bunches of women always look so pitiful."

On the other hand, when you do find a woman who is mutually congenial, treasure her. She is the one who will worry about you when you are sick, do the errands you cannot ask of married friends (or men), and be an amusing companion when you want to go to dinner, or the theater, or to a lecture. She is the sort who, if you are busier than she is, will be pleased for you. Nor will she quiz you about what is going on. She will wait until you are ready to talk, if and when. She is also the kind who will tell you the truth, as well as she is able, when you ask her advice. But not before.

This female world of friendship is, and has to be, far more grown-up than the girl-chum arrangements you had when you were younger, or even the acquaintances made with other women when you were married. Some of the latter are strong enough to survive your being transplanted into another world; but the affection has to be solid on both sides. Others are based so much on temporary mutual interests that they cannot survive. A recent widow from the suburbs of Boston told me she had to move, get out and find a job because she no longer had rapport with her best friends: "All they do is talk about their husbands. I have nothing to contribute."

The old cliché, after the death of a husband, is, "The wrong one died."

Unless your ego is shining brightly, when you are left alone, you get more and more doubtful about your own desirability as a friend and as a person. If your friendship with a couple was really based on your admiration or enjoyment of the woman, and if it went over and beyond discussing the care and feeding of children and husbands, you can thank your stars and stop looking for imaginary slights and indications you are no longer in favor. On the other hand, if you liked the man better than the woman, you had better forget the whole thing.

At first you have very little to contribute. ("I think I cut my married friends off," a divorcee told me. "I didn't want them to pity me. Now I feel better, I am glad to have them.") It is the good old-fashioned milk of human kindness that motivates the couples who continue to invite you to go out with them, or come to dinner, even in your zombie state. You may even resent happy people who still have each other. Sitting and saying nothing, while a fox gnaws at her vitals, does not tend to make a woman alone very good company. But blessed be the people who were willing to take you until you revived a little.

A woman in Detroit, widowed early and now remarried for twenty years, told me, "I shall never forget the people who continued to be nice to me after Dick died."

It takes the long arm of time for any woman, widow or divorcee, to realize how much this support means to her, and how ungracious she was about accepting it at the period when she needed it most. In most cases it comes from people who either are genuinely kind, or who have been through the experience and are warm and generous, too.

Think back to your own days as a married hostess, when you studied the list of people you would like to invite to a party, and then crossed off some of the women so the affair would not look like an all-girl band. There was always a conflict in my mind between the women who would add something, with ease of manner and wide acquaintance, and the ones who needed social activity. Usually, pressured by the thought that I wanted the party to be a success, I invited the livelier gals.

These are simply facts of life. I have one dear generous friend who is so overflowing with kindness toward women alone that she overclogs her parties with us. The result is that she is not doing anyone, including herself, a favor. Remembering this, I was a little more understanding about something that happened last Christmas.

An old friend, a divorcee, arrived from England for a brief visit in New York. Mutual acquaintances, who knew her less well than I did, were asked to parties in her honor. I was not, which embarrassed her a little, because she suspected I might be hurt. The fact was I did mind—a little. Yet at the same time, I quite understood why I was not included. Any extra men who could be collected and invited were earmarked for my English divorcee; the hostess did not want any of the rest of us hanging around diverting male attention or even cluttering up the room.

If you want the fox to devour a large chunk of your insides, you can say to yourself that people are just being mean, discriminating against you because you do not have a husband any more. You're wrong; there are simply too damned many women around.

On the other hand, it would be surprising if you were to listen with perfect blissful composure while your married friends rattle on about various invitations they have had (and often rejected) or parties they have attended, the invitations that you would have had if your husband had been around. It destroys you to be resentful. But logic has nothing to do with it.

"I am jealous," the most sensible woman I know admitted to me. "I used to come home from an evening with dear old friends and weep with rage. I'd go to a movie with another woman and watch the others coming out, two by two, women clinging to their husbands' arms, women not half as good-looking as I was. I was corroded with envy. Only when I realized it was hurting only me did I begin to get my balance."

Until you do, you can build ridiculous mountains of fabrication about old friends. A widow will decide she is not wanted because she is a reminder of death. A divorcee will get the conviction she is a symbol of universal male treachery. Or you quietly make up your mind that the couple never did like you, the attraction was your husband, or his position in the business world. Occasionally, a woman alone will think that an old friend is jealous of her. (Sometimes, of course, she is right.)

People are not intentionally cruel. The great fault is indifference. In time of trouble, most of them do the conventionally correct thing—send flowers, call, write. With a few notable exceptions, they then forget the woman alone. They are still sorry you lost your husband, whether he died or fell in love with another woman. But they are busy with their own affairs, and with people who fit more conveniently and more importantly into their lives.

I was guilty many times of not being considerate enough of good friends who were alone, and it was only those who continued to call whom I saw with any kind of regularity. So why should I have such pride about having to be the one who keeps in touch? Or feel hurt when I hear of a party to which I have not had an invitation?

Again and again, in talking to other women alone, I hear, "It's like being back in adolescence, with the awful uncertainties and agonies. I keep saying to myself, why should I make an effort? Why should I care? I'd rather stay home."

It is easier to stay home; there are women alone who do, who stay in bed until noon and never get dressed all day. Their lives, if you can call them lives, are spent on the telephone. When my stomach is churning before some party I have talked myself into on a fighting day, I envy these ladies. And yet, and yet . . .

You have a certain number of years ahead of you, and nobody really cares what you do with them except you. Living as a woman alone is hard. You get used to it, just as you get used to anything if you live long enough. There are moments when it is bliss to go home alone and close the door and not have to account to anybody. But it takes time to make what other people will refer to as a "good adjustment." It takes courage. You have to put yourself in other people's shoes occasionally and, as the old saying goes, try walking five miles in them before you judge their behavior. And you have to grow a reasonably thick hide.

When I first started to do interviews for this book, I met an exceptionally attractive woman executive, never-married, whom I enjoyed very much. I would have liked to have seen her again. But when I suggested another meeting, she grinned and said, "I need another woman friend like a hole in the head."

She, like many another woman who never married, has learned the ground rules so well that she does not fool around or fumble when she sees a situation which is not for her. The widow or divorcee may have some built-in advantages; when it comes to marriage, she has had experience and is a more likely prospect than the lady who has never arranged a household to please a man. But, in the role of extra woman, single woman, or what-have-you, she is a novice, and each time she turns around, she finds another hurdle.

Last year, there was an article in a Sunday newspaper magazine section entitled "The Neuter Women," by Phyllis Battelle, a wife and mother. She wrote, "As is the pattern of most neuters she (the neuter woman) calls upon a retinue of men (unmasculine, safe men: often acknowledged homosexuals) to take her out." The article also mentioned that this "non-woman" clicking along the New York streets, high-salaried and respected, also often pays for the theater tickets when she has these safe men as escorts.

Married women, friends of mine, have barbed things to say about the widow of a mutual friend who is hostess to a group of homosexuals. Even people who are less critical of non-heterosexual males frown on single women going out with "the boys" because it is an admission that you have given up all thoughts of marriage with a normal man.

Perhaps it is. Perhaps having homosexuals around keeps other men away. But in New York particularly, and also California and some large cities scattered between the two coasts, I have found that experienced single women—either those who have never married or have been alone long enough to have established social lives—have reached a kind of adjustment with homosexual men. They are friends who can be conscripted as escorts without embarrassment, who fill in at dinner parties amusingly, who can be counted on to occupy lonely hours as readily as other women alone, and who do not make emotional demands. Of course, in metropolitan areas, the acceptance of homosexuals is more casual. Husbands do not cringe at shaking hands, nor do respectable ladies refuse to be introduced socially—although I do know a *grande dame* in Arizona who refused to play cards at the home of another woman alone because one of the foursome was a homosexual. ("By acknowledging these people, you only encourage them," she told me.)

As a wife, I never thought about whether I was a good guest or not; being invited back was not a concern. In fact, I was more interested in helping my husband enjoy himself than in what I contributed, if anything. Most wives feel this way. In other words —they are secure. Not the single woman, though. She's on the spot.

Several years ago, from the smug superiority of my position as wife-hostess, I wrote an article about the Extra Woman which appeared in *Good Housekeeping* magazine. Some of my friends did not like it much; one in particular, a recent widow, was rather sharp about some of the things I said. I did not hear from my long-term single friends, to whom I was presumably talking. Either they did not read the magazine, which was after all directed toward married women, or they were being tactful. I rather suspect the latter.

I suggested all the obvious tricks to endear you to hostesses, including walking the dog, being helpful with the children, and bringing flowers or hors d'oeuvres. I also advised the woman alone not to monopolize the male guests or to be so bloody useful she made others think she was there as an unpaid servant. I also mentioned returning invitations, and made a rather blunt suggestion that the lady alone take care that she gives her guests enough to eat. I cited a case when I had taken my husband and a bachelor home from a dinner party given by a lady alone, and fed them peanut butter sandwiches. (The main course had been fish and the portion given the bachelor had been so dainty in size that he had mistaken it for a first course and had only one bite, not caring for fish.)

Right now, I cringe at my smugness. As a woman alone, surrounded by others in the same fix, I see the mistakes of being overhelpful, or overpally with the gents, as a result of simple embarrassment. We try so damned hard to be good guests that we can be pains in the neck. We are so agreeable to the bits and pieces of extra men invited for us—to show our hostess our appreciation—that we make them nervous. And, unused to cooking for anyone else, when we invite back we forget about the size of male appetites, particularly healthy men under fifty.

I have learned the hard way—watching lean and hungry guests —that when a single woman entertains, the emphasis should be on quantity, not variety. Simple hors d'oeuvres are fine; the healthy young people who come from offices or a day in the park with young children are always starving. But a lot of older people will be watching their figures and will not thank you for passing calorie-ridden tidbits dripping with chlorestorol. As for the main course, the object is to keep the hostess out of the kitchen as much as possible. So, even if you have a maid or a caterer, have simple foods which can be prepared in advance and kept warm, or re-heated in the oven. I am thinking of hams, pot roasts, meat loafs, creamed potatoes, or pasta dishes, good plain cooking which does not go wrong if it has to stand and which most men prefer to gourmet meals—especially, I might add, badly prepared gourmet meals.

As for leftovers, if any, try freezing them. Or get a hungry dog.

As for the main question, do you want a social life aside from the girls? The answer, from watching the long-term singles, has to be yes—or perish. Even if you are not interested in getting married, it is more pleasant to have men in your home, to be aware of male conversation. It keeps you in the mainstream of life.

But this means you must think about changing the rules you operated by as a wife, and consider yourself a single woman. I say "think about" because you cannot change your spots in a single week, or in a few months. You have to keep plugging. One woman told me, "My husband has been dead three years and during that time I have made no effort to entertain at all. Occasionally, I send flowers or give presents. But this is not enough and I must start making an effort." Another said, "I tried at first. I really did. I gave big parties and I took my married friends to lunch at nice restaurants. But about a year after Ralph died, I found it was so easy to come home from work and sit that I got into the habit of doing nothing. I even made excuses when friends called. Then one day I telephoned thirty people I hadn't talked to in months and invited them over. It was a wonderful party, and as a result, my social life started again. Thank God— because I was getting sort of strange."

Everyone—or shall I say almost everyone—has dull periods socially. The trick, most women feel in retrospect, is not to worry so long as it does not go on too long. The treatment is to rest, read, pamper yourself with food, stop counting calories, watch TV. One comment: "Act as though you had a bad cold. Indulge all your bad habits. Then one day you'll wake up feeling better and wonder why you ever wanted to lie in bed."

The more you do, the easier it is to keep going . . . unless, of course, you push yourself until you cannot enjoy anything or anyone. You have to get your hand back before you enjoy entertaining and cooking again. Of course it's harder when you're alone, without moral support, perhaps without as much money to spend, and particularly if you're working, with a full-time job. For example, take Mary K. Mrs. K. is the widow of a New York judge, with college-age children. When her son began to complain that his mother never got up until noon, she decided to fill her days and got a job as a buyer for a small gift shop. The work is hard. She has a part-time maid come in once a week, for the heavy cleaning; otherwise she makes her own bed, cooks her own dinners, and washes her few dishes.

A nephew of whom she is fond wrote and said he was coming to New York. She got tickets to the ballet, which she knew he enjoyed, and planned to have dinner at home that night. To make everything easy, she decided on a casserole. The date was for Wednesday evening. On Monday night, she shopped. On Tuesday night, she made the casserole and set the table. On Wednesday, they had dinner and left the dishes. On Thursday, she came home from work and washed them. "Four nights spent fixing a simple dinner for a nephew," she told me. "How long would it take if I really tried to have a party?"

The answer is—surprisingly—not much longer. Another friend of mine, a divorcee, invited me to dinner one night with two other women, to whom she was indebted. "Don't bother to put on lipstick," she said, "it will be all-female." Two days before the date she called to say, "Put on lipstick. I've invited a couple of men to drop in for dessert and coffee." Actually, in the end, she had twenty guests, four women to dinner, extra men and some extra women for dessert. As she started to ask people, she got "in the mood" and even called up one or two men friends she had not heard from for a while. Everything was so much on the spur of the moment that the preparation could not be too time-consuming. She made a few things—she is a fine cook—and bought others. The party was a success, and it brought her back into active circulation after a quiet period.

We all have to do things in our own ways, even when we are trying to change. It is hard for some women to pick up the telephone and make contact; with others it is like breathing. How you entertain . . . what circles you move in . . . what new friends you make . . . all depend on the sort of person you are. One friend of mine, recently widowed, used to complain that she was "pathologically shy." Left without much money, she is starting an interesting and rewarding career for herself as a free-lance editor. She has made herself into a popular hostess by inviting her new friends to tea, because it was all she could afford.

"Lucia," said a friend of hers recently, "loves people. Only she never found it out before."

If you were good at entertaining when you were a wife, the chances are that you will give good parties again, after you feel more secure. But a woman who entertained primarily to please her husband—some of us really did—may discover that she has more to offer than she had ever suspected.

I have collected a few ideas about behavior in social situations during my interviews. Here, for what they are worth, are observations from other women alone.

About dressing for parties. In your own home when you are the hostess, you can and should trick yourself out a bit, wear long skirts, crazy (sexy?) dresses, or pajamas. Your husband might have disliked your making yourself conspicuous but your problem is different now. When you go to a small party, play it cool; don't compete with your hostess. But in a large gathering, such as a mixed affair where you know only a few, or none at all, you can be conspicuous. This may mean a red wig, or a dress cut down to you-know-where. If you haven't nerve enough for tricks like that, try crutches. I heard of a woman on a cruise who parlayed a broken leg into marriage with one of the three eligible men on the ship. This may be going to extremes. But a young woman who attended a Parents Without Partners social holding a cane and wearing a pretty pink bedroom slipper on her foot had four solid invitations of rides home.

About friends. No matter how rough things are, friends help. And a single woman needs married couples for balance and for enlarging her horizons. The relation may not be quite the same as it used to be. A widow told me, "I make it a point never to infringe on couples in the evening. If they invite me over and are having a group that's one thing. But I don't just call them up and say, 'Here I am.' "

I've heard it said of a rather prominent woman in New York that she has "more friends than anyone in the world." When I asked her about it, she said soberly: "I worked at it. When my parents died, I was absolutely alone without family. I simply had to go out and find people with whom I was congenial. Some of them I worked with. Others share my interest in music; I met one dear woman when we were both standees at the opera. One of the great things I've discovered is that age doesn't matter if you like the same things; it even enriches friendship. Another is that, although a woman alone needs friends more than a married woman, it is easier for her to keep them, for she has to please only herself, not a husband."

No one, not even this remarkable woman, has many intimate friends. In a crisis, there are only a handful on whom you can always call. Yet, as a woman alone, you may find that you have more acquaintances than you did when you were married.

About your appearance. I'm not envious of really beautiful women. Like rich people, they never know whether they are loved for themselves or their looks. And it is much harder for them to grow old, to lose the beauty of youth. Yet it is true that appearances count, and more so if you are alone.

It is much harder for a woman than a man if appearances are against her. But it is also easier for her to do something about it, with the camouflage available these days. One woman I know, divorced two years, has changed her hair to blond, her figure to a size-8 through Air Force exercises, and wears false eyelashes, false fingernails, and a blond fall when she goes out in the evening. She also dips her hair in protein rinse, uses a special moisturizer for her skin, and has three kinds of kits she uses in making up her eyes. "The only trouble," she says, "is that it takes me so long I am tired before I get to work." She also added—which is proof her technique may be working,—"The other night when one of our clients made a pass at me, all I could think of was protecting my false eyelashes."

If there happens to be an extra man, invited with you in mind, your hostess does not want you to look like a dog. She is more or less your sponsor. But, on the other hand, neither does she want you to come in like a Playboy Bunny, stripped for action. A divorcee who is spectacularly beautiful used to wear marvelous extreme clothes when she was married to an artist husband. Now that he has left her for a rather stubby little fat girl (which may be a lesson in itself) she makes a point of having a wardrobe that is carefully underplayed to conceal her figure, but in soft becoming colors which, she says modestly, "please men."

Being the type who begrudges time spent sitting under dryers in beauty shops, I cannot be bothered with fancy hairdos and false eyelashes. I also think that too much makeup, especially eye makeup, only emphasizes wrinkles. I am sure I could be wrong. I have been scolded roundly by one of the neighborhood women for going out during the day without makeup; "Look at me," she said, "I am seventy years old and I never go outside my apartment without spending an hour on my face and hair."

I agree that it is good for the morale to dress up in new clothes, and that a change of wig or hairdo may help your spirits. (Everywhere, among the recently alone, wigs are very big.) I also believe you should exercise, keep your figure within the nice-armful category, and be shiningly, scrupulously fastidious about cleanliness. But I do not believe in spending an hour on your face and hair before you go around the corner to buy a tube of toothpaste. Maybe you will meet your Fate on the way. But wouldn't he like you just as well in blue jeans and a plain face?

About your pride. "It took a year and a half before I would go to a party alone," a divorcee told me. "Now it builds up my ego to think people want me; for so long I thought I was invited just because my husband was an artist." Frankly, it is a schoolgirl trick to be coy, to refuse an invitation because it comes at the last minute or because it is Saturday night and you are ashamed to admit that you have no date. The most charming woman I know, whose telephone never stops ringing, is always willing to go anywhere at the last minute; having turned down several offers, she accepts yours, acting as though she has been sitting home waiting for it. Such obvious naïvete takes great sophistication.

About going alone. Of course a woman alone is more conspicuous than if she were with a man, or with other women. But isn't that the point of going out—to be noticed in a nice way? And, whether women know this or not, men are intrigued by a woman who has the courage and sophistication to walk into a room or a restaurant alone. Women (remember that frail female ego) may stare at her out of curiosity, with pity. Men admire her. They will also keep her in mind—pleasantly—or seek her out to discover if she is as nice as she looks.

About your social skills. Bridge, I am told, is the great social common denominator, and the ability to play an adequate game is a must for a single woman. On the other hand, being able to play bridge, unless you are genuinely made for it, can be a trap. A New Orleans widow told me, "I rather like bridge. But when I looked around and saw the women alone who fill their lives with it, I decided no. At home, I told the avid bridge groups I hated it, I had always played just to please my husband. When I go away, if I see cards coming, I just say blandly I don't know a thing about them."

Dancing is another vital skill. As a wife, I found any husband who danced well was slightly suspect; I figured he was going off to a discothèque with some young tiger-cat. Wives remember the days when they loved to dance; husbands tend to lose interest as time goes on—certainly in dancing with their wives. But the odd thing is that, once more a bachelor, the man rediscovers dancing. He often takes dancing lessons and goes on dancing trips and cruises.

A woman alone may find herself in an entirely different world when she starts to recirculate after being married. Dancing is an important adjunct of nearly every get-acquainted affair, whether it is a church, a nonprofit organization, or one that is in it strictly for the door receipts. If you have lost your touch, if you feel rusty or are tense and anxious when you try to dance, a few lessons may help.

The advertised dancing lessons are very much with us, too much with us, in some cases. Some of them also provide social evenings at various hotels, as well as the regular dancing parties in the studios. Others promote dancing trips. A widower cousin of mine went on one of these out of Washington, D.C., to Mexico, and had a fine time. But there will tend to be more women than men in these groups and, as always, it is the eager little blonde early bird who will capture the desirable man, and hang onto him—hard. I have also heard complaints that the pressure to take more lessons and to sign up for trips is so intense that you spend more time arguing than learning to dance. In some cases, unscrupulous teachers make a point of mixing you up deliberately so that you need to keep taking lessons.

Strictly speaking, from the outside, it seems to me that it would be wise to sign up for only a few lessons in advance, and to quit if the pressure gets strong. It is also a good idea not to sign any contract without the advice of your lawyer, for I know of a number of cases where women have been tricked into putting their names on long-term contracts.

I am told that not all schools operate in this manner. But I know of at least two, both national and well-known, that emphasize pressure. Unless you are very sure of yourself, the YWCA or YMCA classes might be a safer starting point. I also know of dance halls, where women and men go separately, that feature lessons as part of their programs.

Like bridge experts, serious ballroom dancers live in a world of their own. Wherever they go, they recognize others and make friends easily. It is a way of life, which includes contests, different styles of dancing, and studios in various cities where a woman alone can go and feel welcome. This might be a good way to meet men, if you are interested in having a spouse who will waltz you through your golden years.

On the other hand, the discothèque type of dancing takes little skill but lots of stamina. You do not need to follow; on a crowded floor, you hardly seem to be dancing with your partner. All you really need to do is relax your inhibitions, and it is fine exercise. Just what the doctor ordered for those heart muscles.

About party manners. Almost the worst thing a woman alone can do is talk too much. If you are too scared to peep, you at least do not annoy anyone except yourself. But talking is a form of disease; the more you talk, the more impossible it is to keep still. You even grow to resent other people who try to say anything. Talking too much can be caused by nervousness. I have also heard it said that women who are alone a great deal begin to babble in company just because they do not often have the chance to communicate. Having observed the habit, however, I can only say it is an absolutely sure way to make yourself widely unpopular.

A Minneapolis woman, a recent widow, caught herself chattering and consulted her doctor. He suggested that she take a tranquilizer before she went out. Tranquilizers are not the universal answer; they have to be given by prescription, and they don't mix with alcohol or with driving. Just listening to yourself might work as well.

A woman who enters a party and begins to complain about her ex-husband can ruin it. "Give me a widow anytime," a realistic hostess told me, after she had entertained such a divorcee for an evening. "She at least still has some social confidence."

Under emotional stress, either lady can be a pain. The widow, in her quiet way, can weep and depress the whole party under the table. If this happens, it is the better part of wisdom for the lady to get up and go home and call the next day and apologize. In grief, there is a role for tears. But you wear out your welcome if you abuse the privilege in public. Of course it is better to weep or curse your ex than to try to find peace and forgetfulness in the bottle.

In the suburbs or country, having your own car is an asset; then you can leave alone if you are not having a good time, and you miss the torrid passes. In cities, you may feel you need a man to help you catch a cab. I used to. Now I have become so competent that even if I have an escort, I am apt to dash out in front of him and flag the taxi before he knows it is there. (Not really recommended.)

Last spring in Hong Kong, I had an experience that completely blocked out any hesitation I might have had before about going home alone. I was staying at the Peninsula Hotel in Kowloon, on the mainland. In order to get to the island of Hong Kong, you take a ferry. It seemed reasonable to me when I was invited to parties in Hong Kong in the early evening, before dinner, that I take the ferry and arrive alone. But when I also found out that I was expected to go home alone, I was astonished. In one case, my host rushed out of a fashionable Chinese restaurant and flagged down a cab, giving instructions about reaching the ferry in Chinese. In another, my escort simply left me at the ferry, after a peck on the cheek.

Obviously, there was no problem getting home. The midnight ferry was crowded with nicely dressed people also returning from parties, and I had a great deal of company walking back the few short blocks to my hotel. But I was a bit mystified—until I posed the problem to a British divorcee who was living in Kowloon.

"Oh dear me," she said. "I'd be very nervous if a man took me home on the ferry—it would mean he expected to be invited in and would try to spend the night. We women always go home alone. It's perfectly safe and we prefer it."

About entertaining. You may be ashamed of your apartment, or think it isn't adequate for the kind of entertaining you want to do. You may fear that, without your husband, no one will be interested in accepting your invitations. You may, and with good reason, feel you have lost your touch in cooking.

Some women will not try to cook for anyone except themselves. This means that, if they entertain, they must do so in a restaurant or a club. A club is more graceful, because a woman can sign the check, to which tips have or can be added. A woman with a full flush of credit cards can do the same thing in a restaurant, or she can arrange that the bill be sent to her, or even pay a certain amount in advance. An old friend—or a male relative—can be given money to pay the check, and be reimbursed later if it wasn't adequate. I also know one lady who slips her billfold into the pocket of the man she has selected as her escort, whether she knows him well or not, and asks him to do the honors.

But it is cheaper and more relaxed if you can bring yourself to having guests at home. Unless you are going to the theater, or on to another party, it is also more comfortable. And, once you are over the first hurdle of entertaining without a host, it is not as difficult as you feared. You may be a little ill at ease. So it will take some of the sting out of the occasion if you have an excuse for the party: someone's birthday, an old friend in town, an anniversary, a new job.

People will come, at first out of kindness; you are being encouraged to stand on your own feet. Later, your parties have to stand on their feet. Someone has said that if you have good food and liquor, you don't need to worry. I think you also have to have an entertaining mixture of people, and not have the same old faces, even if you are under obligation. One or two surprises are all you need, one or two strange faces. They may belong to some of your new women friends—and their escorts.

Two women in Bloomfield Hills, Michigan, who are entertained a great deal tell me that they pay it back each year with a really spectacular tea dance (featuring drinks) at the country club. Where a party is lavish enough and talked about for a long time, this is almost enough. I know one New York executive who each year gives a big St. Patrick's party. Although she does entertain from time to time in between, she hardly needs to, because this party is such a smash. And a widow I met, who lives in New England, is famous for the tremendous Fourth of July lawn festival she gives around her swimming pool. It takes a lot of planning, for she often has two hundred guests, but it is one of the great events of the year. In a college town I met three women who band together to rent a hotel ballroom and give a big Christmas party. The unfortunate result, it seems to me, is that all during the holidays and after, these three are invited to other places as a trio. Last year, they went to Europe together, too; perhaps they have become resigned, but it seems a bit too much togetherness. Despite the fact that it is easier to have another woman share the planning and the expense—and the hostess worries about success —doing it all on your own is braver and better. And here you can call on your married friends to help.

When having a small dinner or drink party, without hired help, some women ask a man friend to fix the drinks. This can be an excuse for inviting a bachelor you like. I think this is a shade possessive, for it puts him on display as a substitute host. Most drink-mixing is so simple that you need no skills. Unless it is too complicated for you to be greeting guests and performing introductions and mixing drinks, I would say that a hostess should start out tending bar, and then let men volunteer to help her.

A divorcee in Detroit told me, "I can't afford to belong to a country club, so I do my entertaining at home. I'm not equipped to give big dinners. But once in a while I have as many as twenty people for brunch; you don't have to make it formal, and some of them sit on the floor. I also give cocktail parties for out-of-town guests, which gives me an opportunity to invite people who might like to know them—people I wouldn't otherwise ask to the house. Very often these people ask me back and it makes a pleasant change."

Giving a brunch has several advantages. It fills what otherwise can be a grim Sunday, and you can invite a mixture of guests who do not know each other. The cooking is easy and the drink-mixing, if you serve the traditional Bloody Marys, can be done in advance. You may also be able to snag popular bachelors who are busy in the evenings.

A real estate woman in Evanston tells me that when she is feeling ambitious she makes several casseroles and freezes them so if the mood is on her she can ask friends to drop in for dinner. A divorcee in the suburbs gives spur-of-the-moment poker parties; the refreshments offered are coffee, beer, and, at the conclusion, cold cuts and cheese from the delicatessen. Sunday night suppers of soup and salad are a speciality of a suburban widow with young children. They are inexpensive, because the food is cheap and the consumption of liquor tends to be small, after a big Saturday night. And they give her and the children something to look forward to. A single woman who free-lances and works at home, has drop-in cocktail parties twice a week, where a certain circle of friends are always welcome. In addition, she sends out cards to others. This is a good way, she says, to include men she has met casually and would like to see again.

At a sitdown dinner, it is customary to have a balanced number of men and women. This can present problems for a single woman, if she does not have one or two reliable bachelors to whom she is obligated. Rather than invite a stranger, experienced women alone tell me they prefer to have an uneven number.

Big parties can, of course, be much more casual. It is a nice gesture to include some of your single women friends at these, which means you will ask all the unattached males you know, and some who are only casual acquaintances. The principle is fine, but be prepared for what may happen. For many women alone, the only opportunity they may have to meet men is at parties. Consequently, no matter how charming and considerate they may be at other times, they come into all parties like man-eating tigresses. Just recently I heard a girl say to her hostess, also single, "Don't bother to introduce me. Just point out the single men."

Of course, if you have a beau who is fairly faithful, he may have already been exposed to so many women that this will not bother him. On the other hand, you do invite certain fundamental risks. I heard about a Christmas party, given by a Miss G., the copy chief of a large Chicago advertising agency. (Miss G. is a widow of some years, and a very forceful blonde.) One of her copywriters, Jean H., had just been through a painful divorce and Miss G. was being of great help to her. Part of her therapy was coming to the party.

Jean H. did not have a very good time, so she left early. As she was getting her coat, a young man she had noticed asked if he could take her home. Since she lived only two blocks up the drive, she explained she did not need an escort. He said he was leaving anyway, so he walked along with her. She had hardly reached home, leaving the young man at the door, when she had a furious call from Miss G. The young man in question had been a new beau, and she accused Jean of stealing him. Jean tried to explain how innocent it had been, and that they had made no future engagements. It did no good. She was permanently in Miss G.'s Black Book and eventually she had to get another job.

Some women alone have no social lives—by choice. One told me that after living a frantic life with children and jobs and in-laws, she relishes being by herself.

Most of us, however, need people. And you cannot sit facing four walls and expect the telephone to ring. A priest told me that he had a call from a woman who was doing just that, after being divorced for seven months. She said, "People are talking about me." Actually, the priest told me, they were not; they had forgotten all about her.

The president of a large women's organization said that many of the women, particularly the widows she encountered, were lonesome simply because they expected things to be done for them, instead of doing them for other people. This busy, energetic president would take time off from her many affairs to suggest various activities, only to be told by the lonesome ones that YWCA work, charity activities, going to adult education courses were "not for them."

People who are doing nothing do not get talked about; they are not interesting enough. And just by doing, not by having something done for you, a woman grows, matures, and becomes more interesting. I found any number of women who told me that when they were left alone, either through death or divorce, they had no friends at all outside their husbands' contacts. Some of them had young children, which imposed a greater burden. For these women, there are singles groups, church organizations, political organizations, civil rights, and the like: "I'd rather die than go to anything like that," one woman told me. "I'd rather sit in a bar."

The trouble is, women who feel like this do not sit in bars, either. They grow in on themselves, until they don't have contacts even with other women. Staying home can become a habit, such a bad habit that you resent, rather than welcome, intrusions.

A divorcee who goes through occasional periods like this will pick up the telephone and say to a friend, "Come and see me. I'm afraid I'm getting invisible."

You can also begin to feel very sorry for yourself when you are too much alone. And that is even worse than having people feel sorry for you, which must be taken with a pinch of salt and a large grin. I am thinking of a large engagement party that I attended recently, where I met a woman who first asked where my husband was and then said, "My, I think you are brave to come."

Perhaps she meant well. But there are women who do not, and the best thing a woman alone can do is take the drippings from their acid tongues as a compliment. Because they are either a bit afraid of us (consider this praise) or they envy us our freedom.

And once the shock of being husbandless has been absorbed, there are compensations. It is fun to be able to flirt a little with an attractive man at a party without worrying about a husband glowering in the background. There are nights when it is bliss to be able to go home and fall into bed alone and not give a damn about someone else's fatigue or comfort. Sometimes it is a relief not to have to account to a husband when you have made a mistake or done something stupid. Most of all, when I see a couple backing into one of those routine family back-biting arguments, I am glad I am free to jump into a taxi and leave it all behind me. And this, of course, is why wives are a little jealous of us.

A young widow from Florida told me, "I had to have a job after my husband died—it was a matter of economics. By luck, I managed to find one modeling and selling in a shop that catered to tourists. It was no joke. I had to leave the children with my mother and pick them up and fix dinner for them at night, when I was often too exhausted to eat myself. But because of the job, I had to pay attention to my looks, and spend more at beauty shops and on clothes (even with my discount) than I ever had in my life. And do you know what happened? The damned bitchy wives who used to be my good friends got jealous because I was leading such an exciting life while they were tied down to kids, PTA, stoves, and dull husbands. While I'd give anything to have those things back again."

I talked with a mature woman in California who had a similar experience. Shortly after Mrs. F.'s husband died, she went back to work running the public relations firm her husband owned. She hadn't been in business for twenty-one years and it wasn't easy. Her hours are long and her problems extensive; some of the men who had been hired by her husband have not been able to take her as a boss, and she has had to hunt for replacements. Her married daughter, Linda, lives with her husband, a college professor, in a California town some fifty miles away, and Mrs. F. has spent weekends with them and the children, but she has not been able to have them back very often because of her schedule.

One Friday night, however, she managed to cook dinner and invited some of the younger men from the office and their wives, and her daughter and son-in-law. Although the son-in-law had to leave early because of an eight o'clock class, Linda stayed overnight. The next morning, she wandered around the apartment restlessly until Mrs. F. asked what was wrong.

Linda said: "It doesn't seem fair. I feel as though you were the young one, having fun and meeting new interesting people. Ron and I see the same ones day after day. When I talk about taking some courses toward my doctor's degree, so that I at least won't stagnate, he reminds me how little Ron nearly drowned in a neighbor's pool last spring when I left him with a student while I went off to a graduate class. Does that mean I am going to be cooped up with the children until they are ready to go off and get married?"

Mrs. F. said to me: "I guess I forget how tied down I used to feel, not able to go places because of the children or because my husband was so tired. Now all that glorious uncomplicated life seems like heaven. I never know when I get up in the morning whether it will be one of those godawful dreary I-want-to-die days or whether it won't be so bad. I loathe this crazy mixed-up life. Yet my daughter would like to trade places with me."

All of us, married and single, have moments of desolation when we think the grass looks greener in the other pasture. There are compensations—not many, I grant you—in being alone. But, unless you are prepared to be alone permanently, and take bleak loneliness by the hand, you must have social contacts. And, as the ladies who know advise, you have to work at it, harder than any married woman.

A Connecticut widow: "About two months after John died, I received an invitation to a big wedding. I didn't want to go, and I told my sister. She said, 'Of course you can say no, and people will understand. But this is the time of decision. You either try to make a new life for yourself or you fall by the wayside.' I went—and to my surprise had a good time. Instead of avoiding me, people went out of their way to be nice."

A California divorcee: "Age makes no difference when it comes to having friends, and going out. Attitude does. I see some women whose horizons are so limited now they are alone that they have only two subjects—their children and 'poor me.' Both subjects get very dull after a few minutes. The woman who gets invited back has something to contribute, both in her house and in yours. You're sorry for the first kind, but you like the second. And the women who get repeat invitations are the ones who are likable."

5 WHERE THE MEN ARE

Our church has a young adult group. Once in a while one of the members will have a "Bring your own bottle" party for the singles. This is less humiliating than being invited to dinner by a married friend to meet somebody. You feel so much less in the market place because everyone is single.

NEBRASKA DIVORCEE

If you want to meet men—as most women do—a few friends will try to find dates for you, but mostly your married couples will say they don't know anyone good enough or nice enough and let it go.

MICHIGAN WIDOW

I asked about the Grosse Point chapter of Parents Without Partners and was told they were a bunch of snobs. I decided to go there because I wanted to meet snobs. I feel they are the ones who are hurting the most because they won't permit themselves to be pushy. I think when you give something of yourself anybody will respond.

DETROIT DIVORCEE

A widower in my building invited me to go to the show on Saturday night. I was pleased. Then I found out it was all he wanted to do, go to the movies on Saturday night, that one night. It got terribly dull and I gave up. So he started taking another girl. Now they go every Saturday night, I see them—except for one Saturday night when they were married. Then they went to the show on Friday night. She can have him.

FLORIDA WIDOW

If I knew how to meet men, I wouldn't be talking to you.

NEW YORK DIVORCEE

"ONE night about midnight I was lying in front of the fire, feeling sorry for myself. I'd been divorced two years, and after trying to make it in the city, moved back to our old house in the suburbs where the children had been born and I had friends. But so many people thought of me still in connection with Paul that they never asked anybody for me when they gave a party—I went alone and some couple took me home. The telephone rang and I jumped up, hoping for a miracle. But it was only a married friend. She asked me how I was and I was depressed enough to say, 'All you married girls must know at least two unattached men, or your husbands do. Why don't you think of me when you see them?' "

A divorcee who lives outside San Francisco is talking. She is thirty-two, the mother of three young children, and extremely attractive. She goes on, "An hour later, I was in bed when the telephone rang again. I was nearly asleep but I was glad to hear my friend's voice—she had somebody she wanted me to meet and made a dinner date for the next week. That was how I met a man I went with for six months. He and I weren't right for each other, but through him, I met a man who is—I hope."

The most pressing need of most women alone is to meet men. It does not matter whether the lady has matrimony in mind or simply likes male conversation or wants an escort. But it isn't easy. I know a beautiful actress, whose name is a household word, who was so painfully lonely for male companionship after her husband's death that she would invite the newspaper men who interviewed her to dinner. A chic divorcee from a prominent California family confessed that she picked up dates with some regularity in hotel lobbies when she came to New York. Others go to bars and restaurants and sit alone, hoping there will be a lonely man at the next table.

It is no fun, most of the time. It is often embarrassing. A go-getter widow I know has tried everything from night school to investment classes to bridge clubs and still has not found a husband. Many go into politics, do volunteer work at night. Others travel endlessly, restlessly; but a widow who admits she has "a lot of money" told me that the men who look good in Spain do not necessarily stand up so well when you get them back in the U.S.A. Lots of women join singles organizations or go to parties catering to singles. An appearance at such a function or club is tantamount to wearing a sign saying you are man-hunting, according to one women, but "at least you can be reasonably sure that the men you meet are eligible, not wolves on the prowl looking for a one-night stand."

Probably the best, and safest, way to meet men is through friends who know both of you. But it takes time for friends who knew you as part of a couple to stop associating you with your husband. It also takes time for wives to appreciate that you are lonely, that you want a replacement. Some think a woman alone —this goes for a divorcee as well as a widow—is "insensitive" to want to go out. Others decide she is still smarting over her loss, and will not be good company. One divorcee told me: "I will admit that when I was married, I didn't knock myself out to find men for single girls. In fact, I thought they were rather a nuisance. Now I know I must have married women on my side like mad, so I play the role of 'poor, pitiful Pearl' and tell them the celibate life is killing me."

A widow, living some two thousand miles removed from the divorcee but also in a suburban community, has a similar problem. "Soon after Gordon died, I was invited twice to dinner with single men—one was a bachelor who had been on the loose forever and is so attached to his ulcers he can't see females, and the other was a widower who made my flesh crawl; he even had awful table manners. After that, the wives decided I was hopeless and let it go at that. Once in a while, I'll ask my good friends if they know anyone I could meet and they'll say no, that is, nobody 'good enough for me.' I'll suggest mildly that I could be the judge, but nothing ever comes of it."

A single girl who is just over thirty wrote: "Let me, as a veteran, give you a rundown of the helpful wives. First, there is the married friend who invites you to dinner only when her husband

is out of town. Then there is the wife who apologizes for not inviting you because she 'just doesn't know any unattached men.' And
then there's the wife who does invite you, and you spend all evening fending off her husband's passes. Every time she leaves the
room, it is his cue to dash over and try to do a quick rape. A lot of
women know this, I'm sure, and figure it's better if it happens
under their noses. One even said to me, 'Oh, honey, don't be so
prudish. A little bit of sex will loosen you up.' "

Good friends keep you in mind, if they come up with what they
consider a presentable male. But many a wife enjoys having an
unattached man around, flattering her in un-husband-like ways,
and prefers to keep him for herself. Or, as a Kansas City divorcee
complained, "Of course, if you've made a pitch for help and some
wife scraped the bottom of the barrel and comes up with some
terrible creature, she blames you if you aren't grateful. Then you
have to apologize for being so choosy, and you blow that source of
men. But the end, the really bitter end, is when they produce one
of their single men and he gives a look and turns up his nose at
you. It's always your fault. Either you didn't make an effort, or
you put on the wrong dress, or you chewed gum. Or you wouldn't
go to bed with him."

Blind dates are hell. The woman arrives feeling as though she
is on the auction block and the man has a chip on his shoulder.
But they are necessary evils, and you never know when the most
unlikely friend will produce a smashing single man—who will go
for you. So you have to keep putting on a bright smile and trying.

An attractive man, a widower from the Midwest, described
how he met a widow he later married. "I got sick and tired of
having all my friends throw women at me. But I didn't do so well
on my own, either—a yachting magazine cruise produced only
married women and four old bachelors like myself, who played
bridge most of the time. So I decided to hell with it, I had my
dog, a good housekeeper who cooked well so I could entertain,
and my children and grandchildren. Then one day, when I was
going out to my boat in the dinghy, alone with the dog, a young
couple saw me and felt sorry for the lonely old guy. They invited
me to dinner with a widow they know—when I arrived, she was

sitting there with the canapes. I immediately decided she wasn't for me. The evening was pretty dull. Next day, I called my hostess to say thank you and, just to be polite, I called the widow, too, and asked her to go to the movies the next week. To my surprise, I found out that without an audience, we did much better. In fact, I found myself liking her a lot."

A Detroit woman told me: "Just last week, a client called, a sweet guy, and asked me to come to dinner at the Boat Club with him and his wife, adding, 'We've found a very nice man we'd like you to meet.' I suppose he was nice, but he was at least a foot shorter than I was, and we were both self-conscious. He didn't ask me to dance and I kept avoiding his eye for fear he'd feel he had to. It was a horrible evening. Maybe if I'd just met him at lunch, we wouldn't have minded the difference in height. But he felt stuck and so did I."

The alternative is to do-it-yourself, see what you can manage on your own. This is difficult, unless you are by nature an extrovert. (And even extroverts get tired of pushing themselves to attract the elusive male.) But at singles clubs, at church organizations, at dance groups, at parties that cater to singles, you can attend without feeling like a misfit. Everyone present is lonely, and you can be sure that most of them are as ill at ease as you are—and some downright miserable.

Even if you do not meet men—which is the primary aim—you will have no trouble finding women who want company, and they may introduce you to their prospects—or discards. The only trap is in clinging to these organizations too long, in letting them become a substitute for a normal life or a normal relation to a man. One pretty Chicago divorcee summed it up: "For the first year, you are impaired, you don't belong with the rest of society. Then a singles group can be a crutch. You learn not to be so sorry for yourself, there are lots of people in the same fix and worse. But you can't lean on the crutch too long or you may become a permanent invalid. After a year and a half, not more than two years, throw away the crutch and return to the human race. Keep some of the new friends you made, but graduate to a new maturity."

The largest and best known of the singles organizations is Parents Without Partners, which has over thirty-five thousand members in three hundred chapters all over the United States. It is nonprofit and its purpose is to help single parents adjust to their new status. But it is more importantly a refuge for men and women who feel painfully alone—and want to meet people of the opposite sex. PWP holds conferences at regional and national levels, giving opportunities for members to travel, and meet single people from other areas. Besides group meetings and big dances, each chapter holds small affairs where you pay a fee at the door, bring your own bottle or (in the case of women) a hot dish, and mingle in an apartment or at the house of one of the members. These are less awkward because a hostess performs introductions, and conversation is more or less general. But you may get stuck at a party where there is a massive surplus of women—plenty of hot dishes and few bottles and no chance to get near the rare man who has turned up.

Church and YWCA "over thirty" clubs also divide into splinter groups for Christmas parties, nights out for widows and widowers only, fancy dress parties. They try to balance the sexes by accepting the first fifteen women and the first fifteen men who call, but the rub there is that sometimes fifteen men do not call, and the hostess is left with many more women than men. On the other hand, an imbalance with more men than women is even more deadly, because the men will withdraw and play cards or talk sports, leaving the few women to spread their feathers in vain.

A friend from the Peace Corps who was stationed in Central Africa, in an area where there were at least five men to every woman, told me, "After one party, the girls discovered they had to import girls or they would never get any attention . . . the gathering degenerated into a stag party with the females on the outside, onlookers."

The best way to meet men, and have first chance at the most attractive males, is to give the splinter-group party yourself. As hostess, you can circulate and you are supposed to make advances. The worst way is to go with another woman. Of course it gives you confidence, and if you have made plans in advance, her presence keeps you from changing your mind at the last minute. But where singles are concerned, two is a crowd. Men may come in pairs, or even clusters, but as soon as they enter a singles party, they separate, and prowl on their own. Two girls sitting on the sidelines will not be approached, whereas a single girl, sitting at a table smiling, or standing near the dance floor looking not too forlorn, will be.

Except among young people, who treat singles parties casually, there is a natural reluctance about admitting the need to attend. A Minneapolis executive of thirty-five, who has never been married, told me she wanted badly to meet new men but she would not dream of going to an organized single affair, "because I'd see my secretary." A man of fifty told me that he would not join PWP because "I wouldn't find any of the kind of girls I'm interested in." A divorcee a bit younger than he, and whom he has been taking out, said, "I've gone to PWP. The girls are nice but the men are drips. The attractive men don't need to go."

There can be an air of desperation about a singles party, I have to admit. I went cold to one, which advertised for formerly married men and women with college degrees—or the equivalent. It was held in a club on New York's East Side, from 7:00 to 10:30 on a Friday night. I went along about 7:30 and found a scattering of men and women sitting forlornly around the walls, with a record player struggling away at shades-of-1940 music. The men were World War II vintage, although some of the women were younger.

Admission was $3.50 each, with cookies and punch offered. There were few takers for the punch, and fewer takers for the alcoholic drinks which were being sold at $1.00 each. But the air was blue with cigarette smoke. Nerves, of course. One man, who was puffing like a steam engine himself, told me, "It takes courage for a woman to walk through that door. For she's admitting she hasn't a date on Friday night. Myself, I only drop by because I go to the executive health club at the YMCA every Friday evening."

Mrs. Ellie Bragar, who started the group and was on the door taking money, told me to introduce myself, but I was the only woman who did. Most of them were sitting in pairs, chatting too brightly to each other. After my little circle of the two rooms, shaking hands, I ended with a widower from Brooklyn, who asked me to dance.

As we went around the floor, with one or two other couples joining in, he told me he was a pharmacist from Brooklyn and his wife had died last year. His children were grown, so he was hoping to get married again, or at least find some congenial girls at the party. He was such a likely prospect for someone else that, after about fifteen minutes, I suggested we introduce ourselves to other people. Afterward I noticed him dancing with several quite pretty girls. But I made the mistake of accepting an invitation to sit down beside a man on the couch. He told me he was a stock broker; two seconds afterward I found I was stuck with a compulsive talker.

I couldn't stop him long enough to excuse myself. Later, Mrs. Bragar told me I should have said, "Sorry, I came here to meet people," or, failing that, simply have smiled and walked away. I didn't have the know-how. After what seemed like hours, and was probably closer to an hour, I fled in the middle of a sentence.

By this time, the party was livelier. There was so much conversation you could not hear the music and quite a few people were dancing. Mrs. Bragar told me she had nearly seventy customers, up over the last affair. She also told me she keeps the ratio of men and women even by inviting four times as many men as women. Women pay $5.00—if they are accepted in the club—just to get mailings of events. Men get the mailings without paying. "It's the way life is," Mrs. Bragar said.

Leaving, I met two women standing outside. They asked me if they should go in. I said honestly that it was fairly lively and, in answer to their question, that there were about as many men as women. "Then why are you leaving?" one girl asked sharply. A little apologetically, I explained about the compulsive talker. They agreed the only thing I could do was to leave, and they went in, paying $3.50 each for the hour that was left.

The next Friday night, Mrs. Bragar suggested I might be interested in one of the smaller meetings. Discarding groups featuring bridge lessons and ensemble singing, I joined a "discussion group" in the home of an engineer at London Terrace, a large apartment compound on the West Side of Manhattan.

There were eight of us—seven women and our host. Although we waited an hour before starting, drinking coffee in paper cups and eating cinnamon buns which Mrs. Bragar had brought (door fee, $1.00), no men turned up besides our host. This was the first time for three of the women and Mrs. Bragar described the social evenings (like the Friday one I had attended), adding, "Don't worry about coming alone. There's always a first time for everyone. And don't take a negative attitude. Expect to have a good time and wear your prettiest dress."

The discussion subject was Jonah, on which our host had done his thesis. I was more interested than I expected. The seven other ladies seemed fascinated and would have gone on talking all night (about Jonah and then about Being Alone and Men and Sex) but our host glanced at his watch and said it was getting late, 11:30. When six of us got out on the street (Mrs. Bragar stayed behind to help clear up) there wasn't a taxi in sight. The rest were going either to New Jersey or Long Island, taking the subway. I did not feel particularly eager to take the West Side subway to Times Square, and then shuttle across to the East Side, that late at night, so I waited for a bus. The bus never came but eventually a taxi picked me up. The driver asked, "What are you doing all alone over here?" Frankly, I was beginning to wonder myself.

Now that I have done more research, I realize that I had the typical "first time" reaction and that, as a widow, I was also running true to type, being less willing to participate and enter into things than the divorcees. It may take several visits before you feel comfortable. But if you are painfully lonesome and need contact with other people in the same situation, these various clubs and singles parties can be helpful.

A Rutherford, New Jersey, widow said: "I was so humiliated at the idea of having to find companionship that way that I went to my first meeting of PWP in New York, rather than the suburbs, and to my surprise I met two nice men. They didn't want anything more of me than friendship and a dancing partner. In fact, one warned me against a man at the party who had the reputation of a wolf. I really had a good time.

"At the recommendation of the second man, I went to a Valentine party in the suburbs, and he introduced me around, I had a ball—I felt like a young girl. Of course I love to dance, and that was part of it, and I made sure to leave early and alone. I don't think I'd be interested in marrying anyone I've met, but it is nice to hear the telephone ringing and be asked out to dance. It could happen to anyone, I am sure, for I'm no chicken—I have three big teenage sons."

The woman who is a good dancer and obviously enjoys it has an advantage at these social gatherings. Other women are happier at singles gatherings that focus on bridge, or on sports events. But the whole trick is to participate, not to hang in the background.

One of the most admirable—and likely to succeed—women I met is a fitter for a big Detroit department store. She said, "As a woman alone, you have to be extroverted. I was so strictly brought up I wouldn't even dance with a friend of my husband's, if my husband weren't there. I heard about PWP when I was fitting one of my customers for a dinner dress; she was going to wear it at one of the parties. I hadn't gone out once since my divorce because I didn't know any men.

"I asked about PWP in Grosse Point and was told they were a bunch of snobs. I decided that was for me, because I could help snobs. Snobs are the ones who are hurting the most because they won't permit themselves to be pushy. I think when you give something of yourself, anybody will respond.

"I have worked with widows and divorcees at the store a great deal and observed how they act. I've come from complete withdrawal, such as that dancing incident, to being fairly outgoing. My hurt when I discovered my husband had another woman was bitter, but I said to myself, all my life I have given every effort to my marriage. I was a good wife but didn't fulfill what he wanted. And what I have left, after all those years and two grown sons, somebody else may want.

"My first trial experience was at a 'thirty and up' dance at the YWCA. You should have seen me—I sneaked into the lobby feeling like a lost cat and there was a man looking just as miserable as I felt. So I spoke first, asking him if he was going to the dance. He was so delighted I spoke to him that now I'm always the one who speaks first. The only problem is—you'll find these men so grateful you will have a hard time getting rid of them to meet anyone else."

Some women will never fit into these organizations. At one Midwestern singles meeting, a widow who had been brought by a divorcee neighbor spent most of the discussion period in the washroom being sick. Yet a widow who is now president of a church group of "mature singles" told me, "It took me two years before I would attend a meeting of the club, although my pastor kept inviting me. Even when I did, I kept thinking of the other people as different from me, as 'they.' One night, when I was hurrying out as usual after the talk, not waiting for the social period, a man said to me, 'Are you too good for the rest of us?' First I was mad, then it set me to thinking. I wasn't any different from the rest; if anything I was lonelier because I was afraid to mingle. Now I have found that by being nice to other people who are shy, I've overcome my own timidity."

A divorcee from the North Shore of Chicago who teaches bridge at a Senior Citizen's Club told me, "We all crave affection. Many men who are alone really don't want to get married—they just want attention, somebody being nice to them. I don't want to remarry; I'm too old. But I do want friends. And by giving affection, and interest—which is all I really do in the bridge lessons— I feel important, wonderful, needed."

A New York divorcee told me, "My husband left me for another woman. It undermined my confidence. Some of the girls at the office go to a restaurant where singles pick each other up and dance. I told them I wouldn't dream of going, I was too well brought up. 'You mean scared,' one of the girls said. And I said yes, I guess I was scared. Just admitting that helped me. The next week I went, and some of the girls fixed me up with dances. I haven't met anybody I really like, but this gives me something to do on Friday. And once in a while when I see a woman alone and looking like she wants to escape, I go over and sit with her, and introduce her around. I've met some very nice ladies that way."

Any new experience is an adventure, and any first time—from the first day in kindergarten to your first entrance alone in a social gathering after having lost a husband—is rough. But it is a way to get started. Once you learn the ropes and know your way around, nothing is quite so hard. You don't need to join clubs if you don't want to, or if you really feel you wouldn't fit in. But, unless you have something better to try, don't knock them. They serve their purpose. For the woman who wants to meet men cannot sit home, as one of them told me, "and wait for someone in a white Cadillac to ring the doorbell." She has to expose herself.

There are other do-it-yourself ways to meet new men, of course. Some of them work, some do not. A divorcee told me, "I took a course in stocks and bonds, hoping to meet a rich man. The only people there were silly old ladies and decrepit men in their dotage. Then I volunteered to be on the reception committee at my club. I went to one meeting, and was never invited again. I don't think there is anything I haven't tried, from collecting funds for charity to taking adult education courses. The only men I've had passes from are those I meet on the street, and I'm afraid to encourage them."

Once in a while, you meet a nice man in the most unexpected place. You can't count on it, however, so many women take the precaution to go only to places which interest them (the same goes for courses or fund soliciting). But you sometimes hit the jackpot unexpectedly.

A Massachusetts widow of seven years wrote me, "Last year I got an invitation to my husband's reunion, saying they were inviting all the widows. I was horrified at the idea and laughed when my son suggested that I go. Finally, I went, just to satisfy him. And I met a widower, a classmate of my husband's whom I am marrying next month. You'd never believe I could meet a nice man at a Harvard reunion, but I did."

Shortly after that, I heard of the widow of a prominent Princeton alumnus who had married a widower in her husband's class.

She told me, dimpling a bit, that she made it a point to continue to have Open House on Saturdays after football games, and to send particularly warm little notes of invitation to the men she knew who were widowers or divorced.

All these efforts take patience, courage, and a faith in your own luck, which will get you started and keep you going. As an Oklahoma widow put it, "It's simply a matter of exposure. Most of the time you'll be bored witless. The men you meet are such awful jerks you are happy to go home alone and double-lock the door. But once in a while, when you least expect it, you will go someplace, and there will be a real nice man."

An Idaho woman told me, "I had invitations to visit several old friends after my husband died. Each time, just as I was packing, I would get sick. Once I decided I couldn't go because it was my little granddaughter's first birthday. Then my sister said to me, 'Remember Mother after Dad died? She would get dressed to go someplace and then have such violent hot flashes you and I used to have to pull her clothes off and put her to bed.' Suddenly it dawned on me I was doing the same thing. I determined I wasn't going to hide behind the menopause or my grandchildren. Much as I dread starting out by myself, I do it. After you have made an effort, you feel better, have a certain pride in yourself. I even talk to men in planes. On a recent trip, I met a young man who invited me out to dinner the next night. I was old enough to be his mother, but I decided if he didn't care, I didn't. So I went and had a very good time and he seemed to enjoy himself, too."

A widow whom I remember as one of the prettiest girls in college told me, "If a widow is in an environment where she has lived many years and where she and her husband had become associated with a group of friends, she will continue to fit in and not feel so much like a fifth wheel. But if she has lived in many places and has to decide which one she should return to alone, it is much harder.

"She will find that while all her friends in whatever place she selects will be wonderful to her, she will not really be a part of any husband-and-wife group. It's a whole different life, being alone. Children (and grandchildren) help a great deal, but they will respect you more, as well as appreciate you, if you go your own way. A woman with a job or hobby is fortunate. If not, it seems to me that the best way is to do the things that have always interested you, and you were not able to do before.

"I returned to my home town, where I soon realized I didn't fit as I had thought I would. The weekends and holidays were terrible. I'm not a party-giver or one for great groups of people. I didn't like to be taken by friends or to go alone, so soon I wasn't going at all. Of course that was my fault.

"I thought it over and decided what I wanted to do most was travel, so I rented my house and went to Europe. That put me on my feet. When I went home, I didn't care so much what my friends were doing. I knew I could get along by myself and I also had more respect for myself. After seeing some other women alone, I also learned to count my blessings, that I had so much to be thankful for."

Shortly after she returned from one of her trips she met a widower she married—she met him at dinner, at the home of an old friend. She added, "I doubt if I would have attracted him if I had met him earlier. I was too miserable, too sorry for myself."

Travel is a way of exposing yourself, particularly if you feel you have exhausted the possibility of meeting an eligible man in your community. But, although you hear about women going in pairs to places like Bermuda and Miami Beach and meeting men who were lonesome, and single, the chances in a resort area tend to be slim, and the competition is fierce.

A friend who has a house in Mexico wrote me, "Widows and divorcees by the carload—and the troubles they have. A kook of some sixty years, a widow whom we've got to know since she moved here full time, aimed to marry a nice improvident piano player in Mexico City half her age. That fell through, so she now plays bridge all the time. Last year we knew a very handsome feckless bright crazy painter, who was living with a beautiful young woman. She left him, which meant he was the only eligible male in town. Competition was incredibly savage for his favors. Six good single-type lady friends all fell out and became bitter enemies, competing. . . . There's another local breed of female alone, too; foreign usually, with shops or night clubs or some kind of business, bright, capable, good-looking, all divorced, all looking for men—they can't live with them or without them."

Dancing clubs, sailing, sports of all kinds, bird-watching, even walking clubs can give you a chance to meet men; attractive men, perhaps, if you're lucky. Some of these activities take no money at all, or very little—a well-known radio commentator, a divorcee, met the man she's been dating regularly not in her job but on the public tennis court one Sunday afternoon.

A New York divorcee, separated from an art teacher, tells me she has met several interesting men, whom she continues to see, at museums. Her knowledge of art, gained from her husband, enables her to make intelligent comments if she spots an attractive man, also alone. Music can also be a wedge. A pretty divorcee, coming cold to New York after she left her husband, found a group of friends by taking guitar lessons at a YMCA. A married friend from Pennsylvania, who plays the recorder, told me she has introduced several single girls to an attractive man she met at one of the local recorder sessions. None of these introductions worked out; he married a girl he met at a recorder convention in New Orleans and he is now president of the local club, while she is secretary.

I understand that romances sometimes develop between serious dog fanciers who travel from place to place showing and, eventually, judging. Like bridge, this is not for the dilettante; dogs or games have to be a reward in themselves if you do not happen to meet anyone you like.

There are also the vast networks of computer "meet your mate" services, dating bureaus, advertised singles parties. The dating bureaus and marriage clubs are, in my experience, suspect. They often charge high fees and prey on unsophisticated people. The commercial singles parties for "over thirty" are respectable, per se; but they can be painfully dull. Even as a spectator, I found an hour too long to spend at most of them. As for the computer dating services, which started as a joke among young people, I can only say from outside observation that they are fine for young people, and for a gag. Taken seriously by older people, they are not funny and the results are even less amusing. Some of these cost considerable money; while these may be more accurate than the $3.00 or $5.00 questionnaires, they seem to me to be infinitely more depressing. The value of the computers is in the light-hearted, tongue-in-cheek approach.

My informants report that there are many lonesome men, that men's clubs are filled with men drinking and eating alone, night after night. Are these the men who are so conditioned by mothers —and wives—to having things done for them that they can't make an effort? Perhaps. It also could be that these men, after a while, come to the point where it is too much of an effort to go out even when they are invited.

I do believe that men, on the whole, are less brave about accepting adversity and making an effort to build a new life than women. They often take the easy way out—marrying the first woman who attracts them. I was told that (1) they complain more than women; (2) they feel sorrier for themselves; (3) they are less disciplined about grieving for a dead wife or complaining about a live ex-wife; and (4) they bury themselves in drink and lost weekends after a severe blow, instead of fighting back.

Some men want to remarry quickly—or think they do. (They have young children, they hate eating in restaurants, they don't like sleeping in an unmade bed.) With a man like this, you have to be conditioned to fast moving and fast thinking—getting him before the widow next door has him tied up and persuading him to hang on until you make up your mind whether or not you want him on a permanent basis.

A widow in New York met an attractive widower at the home of her lawyer. He drove her home, from Central Park West to her apartment on Park Avenue and Thirty-sixth Street. In the course of the drive, which took about twenty minutes, he told her: "I plan to get married again . . . you are under consideration if you do not object to my being Jewish . . . I have two married daughters but one, who is eighteen, would live with us . . . I am an enthusiastic golfer and would expect you to play, also, or allow me to spend my weekends and holidays playing." In front of her apartment, he parked the car, kissed her, and ordered, "Say yes or no."

She was in such a state of shock she said no; now she regrets not having temporized, because she liked him. But she has not had the courage to make contact again.

A divorcee with three boys from Nebraska told me, "The first man I dated was a widower, whose wife had died of a brain tumor about three months before. We'd been out four or five times and he proposed. I said I didn't know him well enough and he said, 'I want you to know one thing—you've had your chance and muffed it.' I just gasped at him. But he never called me again, and I read in the newspaper that he had married a widow. Their combined six children went on the honeymoon to Florida with them."

If you are uninhibited about hunting men, here are some other methods I heard about. Several women admitted that they attended meetings of Alcoholics Anonymous, pretending to have alcohol problems; but they warned me that ladies on the prowl should be careful to select chapters in better neighborhoods, where men supposedly have incomes or still can earn good salaries. There are also women who follow the obituaries and write letters of condolence, whether they know the men or not; I heard of a lady investor whose letters caught the chairman of the board of a big company while he was still presumably bereaved. I met a widow with a master's degree in English who took a job as a waitress in a Wall Street restaurant catering to men. (Unfortunately, she gave it up before she met anyone interesting; it was too hard on her feet.) I also talked to a divorcee who told me that she and another pretty woman alone went to bars of hotels where there were conventions. So far, their high spot was a medical convention of psychiatrists; there she met a doctor she still sees when he comes to Chicago.

Of course any woman on such a kick is taking chances. The clubs and singles dances are strictly policed, brightly lighted, and sufficiently dull so that a man who wants quick action does not patronize them too often. But a woman who picks up a man at a bar, or in a restaurant, or who writes to him blind, can invite unpleasant experiences. I won't say she will always have a bad time, or that occasionally true love won't result from a pickup. (A widow told me she picked up her future husband on a train; now he refuses to admit that even to himself, telling people they were introduced by mutual friends.)

A beautiful divorcee in Los Angeles reports that the men she met in restaurants are much pleasanter and less demanding than the ones she is introduced to by her friends. For example, she cites an experience she had with a doctor friend-of-a-friend who came in for a nightcap, and beat her up when she refused to go to bed with him. A divorced singer agreed, saying that a "charming" lawyer, whom she had met at a cocktail party given by mutual friends, invited her out to dinner the following week. After he took her home he became so obnoxious that she grabbed her door keys and ran next door to her neighbor's, where she hid by the window until she saw him leave.

The Los Angeles divorcee has a pick-up technique that she shared with me. When a stranger approaches her on the street or in a restaurant (she does not go to bars alone), she gives him her telephone number and her first name. If he calls (and he usually does because she is that beautiful), she meets him for a drink, or a cup of tea, far from her home. Sometimes she insists on seeing a man several times before she gives him a date, ". . . and I think that I am a pretty good judge of character."

"My mother would be revolving in her grave if she knew," the divorcee told me. "I don't tell my friends, either. I simply turn up at parties with a new man once in a while and the other gals alone wonder how I can get so lucky. And what's so wrong about it? I see the man before I date him, which is more than women do with their blind dates arranged by friends. And I talk to him long enough when I meet him so I can catch anything which might be peculiar. What's so different with going out with a man who sits next to you in a restaurant and one you meet on a plane?"

She sounded so logical and so pleased with her social life that I was impressed, in spite of the horror expressed by some of my more conservative woman friends—women alone, also. But some months afterward, on a business trip to New York, the Los Angeles divorcee told me of an incident that had rather changed her attitude.

She was alone during the long Labor Day weekend, clearing up some details at her buying office. One evening, too tired to fix dinner for herself, she went around the corner to an air-conditioned restaurant . . . "terribly respectable, almost a tearoom. It was late and the place was almost empty. I noticed a man eating alone, but he wasn't that attractive so I paid no attention.

"I finished my dinner and, when I ordered coffee, a brandy came with it. The waitress said the gentleman across the room had sent it. I nodded at him and he got up and asked if he could join me with his drink. He explained he was in town because of the illness of his sister, and that he had just left the hospital. I knew the hospital, I even knew his sister's doctor. When he asked to drive me home, I said no, I had my car. But he asked if he could take me to dinner the next night and I agreed. He seemed so harmless. I still wasn't attracted very much, but I was lonesome and bored.

"He took me to dinner the next night, and then to another place where we danced a little. About midnight, I suggested we should go home, as I had to work the next day. He drove me home without a murmur, then asked if he could come in and borrow a magazine he'd seen on my coffee table. I never suspected he would be nasty . . . but in the apartment, he turned into a wild man. And when I told him he'd have to get out or I'd call the building manager (which I hate to do, especially at that hour), he said, 'How can you treat me this way after all the money I've spent on you?'

"I happened to have nearly a hundred dollars in my purse. I told him I'd give it to him if he would leave and grabbed the purse (my doorkeys were in it) and ran outside. He followed me and I gave him the money in the corridor and watched him walk down the stairs before I got back to my apartment. It was an expensive lesson, but it taught me there is something to be said for a dull social life."

There are many women who have had no bad experiences—or

good ones, either—because they hesitate to take any chances at all. They have been taught that men are the aggressors, or should be; besides, it is much easier and less embarrassing not to make an effort. But it is also more boring. And one of the painful problems of being a woman alone is that, whatever happens, you have more time to brood than if you had a husband. A telephone call, an invitation, puts you on Cloud Nine; a disappointment, even a tiny one, can color a whole day—black.

A vivacious blonde, a widow, said, "You can't stop because you are tired. You have to take a deep breath, and try a new tactic when something goes wrong. Men, nice men, aren't horrified at being chased a little. It tickles their vanity. Of course, you have to be a little inventive—say you've had theater tickets given to you, or would like advice on some decorating problem, or on some china you are thinking of buying. Some men are such slow starters they need to be prodded into action. And if you're rejected, just scratch the gent in question off. As for the man who gets the wrong idea and thinks you are on the make—honey, tell him off in no uncertain terms. And don't let a man in your home when you're alone unless you are pretty sure he won't cause trouble—or you have a friend alerted to telephone and check on you."

Sometimes you are sure to sit back and wonder why this is happening to you. But then you have to remind yourself that wanting to meet a nice man is a problem lots of women have . . . and it is the early bird who gets the man, no matter how many jokes and wisecracks are made.

It is funny—sometimes. It *is* funny when comedian Joan Rivers talks about the Queen Mother: "She's so cute. I saw her walking in front of Clarence House in her miniskirt. She's looking, you know. After all, she's a widow, the kids are all married now. They've all moved away—Meg, not far enough. Well, it's the old story; kings she wants don't want her. A king her age wants a younger queen. I told her to go to Miami. I said, 'Wear your crown, go sit on the beach, and believe me, you'll meet.' "

There is also the story which you may have heard about the widow going off on a cruise. She buys lots of clothes. All her family and friends come to say "Bon Voyage." They bring champagne. Corks pop, bands play, men and women laugh. Then the announcement comes: "All visitors ashore." Down the gangplank go all the men, leaving three hundred widows and divorcees to sail alone, with a few ship's officers.

The man who told me the cruise story vowed it was true. (The happy ending and moral was that one lady came back and married a man she met in the antique shop around the corner.) I personally know two women who boarded a cruise ship in Montreal and were so horrified by the shortage of men they got off, and sacrificed the money they had spent, when the ship touched New York on the way down the coast.

A widow in my neighborhood said, "I've been alone eleven years and have been on twenty-three cruises. When you dress up at night, you never know whether you are going to have fun or come back to your cabin and want to rip the dress off and throw it out the porthole."

A sense of humor can be salvation for the woman alone. So can the feeling that, uninteresting as your escorts are, lots of women have none, because they are too proud to fight.

A divorcee from Kansas City, a lady of seventy, came home from the movies one night and reported to her son that she had to slap her date's face three times . . . then added, "to keep him awake. He kept embarrassing me by snoring."

A Detroit widow ticked types off for me. "First there are the men who try to borrow money, subtly and not so subtly. And there are the men who have money themselves, but don't want to spend it on you, inviting you on picnics if you bring the food. And the ones who call up just at the moment you're ready to dish up dinner, hoping to be invited. And the ones who have money to take you out to good places but are so feeble you don't feel safe any farther away than the cafeteria at the corner.

"There are the men who make dates and don't show, the ones who take such care of themselves they cancel out at the first drop of rain, the brutes who lie because they have a better offer. *And* the double brutes who tell you they have a better offer, adding, 'You're such a good sport, you don't mind, do you?' "

Is it worth the effort?

The answer is up to you. For most of us, the consolation is that if you don't give up, you will know how to act with a man if a fascinating one should come along. And here we are not talking about remarriage. We are not even talking about falling in love. We are talking about males who are available, with faults and flaws to be sure, but who can add a modicum of spice to the life of a woman alone.

A Colorado widow was invited to dinner one evening by friends, to meet a widower from South Dakota, brother-in-law of the hostess. The widow said, "But I don't want to live in South Dakota." Her hostess said tartly, "I'm inviting you to dinner, I'm not arranging a marriage."

Of course the two fell in love and the widow moved off happily to South Dakota to live. Which proves whatever you want it to.

6 WHERE THE JOBS ARE

Women get anything they want with charm. When they turn aggressive, they rub me the wrong way. Their pushiness stems from men excluding them from the business or creative worlds.

NEW YORK MALE EXECUTIVE

The gals who sit home think working women have all the fun, meeting men, lunching and drinking cocktails with them at night. It is true there are many reasons for working, especially when you are alone and think you face a dismal, lonesome future. But work isn't all laughs and companionship. It's one thing to age gracefully at home, napping in the afternoon, surrounded by people who love you. It's quite another thing to be in an office, with younger people trying to push you aside and the men your own age giving you the hard look, wondering if you aren't getting menopausal symptoms.

DETROIT WOMAN EXECUTIVE

Volunteer work is not discipline enough for many women, especially those who aren't used to jobs. Most women get bored after two years—three at most.

NEW YORK MINISTER

You sleep better if you do things for other people. It doesn't matter what—collecting for the Red Cross, working for your university or church, or just helping a friend who is sick. Being alone tends to make you selfish.

NEBRASKA WIDOW

A paying job is better for the ego than volunteer work— and usually more interesting, for they give volunteers the boring chores, figuring they aren't serious anyway. And part-time work is almost as time-consuming as full-time and pays much less. There are openings for mature, intelligent women in all kinds of fields—nursing, secretarial, laboratories, professional services.

SAN FRANCISCO EMPLOYMENT COUNSELOR

When you apply for a job, if you are over thirty-five, lie about your age. Otherwise, people will turn you down sight unseen, figuring they don't want to hire an old bag. It's better to see an executive in person before you give him a chance to look at your application form. Otherwise, unless you are strictly twenty-one, he will refuse to consider you because you remind him of his dear old Mum.

NEW YORK DIVORCEE

My husband died suddenly at forty-five, so not much was left for me and the children. I had to work, and I decided I might as well go where I could earn good money. So I took a secretarial course, aiming at being a legal secretary. The pay was good, the work was interesting—and through it, I met my second husband.

ATLANTA WIDOW

I HAD dinner a few nights ago with Marjie D., whom I have known for twenty-five years. We met when we were both young advertising copywriters. She was a troubled girl in those days. She wanted to get married; being a virgin bothered her terribly, so she went off on a series of adventures. Most of them ended messily, with wives accusing Marjie of husband-stealing or Marjie getting cold feet at the sound of wedding bells.

I remember well the character of her disappearing acts. A friend had a house on Fire Island and Marjie would high-tail over there and spend the week painting a room or reupholstering an old chair, a glorious splurge of therapy. Eventually, Marjie decided to hell with getting married, took a good solid look at what she could make of her future alone, and quite wisely chose to specialize in interior decoration. Marjie is not her real name; I do not want to use even a correct first name because she is now famous. What is more important, I think, is that she has made a good life for herself, with a circle of fascinating friends gathered from her many junkets around the world.

Marjie is completely self-sufficient and a bit bored with those of us who are not. The future is not a nebulous blank to her. When she accumulates enough money, she intends to retire to France and to write books. And, because she has been able to devote herself wholeheartedly to her work, without the distractions of children or husband, she has made herself a household name. Some women with families have accomplished almost as much as Marjie—but not without considerably more anguish and sacrifice along the way.

Marjie and I both remembered the days when people used to wonder why she was not married. Men, in particular, used to irritate her with their patronizing, "You're pretty enough—how come you never caught a husband?" Now she can laugh about them. She has had a number of years in which to make peace with her own bêtes-noires and to make adjustments. She has never known the joys and agonies of having children or the sorrows of wanting children and not being physically able to have them. She has never had a husband to cherish, and battle, and lose. She has missed all those so-called essential feminine experiences. Yet, when we women who have had them look at the Marjies, it is difficult not to envy them.

They own pleasant apartments or comfortable country houses (sometimes both). They have a well-established circle of friends. (Some of their male friends are homosexuals, to be sure, and some of them are men who have not married for other reasons, but they balance the table at dinner parties.) They no longer brood over sex. Young people are attracted to them not out of duty but because they are interesting. If they ever suffer the pangs of loneliness (and they must) they have long since forgotten what it is to sit and wait for the telephone to ring. But the most impressive thing of all is their quiet sense of importance. They may not have married, but they compete with men in the man's world of business and they are aware of their worth.

Wives often resent these women. And, because we are in a muddled state when first left alone, we think we can get everything these ladies have, without their years of apprenticeship and hard work. It is a common housewife syndrome to daydream while chopping onions and sewing name-tapes on children's shorts. Listening to men talk business, watching them fret about petty problems and personalities, we secretly suspect we could do just as well, if not better, in the business world. Watching women in offices, comparing their nine-to-five jobs with the around-the-clock routines of housewives, we are grimly sure we could be twice as efficient, if God had only given us the chance. So, when God sees fit to do just that, we are not very realistic about our talents or our chances. We tend to look at ourselves with rose-colored glasses and it may come as a disillusioning shock when we find out that prospective employers feel otherwise.

. Sometimes a woman with no experience has the luck to fall into a good job. She is even luckier if she has the discipline and good sense to hang onto it, tooth and nail, asking few favors and expecting none. More often, she falls on her face.

Young personnel directors make us conscious of our years. Our clothes, so right for the suburbs, look dowdy. The executives who were so sweet at dinner parties become ogres behind desks in offices. After a few hard brushes with job hunting, many a woman runs for cover to the safe world of bridge, grandchildren, ladies' lunches, and golf. Unless her economic situation will not allow her that luxury; then, as I have said, she is lucky.

Work can be satisfying, a source of income, and a way of meeting new friends. It can also be dull, time-consuming, and physically and emotionally exhausting. Young girls, who can afford to waste time and experience, often drift from job to job, hoping to meet eligible men or, at least, have more fun. The mature woman, particularly if she needs the money or thinks she does, has to be less impulsive, more careful of the job she takes in the first place. One of the great assets she has to offer is maturity, and maturity does not mean being unreliable.

Part-time employment is often a good starter for the woman alone, because she can move around, meet different people, and work when she pleases. There are employment agencies which specialize in part-time jobs and they tell me they are eager to help mature women brush up on their skills, such as typing or clerical work. Working part-time also means that age is not a factor, as it can be when a future employer thinks in terms of pension plans, company insurance, and retirement. However, just the nature of part-time work gives a woman a feeling of drifting, postponement. Security, so hard to come by in the world of the woman alone, is a job which gives you a sense of accomplishment, or worth, a feeling that you are contributing something to society.

A job—if you have not worked for a long time and particularly if you have never had the discipline of working for pay—is not doing what comes naturally and earning pots of money. Yet it is not an impossible dream. There is a need in the labor market for mature women who are willing to work and are responsible. Running a household is good training, and the things you have learned almost incidentally are often of amazing value in an office. Skills which you did not know you had, or acquired so long ago that you have discounted them, may be of value. I met a widow who took a job as a comparison shopper in a big New York store because she felt, after twenty-five years as a housewife, she had learned how to shop for value. Before her marriage, she had been assistant buyer in a store on the West Coast, but she did not even mention that when she was being hired. However, when she began to work, she found herself able to look at merchandise from the point of view of the retailer, as well as that of the shopper. Her reports were so concise and helpful that she now has been put in charge of other women in the field, while she stays at a desk and edits their reports. She tells me she is in line for promotion to head of the department.

I am a great believer in taking a chance on yourself. A Honolulu divorcee with three children was determined to go into real estate when her husband left her with few resources. For a time, while she took courses, she "house-sat" for various friends who were traveling and did not want to leave their homes unprotected. She tells me that she and the children lived in twelve different places in two years. But now she is making enough money selling real estate to afford what she considers her dream house on the big island of Hawaii.

When and if you have long cherished a desire to do something, whether it is learning to play the organ or taking up painting, the time to consider doing it is when your world falls apart, and you have to remake it. You can not tell unless you try. It is more fun earning a living in a field that interests you enormously, if you can do it. And even if you cannot, you have grown a little, learned something for future reference.

I believe in work. It has the blessed quality of forcing you to think of something besides your own miserable little world. However, in the first few fuzzy months when you are alone, it is easy to make mistakes.

Returning to a familiar job is good therapy for a woman newly alone, and it can help her over the early feelings of being lost, of not belonging anywhere. All the experts advise that this be done as soon as possible. But even here, you can find yourself operating at something considerably less than peak efficiency. And sometimes a desperate or desperately lonely woman flings herself into work so violently that she destroys herself. I know one widow, already exhausted from her husband's long terminal illness, who took up the family business upon his death and in nine months worked herself into the hospital. Another young woman, whose fiancé died three weeks before their scheduled wedding, ran away from friends and got herself a demanding government post. Determined to succeed, she worked blindly and selflessly. Then, on the anniversary of her fiancé's death, she swallowed the contents of a bottle of sleeping pills.

When I was first alone, I did not think I could bear to continue as a free-lance writer. At best, when you expect someone home at night, when there is always a husband you can telephone, it is lonely work. So I toyed with all sorts of other ideas, going back into copywriting, joining the staff of a magazine, or—and I must admit this fascinated me most of all—changing my profession completely and going into social service work, where my main concern would be people.

I discovered, some months later, that free-lance writing, which seemed the sensible solution when I was married, was still my best bet simply because it was a career I had followed for twenty-odd years and in which I had made my own small reputation. I did not have recent experience to offer for copywriting or editing. There was no doubt in my mind that I could adjust quickly, but there was distinct doubt in the minds of other people. So far as social service was concerned, I might have been a female from Mars. My qualifications even as a volunteer looked pretty dim. I looked reality in the face, dusted off my typewriter, and continued to do what I am best qualified to do.

I shall never forget an afternoon some years ago when three of us married women sat around the fireplace in the home of another friend whose husband had just died and considered what we might do under similar circumstances. Shirley, who had young children still in grammar school, said she would start her own private school, using mothers as teachers; she was fed up with professionals. (Shirley had left high school in her junior year to go on the stage.) I opted for social service; instead of writing about people, I wanted to help them, to share their lives. Elsie, a British journalist who is very much out of the top drawer, said she was sick of being a hack writer; she would get a job as house-keeper, taking care of some nice old couple, and perhaps after a while they would notice what nice table manners she had and invite her to share meals with them. The odd part of this conversation was not that it was quite serious, and it was, but that each of us had spent some quiet time of our own thinking about the question.

I have not had the chance to talk intimately to either of these women since my husband's death, but I suspect my experience has not made a dent on their own equally unrealistic schemes. Necessity is a great partner. Many a woman who thought she could not possibly tackle a job, or a problem, discovers that when the chips are down, she can manage. A friend of mine, a single career woman who is an editor at *National Petroleum News*, recently sent me an article she had written about widows who have stepped into their husband's shoes as oil jobbers, a rough-and-tumble business that entails not only supervising men but getting and keeping male customers. Most of the women had worked only in the home before. One of them, no matter what the weather, insisted on driving the truck and delivering fuel herself. Of course, as my editor friend pointed out, other widows had tried and failed at the same kind of jobs.

I know a woman in the fashion business today who would not have been there if her husband had not died relatively early in life of a heart attack. Norma, we shall call her, had always been very chic. She married young, had children, and her husband, a brilliant psychologist, encouraged her to be "all woman"—which meant he wanted her at home, taking care of the children, being a perfect hostess or guest, an ornament to his career. He had never suspected his heart condition, so his sudden death left the family a great deal worse off financially than he had planned. It was not strictly necessary for Norma to get a job, but she knew she could not continue to keep her children in their expensive private schools unless she worked. Besides, deep in her heart, she had always resented being brushed off as "just" a decorative wife.

She did not say exactly that to any of her husband's old friends when she started out hunting for a job. She merely said that fash-

ion interested her and that she thought she would have a contri-
bution to make in that field. I am afraid not many of us took her
very seriously—we had seen Norma too long as the doll-wife. One
man in our group did. He admired her for her spunk, and he
helped her get a menial job in a fashion publicity agency.

She could not type or take dictation. So she ran errands and
became a glorified office girl. She never complained about the size
of the bundles or the number of trips she was asked to make, no
matter how hot it was or how hard it was raining. One Sunday,
the head of the agency came by and found Norma in the office
shampooing the rug in the reception room—a task no one had
assigned her. Bit by bit, she was given small decisions to make,
and she made them well. So she moved on in the job.

Now, remarried and a grandmother, Norma is encouraged by a
proud second husband to give fashion shows, take on free-lance
publicity accounts, and appear on television panels. She has no
need to earn money, but her husband understands the pleasure
and satisfaction she gets from being part of the fashion world. Recently, when I was telling this story to a divorcee who was unwilling to do anything except sit home and complain, she commented,
"Norma was lucky to be still young when she was widowed."

My answer is, so what? She did what she had always wanted to
do, and she destroyed a picture of herself she had secretly resented. And she tried, modestly, doggedly, without false pride.

False pride is a very nasty burden to carry. I don't mean by
this that a woman should swallow her pride and take a job she
loathes just for the sake of discipline, or her soul, or what have
you. But I think it is foolish to refuse to do something just because it is "beneath your dignity"—by which you probably mean
the position you occupied when you were a wife. A brilliant
financial friend could go down to Wall Street any day of the week
—including holidays and Sundays—and find herself a good job;
she is that knowledgeable. However, when her husband died, she
decided to travel. She felt shy about starting alone; her husband
had cared little about foreign countries. So her doctor suggested,
as a start, a job in the gift shop of a big ocean liner. And she, a
lady who could easily have afforded to travel first class on that

same ship, took it. It was very hard work. The shop was open long hours, and after it was closed, she had to keep books and open boxes of new merchandise and price it. She was not terribly well; she had gone through much during her husband's long, agonizing illness. But she kept the job for several voyages and "loved it."

If I had really seriously longed to be in social service, or if I down deep had felt I was a better editor or copywriter than a writer, I might have brushed off rejections and answered ads or pushed my friends until I was given a chance. Actually, as I see myself, I simply wanted a change for the sake of change, and to get away from painful familiar surroundings. That, in itself, is all right; I believe in saving yourself as much pain as possible. But one night my lawyer, who had been a silent witness to my struggles to change my career, said mildly, "Don't you think that any job that keeps you from writing will frustrate you?"

Writing is a profession that looks easy and interesting to many women alone. It seems to require nothing more than a liking for words—which *is* important. But free-lance writing, and creative writing, require discipline. You cannot write when the spirit moves you; you have to keep at it when you have a toothache or feel depressed or long to be out walking in the spring sunshine.

Of course, if you think you can write professionally and have enjoyed writing letters which friends have praised, go ahead. A writing course of some kind is a good way to start, just to get you in the swing, if nothing else. But unless you have a novel you feel you must get out of your system, and you do not mind sitting alone in front of the typewriter for hours on end each day, I would advise trying to get a writing job in an office, where you have a boss to keep you at it.

I happen to work at home, in an office in my apartment, the same arrangement I had when I was married. This is more difficult for me now than if I had to get up each morning and go into an office, where I could talk to other people. But I have disciplined myself over a number of years to keep regular hours, just as though I had a boss, and this has become habit. I go automatically to the typewriter at a certain time and, even if everything in my mind is at a complete standstill, I stay there until a certain hour. I think I can say that when, by some blessed accident, things are going well, I linger longer, because I want to finish a thought or a chapter. But when things are going badly, I make myself sit at least a few minutes beyond quitting time.

My secret weapon is that I do not go out to lunch—or, let me say, I go out to lunch very seldom, only on special occasions, with friends whom I want to see badly or when I am talking business. I also have another rule. I read the New York *Times* in the morning, at breakfast, but I do not allow myself to read any other printed word, even a fascinating catalog, until I have finished my own writing stint for the day.

Unless I am sick, really sick in bed—not just sneezing, not just feeling tired or sorry for myself—I would no more read fiction in the middle of the day than sit down and work my way through a box of chocolates. I have also found that the best way to fill weekends, which tend to be my worst time of the week, is to keep working hours as usual. I learned this from a best-selling author when she was between marriages. Although she is strikingly good-looking—a male friend of mine once said, "She is the kind of girl I always hope to sit next to on an airplane"—and lived in a magnificent apartment which her novels furnished in deepest luxury, she found weekends hung heavy. So she adopted the custom of working on Saturday and Sunday, and allowing herself to take time off in the middle of the week if someone interesting (in her case, a fascinating man) wanted to lunch or she needed to shop for clothes.

Of course, this is a personal solution, cut to my pattern, and it would not suit everyone. Another friend, who also is a free-lance writer, prefers to get up lazily, go out for lunch, and work late at night. But she also finds reading an indulgence, and a temptation, so she will never permit herself to read lying down.

A long time ago a brilliant friend died suddenly at thirty-four of a brain tumor. The lives of three women were changed directly because of his death. His wife, although she had young children, went to work; she still does not regard herself as a career woman, although she holds an executive job. A co-worker left her husband and later divorced him; contact with sudden death had made her realize it was later than she thought, she had no time to temporize with an obviously bad marriage. His secretary quit her job and went off on a series of trips, hunting something she never found.

Any sudden change, divorce, or death, disrupts. Patterns don't seem important. If, as I have maintained, you have always longed to take a certain course, this may be the time to break loose. But I also feel I must honestly strike a word of warning. Most of us do not return to "normal," as far as skills are concerned, for at least several months after a death or a divorce. If you have a regular job, even if it is only volunteer, it often is wise to get back to it immediately and make decisions about future plans later.

I heard of a divorcee who, at her lawyer's insistence, stayed home for twenty-four months while he tried to get a better settlement out of some common property she and her husband shared. Economically it worked out. But the woman was by that time so depressed and unsure of herself, she was unable even to face looking for a new job when the divorce became final.

A widow who holds an administrative post in a Minneapolis art gallery told me, "I worked when my children were in school, I worked even when my husband was ill, because it helped for me to have another outlet. But after he died, I never wanted to see my office again. I was really angry when the doctor insisted I go back the day after the funeral. But he was right. Getting back to my desk, and routine problems, was like putting my hand on something solid and real." An English teacher in a Colorado college said, "I went back to classes the same week Ben died, telling myself it would be only temporary, that pretty soon I was going to take the insurance money, divide it with his son by a first marriage, and go off into the hills to write the great American novel. Of course, I was dreaming. If I had wanted to write, I could have done it at night, in my empty house. Instead, I took on additional classes, so I wouldn't be home alone. I'm a teacher, and I thank God for it, now."

Needing money, being forced to work when you are mature, can seem terrible and cruel. Yet after meeting women who spend their lives doing nothing because they don't *have* to, and seeing how desperately unhappy and bored they are, I think there are worse things than financial necessity. However, many a woman who doesn't really need to work but would like to in order to keep occupied, or to have more clothes, has an inflated idea of herself and her talents. The divorced wife of an advertising man I knew felt she was qualified to be an account executive simply because she had entertained so many advertising men at dinner, and they had all been so nice to her. You cannot assume, simply because you have met captains of industry socially, that you are ready to sit next to them on the board of directors. I remember how shocked a widow I met was when she applied to the president of her husband's old firm for a job as a stylist—and was offered one at the reception desk, replacing a "common little thing of about twenty who was leaving to get married."

"I decided to go into a stockbroker's office," a handsome widow told me. "I've always been very good at handling investments. But when I found out that I'd have to take training, and pass examinations, I laughed at them. Now I'm taking a writing course at the university, but I have so little time to practice writing. I entertain, my friends invite me back, I go shopping, I do volunteer work at the hospital. Yet it is all so stupid. What I would really like is a *Career.*"

I met a Detroit divorcee who said cheerfully that she gave up a job selling real estate because it interfered with her golf. A widow in Texas sold better dresses in a fashionable department store to supplement an inheritance she thought was inadequate. But the customers—"the dirty, sweaty pigs"—so distressed her she sold her home and moved east to live with her son and his wife.

However, often what seems like a small talent or a knack for doing things can be of great help in the business world. A divorcee with three young children tried working at a variety of jobs, but always had to quit because she paid out more in baby-sitters than she took in. But she had always been clever with her camera and she was, of course, used to taking pictures of her own children. So one day in October she approached the mothers at the playground, suggesting she take children's portraits for Christmas presents. She is prospering so much now that she can afford a full-time housekeeper. And she has a studio in her home so she can keep a watchful eye on the children.

A woman in Illinois, whose lawyer husband's death left her a widow with three teenage sons, asked the rabbi to help her find part-time work. She had worked as a secretary before her marriage, but not since then. However, she had been active in many charities where her liking for figures had made her useful in volunteer jobs. In a few days, the rabbi called and told her a Catholic boys' school needed someone in the comptroller's department. Her immediate reaction was no, because it was a full-time job, which she did not want. Also it was among Catholics, and she was Jewish. And it was in another community. But she forced herself to apply, got the job, and finds she is good at it because she likes boys, and figures, and the teaching Fathers are kind and considerate. More important, she is so busy she has no time to wonder what her married friends are doing. And her sons are very proud of her.

Many times a job that sounds dull isn't—and vice versa. On the other hand, a woman sometimes needs or wants a job so badly that she talks herself out of it. The head of a company told me that he had seen the widow of an old friend but "I couldn't bear the idea of putting her into my organization where she'd have to come in contact with the public. She couldn't stop talking about how awful her financial situation was, and how much she needed work. I sent her out to a nice woman who is in charge of personnel and the widow cried all over her. Finally I said she'd hear from me. To get her off my conscience, I wrote her a check and gave her some people to see, in jobs where she wouldn't be meeting clients. But she still is out of work. I know other people are giving her money, too—but we can't hire her."

When death has happened to a man in the course of his business, a wife naturally feels his company owes her something. Quite frequently, the executives feel the same way. A young man was killed with three other employees in an industrial accident at the plant. The two older men had pension plans and insurance for the wives. Marie F. was left with very little except workmen's compensation and social security. She needed a job, so the company took her on as a saleswoman at a rather substantial salary. Marie was painfully shy and very bad at arithmetic. She tried hard, but she loathed pushing herself, and every morning just getting to work was a form of torture. And her employer, worrying for fear she might not be able to get another job if he fired her, continued to carry her, although she was not earning her salary and it was unfair to other employees.

A shakeup in the company made it necessary for a large number of employees to be fired, Marie among them. She took her severance pay, collected unemployment insurance, and studied typing and stenography. The job the school got her was in a library. It did not pay much, but it was among people who were kind and undemanding. For the first time in years, she began to feel important in her own right. And, although she had to lower her rather high standards of living, she is more attractive now than she was as a young woman. Both children are working their way through college, and she is now in charge of a small staff of young girls. A gentle person, she is thoroughly competent when surrounded by other gentle people. But she never could have been a success in competitive business.

There isn't a perfect job for every woman in the world any more than there is a perfect man for each woman who wants one. But if you are really serious, and are capable of doing a full day's work, week after week (Be realistic about this!), there are jobs available. Don't, however, be discouraged if you find certain qualifications just aren't your particular forte. As we know, one of the great needs today is for competent, reliable secretaries—and typing and shorthand skills work wonders in getting a woman into the field she prefers. When one of my husband's colleagues died of cancer some years ago, leaving a young wife and daughter, I made a point of urging the young woman to study typing and shorthand. Although she is a bright girl, with better than average background of education and breeding, she could not master shorthand. She stopped listening to the rest of us and got a job in personnel work, where she is doing exceptionally well, and whenever I see her, she has had either a raise or a promotion.

On the other hand, even if a woman finds a job uncongenial,

experience of any kind is important when applying for work. And it is not enough to be deserving; you have to be willing to work hard, sometimes under conditions which do not seem particularly pleasant. One of the women I talked with when I was starting research for this book was Mrs. F., who came down to my house after doing a full day's work and spent three hours telling me her story because she felt it might help other women in similar trouble.

Mrs. F. was divorced after twenty-three years of marriage and four children. Her husband was an alcoholic who could get jobs, but not keep them; they had moved so many times she could not call any place home. The two girls were grown and married, but she had two boys left at home, aged fifteen and nine. Her only training had been a brief period as a salesperson at Macy's before she married, and part-time employment at a woman's specialty shop, which enabled her to get clothes for herself and her daughters at a discount.

Her husband had moved the family to New York in June. By September, he was out of work and violent. Afraid of what might happen to the boys, she left him. For a month, while her small supply of money dwindled, she sat and wept, and went from 134 pounds to 99. By the time she knew she had to get a job, she was so thin that she looked much older than she really was. She read want ads, pounded pavements, sat in line at employment agencies, and listened to the bright young women finish the interview by saying to her, "Now, if my mother were looking for a job . . ."

In the beginning, she had determined to do everything by herself, not to call on mutual friends, for fear of spoiling her husband's chances of getting another job. But one day, discouraged to the point of desperation, she picked up the telephone and called a friend in an advertising agency, a business far removed from her husband's field of engineering. She asked, "Where does a woman my age [she was forty-three] get a job? I have no typing, no shorthand and the receptionists I see are all under thirty."

Her friend had just called an agency to find a woman who would do temporary work on a survey for six weeks. She said,

"You can do it, I think. Afterward, you can say you've had office experience."

Mrs. F.'s boss was a young girl who had just graduated in marketing research. She accepted her temporary assistant grudgingly —"I could just feel her wondering why the poor old thing didn't go back home"—but Mrs. F. was unable to afford pride. She asked questions. She studied. At the end of the survey, she was asked to stay on and do another. Finally, in one of the shakeups that occur in advertising agencies, she and a young boy were the only ones left in the marketing section. He gave her books on marketing, and she took courses at night: typing at the YWCA; educational psychology, marketing management and statistics at New York University. "I kept thinking I must be ready when this job was finished. At night, I fell asleep reading want ads."

She was able to afford classes because her husband was working again, and gave her money for the rent and to hire a housekeeper. He was also on the wagon and going to Alcoholics Anonymous; he begged her to come back to him and stop her job. But she was afraid; she had heard his promises before. Her daughters wanted her to go back to their father, but they did not know how bad the situation had been. Her sons did. In order to pull his weight, the fifteen-year-old sold dictionaries door-to-door on weekends and during vacations.

A year after the separation, the divorce became final. Her husband remarried and started to drink again. He lost his job and could not pay her alimony. The rent was due. Her older son had earned enough to pay his own school tuition but the $400 tuition had not been paid for the younger child. The housekeeper wanted a raise. Mrs. F. sat down one night after the children were in bed and balanced her checkbook: she had 34¢ left.

She knew she had to rearrange her life. It was no use counting on her husband, and she would not ask her married daughters for help. She could get a cheaper apartment and give the housekeeper notice. But she needed money for past bills, for tuition, for a deposit on the new apartment, for moving. She called her widowed father. He said, "How much do you need?" She said,

"Twelve hundred dollars." Although he was ill, and living on a pension, he borrowed the money and sent it to her.

"It was my low point," she said. "That night, before I called my dad, I was tempted to stop struggling. It would have been so easy to have gone in and taken all the sleeping pills I had left. I told myself that the boys would be better off without me; their father and the new wife would take them. But I didn't want the people at the office to think I was a quitter, another gutless woman alone."

That was ten years ago. Her older boy is married and the youngest is working his way through college. Mrs. F. is now head of the marketing department in a small advertising agency.

She says, "My children aren't my life. I am proud of them, but I can't hang on to them any more. They have to stand on their own, without me. Work is what I live for. Perhaps it is too important to me, but I don't think so. My ex-husband is dead now; what money he had went to his second wife. My father is dead, too; the little he left I used for my younger boy's prep-school tuition. While all this was going on, I'd push my troubles to the back of my mind at the office. Once a boss made a pass at me. I said, 'Do you think I'm going to endanger eight years of hard work by letting you kiss me?' He wasn't mad—he thought it was funny.

"Later the agency merged and my job was eliminated. The man who'd tried to make a pass lined me up with this job. He said I deserved it. I don't know what I am going to do when it's time for me to retire. My life is all mixed up with the people I have met in business. The girls talk more freely to me than my own children. They call me Auntie Mame and invite me to their parties and ask me for advice. I'm happier and more real than I ever was in my marriage . . . and sometimes I feel guilty about that. But not for long. I don't have time."

Volunteer work is the answer for many women who do not need to earn money. It can be rewarding emotionally, time-consuming, and a step toward a richer social life . . . usually with other women. In Bloomfield Hills, Michigan, the women alone work together weekends in the hospital, calling themselves the "Widow's Brigade." This not only meets a great need in the community, it also gives these women a purpose and a way of filling weekends. And when they finish work, they usually go someplace to eat together. An ex-actress I met, who has a full-time job, devotes one night a week to a group that tours veterans hospitals. The group is limited to five or six men or women. "We have rapport, not romance," she told me. "But this kind of friendship and work takes the place of romance in my life. I don't need anything else."

Sometimes when a woman discovers she cannot make a living in the field she has aimed at, or she is too old to be paid for her services, she can become a volunteer worker in that field, and derive satisfaction from it. An amateur painter, for example, has great fun decorating the children's wards at a hospital on holidays. A frustrated model works in a settlement house, helping girls prepare themselves for jobs. A woman who has always longed to be a doctor, but is realistic enough to know it is too late for her to take training, does volunteer work in a rehabilitation center working with physical therapy patients.

However, unless you are very selective or really dedicated, volunteer work does have flaws.

For one thing, volunteers tend to get the dull, "dirty" jobs that paid workers hate. Even in an exciting institute which is doing important research, volunteers are often so far removed from the action that they yawn over their tasks of addressing envelopes, emptying wastebaskets, checking files. This is partially because volunteer workers are less reliable than those receiving salaries; but volunteers tend to be less reliable because they know their jobs are unimportant. I think many big nonprofit organizations are aware of the problem and are trying to remedy it. But it is difficult to solve. I have been told frequently by administrative heads that unless a charity worker rises to a position of responsibility (and power) in an organization, the span of valuable service is about two years. Oddly enough, the women who do stick, and are willing to do dull jobs, are often the ones who have full-time paid positions elsewhere; there is something to be said for the old adage that the more you have to do, the more you can accomplish. It is also my conviction that, if you are earning money for your talents in a specific field, such as acting, writing, financial work, it is more satisfying to do something completely different when you are working for free. You will regard what you are asked to do as a challenge, instead of a rather dull extension of your regular job.

I know a brilliant public relations woman who offered to take over the fund campaign for a church organization that had a school for handicapped children. Her ideas were sound, and she worked very hard on the first presentation. But her aides were volunteers and inexperienced people, and she encountered so many unprofessional obstacles that she simply got tired and gave up. She admitted to me that she would have been much happier doing something new, like teaching music, about which she is knowledgeable. And she is sure that a music teacher by profession would have had much more fun working on the fund campaign. Once you are an expert, it is tiresome to have to deal with nonprofessionals on a project.

Besides, for the woman alone, unless she has young children who demand her being home at regular hours, the paying job is better for her ego. She may not keep much more money than if she were working for free, but she is in a new world and working side by side with younger people is great stimulation. We all tend to get stuffy; even women executives who do not have to listen to the chatter of their young help can be pretty set in their ways. The woman who is put down in a new milieu, and has to adjust, can learn a great deal about herself and, incidentally, her children. She finds herself growing younger in mind and more elastic. Her friends and neighbors respect her more. And gradually, instead of being ill at ease, she finds herself flowering.

Incidentally, the old excuse that you should not take money unless you need it, is simply an excuse. There are more jobs available in the labor market today than there are women to fill them, and many organizations employing a large number of women sponsor women's conferences in the hope that they can lure competent, intelligent mature women back to work.

Of course there is still some prejudice against age. It would be

foolish not to admit that men regard themselves as peren-
nial swingers, while taking a dim view of women their age, or
even younger. (A young man who is running a club for singles
said, "They have to be twenty-one to get a drink and be out of
school, we figured. And we decided that thirty-five ought to be
about right at the other end of the scale. We do have a number of
guys who are closer to forty, I'm sure, but they're still swinging.
However, by the time a girl gets to be thirty-five, she's not swinging much any more.") Of course you have to give your age on
official papers, and it is better not to lie about it verbally when
you are being hired. However, your attitude toward yourself and
other people makes more difference than wrinkles or gray hair—
although employment counselors do recommend discreet hair-
tinting if you need it, and there are no scruples against face lifting or other plastic surgery if you can afford it and think it will
improve your morale. And you don't need to continue making a
big issue, or apologizing, about your age after you're hired.

I have a friend who, when asked a leading question, such as the
year she was graduated from college, answers quickly, "Back during the Civil War." I had a smashingly beautiful great aunt who,
when asked her age, smiled disarmingly and said, "I don't remember." Actually, if you lie about your age for any length of
time, and skip birthdays officially while encouraging friends to
remember to the extent of little gifts, you probably will be telling
the truth when you say you don't remember.

If you have never worked at a paid job, or if you definitely do
not want to return to your previous employment, it is a good idea
to take advantage of the many counseling and testing services
offered us today. Ask the college or university nearest you if it has
such a service. If not, write your State Committee on the Status of
Women asking which agency near you does provide courses of
retraining and testing. Specifically, there are three schools which I
know of which have centers aimed at retraining and motivating
mature women: The New School for Social Research in New
York, 66 West 12th Street, has a Human Relations Center; the
Continuum Center for Women, Oakland University, Rochester,
Michigan, offers counseling, and testing, with off-campus courses

in Grosse Point and Birmingham, Michigan; and Barnard College, 606 West 120th Street, New York, has a Commuity Service Workshop, financed by a Federal Higher Education grant which is also extending help to other colleges.

High schools, vocational schools, and adult night schools often offer excellent training and retraining courses; so do labor unions, churches, and business groups. Usually, it is just a matter of making a few inquiries to discover one near you. If not, the U.S. Department of Labor, Women's Bureau (Washington, D.C. 20210) can tell you of continuing educational programs available in your locale.

Mary Dublin Keyserling, director of the Women's Bureau, spoke recently at a seminar for mature women at Stern Brothers, a department store in New York. The huge auditorium was jammed and the meeting was twenty minutes late in starting while the store struggled to provide chairs for the women who were standing in the line outside hoping to get in. She said such a response is not unusual; whenever meetings of this sort are announced, great groups of women respond—and, if I may add a personal observation—good-looking women. If there is such a conference in your area, I urge you to attend. There will be no question left in your mind that there is a place for the mature woman in the labor market today. Almost four out of ten women workers are forty-five or over. Since 1940, the number of women workers from forty-five to fifty-four has almost tripled; and the number from fifty-five to sixty-four has almost quadrupled. In addition, even if health does not permit you to take a permanent job, there are many agencies that specialize in temporary help. Just reading the want ads will lead you to one—and sometimes the qualifications are no more extensive than an ability to write clearly, greet people pleasantly, or add and subtract.

If you wish additional information, the Government Printing offices in Washington, D.C., 20402, will send you a list of bulletins on opportunities for women available and the Women's Division of the Institute of Life Insurance, 277 Park Avenue, New York 10017, has a working-women leaflet and a "financial worksheet" that may be helpful. The Office of Economic Opportunity in Washington sponsors Foster Grandparent programs throughout the country. The one at New York Foundling Hospital has been in operation since 1966. After two weeks of training and orientation, qualified older people make $1.60 an hour and work twenty hours a week. If there isn't a program near you, baby-sitting is always a convenient source of income and you can work as you please—but it is wiser not to try it on your own, but sign up with a registered agency which will insist on stabilized fees and clearly defined duties.

If you are interested in becoming a college housemother, and live near a college, inquire at the office of the dean of men or dean of women, or check with the housing director. There are positions open in dormitories that are more challenging than those in fraternities and sororities, particularly if the dormitories are coeducational. A woman who has investigated the subject recommends good health and the disposition of a drill sergeant if you tackle one of the latter. There is also a book, *The College Housemother* by Helen Reich, which your library may have. If not write the Interstate Publishers, Danville, Illinois.

Employers today recognize that women in the middle-age range are a more stable group, with a record of less absenteeism, than either men or women under twenty-five, and that women who enter the labor market in their forties show very low turnover rates compared with other women. The largest category in which there are jobs available is clerical: clerks, secretaries, bank tellers, receptionists, and the like. But there is also great need in other categories: aids to professional people, like schoolteachers, researchers, scientists, and in the service fields—salespeople, beauticians, and people who prepare and serve food in hospitals, restaurants, hotels, etc. The figures indicate that there will be 17 per cent more women employed in 1970 than in 1960, and many of these will be in the areas of service, doing desk jobs previously executed by men in uniform.

There are really only three big obstacles facing a woman when she decides to work outside her home. The first and most important is health. It is probably wise to have a checkup before you look for work. Most large companies today insist on one for new employees and you can avoid what might be an unpleasant shock.

Divorce and death bring more emotional strain than most of us realize and, like the Red Queen in *Through the Looking Glass*, we think we have to keep running to stay in the same place. A period of retraining, or going back to school, can be a welcome bridge both emotionally and physically between you and a full-time job. If you do discover that you have one of the chronic disabilities that old age unloads on us, don't dwell on it but be realistic in deciding how much it will hamper you. I met a woman who was hospitalized for nearly a year in the accident that killed her husband; from her hospital bed, she did so much telephoning and writing for the PTA that she was elected an officer before she was able to go to a single meeting.

The second obstacle is young children. The disruption of a regular home life is hard on them, and a mother may feel she should not hurt them more by absenting herself during the day. This, however, seems to be a specious argument. Children, after the loss of one parent, fear the loss of the remaining one. But they are more apt to be upset by having a miserable, self-sacrificing parent hovering over them than by having one who goes out to work.

A divorcee in Minneapolis told me that her twin sons, fourteen years old, have learned to cook since she was gone back to work, and often have dinner started for her when she gets home. She said, "I was tired and cranky when I tried staying home after my divorce. The children were so young I thought they needed me, but there is nothing harder on a woman than the conversation of children all day and all evening, without a break. My priest was the one who convinced me it was better for all of us if I had an outside job. And I can afford now to hire someone to do the heavy cleaning." An Illinois divorcee, whose now-grown son has made a brilliant record in college, told me, "He was nine years old when his father left us. He understood how hard it was. We had nothing except debts. I worked for a doctor during the day and at nights he and I used to bake cakes and make jelly, which he sold door-to-door. I guess some of the neighbors thought I was an awful mother. And it was hard on Danny. But, in a way, it brought us closer together. I didn't feel guilty about him because I was working so hard, and he knew the reason I was making sacrifices was so he could have an education. And now he's turned out better than the boys who had it easier—and he has a great sense of fun, despite his unusual maturity."

The third obstacle is fear, which is the hardest to conquer and to recognize in yourself. It is difficult to talk yourself out of fear, but there are a few simple things you can do to mask it—once you have squared your shoulders and made an appointment for an interview. First, dress as comfortably as possible, never in a new dress, never with a new hairdo, never with experimental makeup; you must not feel artificial. Second, stand up, take a deep breath, and try to smile, no matter how nervous you feel. Third, don't make more than two appointments for interviews in one day, well spaced so you don't have to rush and will be on time. Fourth, don't decide in advance you won't do a certain type of work, go into a certain area, or keep certain hours. Be flexible; rigidity is a sign of age. Fifth, don't talk too much. Answer questions briefly; be prepared with itemized information about yourself, past experience and recent training. Mention your status as a widow or divorcee if you are asked, but don't elaborate. As references, use people who know something about you as a worker—the head of your local Red Cross, your pastor, your PTA president, or a past employer. Don't ask friends who know nothing about your business ability to recommend you. Above all, try not to use the husbands of friends unless you have to; remember that their wives can help you. Once my husband had an opening that could have been filled by a single woman we both knew well socially, but he disliked hiring her because of our friendship. I felt he was being a little unfair, but I did not argue with him; I simply waited until he was in a good mood one night and persuaded him to let me call her and tell her to apply.

Work can be a way of meeting men, but it's better if you don't count on that, or at least don't count on getting anything more than a chance at being with men and listening to male conversation. I talked with a schoolteacher who gave up her job to sell cars, because she thought she would meet fascinating men. She did—but they were all married. She also discovered she hated selling, so she went back to teaching after six months.

Certain kinds of jobs, which expose you to the public, can mean dates. A divorcee of considerable experience told me that gift shops in hotels are good hunting grounds because there are so many men traveling alone; of course, these men are usually married, but if a woman wants only dates and free dinners on the expense account, she will have plenty of offers. Travel bureaus, service positions on ships, and jobs as travel guides also expose you to men. If you are leading a tour, you certainly have first chance at a desirable man. I heard of one where the leader of the tour spent most of her time and energy on one gentleman. They announced their engagement near the end of the trip and she apologized to the others for her "unusual conduct." Even the other women admitted they did not blame her.

Try to be as realistic as you can. Don't rush off in all directions, tilting at untried projects, unless you are sure you won't collapse under the weight of new responsibilities. On the other hand, don't sit home and wait for a miracle. Put out feelers. Go back to school. Go to lectures.

Of course, take all the help you can get. Listen to advice and discard what you think is worthless. The important thing to remember is that you are on your own, alone, and you do not have to please anyone except yourself. And if pleasing yourself means going off to Africa with the Peace Corps ("At her age!") or taking acting lessons ("Who does she think she is?"), more power to you.

It seems easy, although perhaps not as easy as people who do not write professionally think, to sit behind a typewriter and say these things. But I did not reach these conclusions alone, or without the help of many professionals in various fields. I also want to add that I have made a few tries and fallen on my own face, so I know what it's like. It is part of living, and especially part of living alone. And it is a lot better to be in there fighting, sometimes winning, sometimes losing, than to stay out of the action.

7 MONEY, THE MALE MYSTIQUE

Happy? I'm not happy most of the time. But who is, after you have reached sixty? Thank God I have enough money to feel secure. I tell you, I can think of nothing worse than to be getting on the oldish side when your services are not too much in demand and not have what it takes to live decently. My dear old mother used to say, in her old age, that she didn't do much, but just to have her own little house with comfort close at hand, and to know that if something happened, her children would take care of her, made her feel every day was Thanksgiving.

NEBRASKA WIDOW

If you didn't know how to handle money before you were left alone, you'd better darned well learn. All these kind men are out to rook us.

HONG KONG DIVORCEE

Learn to say no to children, relatives, and all those eager beavers who want to sell you oil stocks and shares in plays, to make you richer. Learn to say yes to what you want out of life, even if it is a crazy idea like going to live in Alaska.

LOS ANGELES WIDOW

The only advice I have to women is, don't hide your money in a sugar bowl. Inflation is a fact of life, like death and taxes. The only way you can have the same buying power ten years from now as you have today is to increase your income.

DIVORCED NEW YORK BROKER

I used to buy stocks the way some people bet on horses, if I liked the name, or if I had a hunch. My husband thought I was crazy. Now that he's gone, I'm too scared of losing money, too conservative. I made more money the other way.

COLORADO WIDOW

KATHLEEN J., around fifty, has been a widow since she was thirty-seven. She lives in a pleasant Midwestern suburb of a large city, is attractive, slim, pleasantly chic, and is admired by both men and women because she is so self-sufficient. I was encouraged to talk to her about a woman alone handling money because, I was told, she even did her own income tax.

Mrs. J. corrected me: "I did do my own income tax—until two years ago. Then a power line was coming through some of the farms I own and they tried to cheat me because they didn't like dealing with a woman. Men don't think managing money is woman's work and resent us if we are too efficient. So now I hide behind my lawyer. I tell him what I think should be done, and he puts up the front."

A sophisticated high-salaried New York executive, who manages a department of a big company, has handled her own affairs financially since she was divorced at twenty-three. She deals shrewdly in properties worth thousands of dollars. She also lives well, with a home in the country, an apartment in town; and her clothes are geared to her important position. On a plane flight a few years ago, she met a high government official. It was love at first sight. He took steps to get a divorce from his wife of twenty-five years, and she notified her company that she was retiring and would live in Washington and devote her life to him.

The marriage fell through. Later she told me why: "He came to New York for a weekend. I was giving a party, and had been rushed in the office so I had caterers take care of everything, even bring the food. I put on a new dress I'd bought at noon, a Norell, to please him. But I noticed he was reserved during the evening. When the guests and servants had left, he said to me, 'You spend a lot of money, don't you?'

"I was a little surprised, but I shrugged and told him, 'It's my own.' Then he said, 'Well, when you are spending my money, you won't be so extravagant. Women are fools about money.' "

Money is a male status symbol, and I fear that the reason men make such a fuss and mystery about it is that it is one of the few powerful weapons they have left in an increasingly frustrating world. (During my research, I was horrified to find out how many husbands—supposedly nice men in good positions—are unable to control themselves and take out their frustrations by beating their wives and children.) So it is not surprising that men cling desperately to the idea that women cannot handle money, do not understand it, and never will.

The divorcee who broke her engagement shortly after that conversation about money horrified the man in question, and many of her friends, who declared she would have been better off with love and less money. Knowing the lady, I can only say she made the right decision. She could not have been happy living with a man whose ideas about money were so different from hers. And, although she is definitely a very female female, she was not ready to knuckle under to her fiance's slant on money just because he was a man and she thought she loved him. She had been on her own too long.

Money is not power, or a weapon. It is simply a means of exchange, and women, being realists, tend to regard it as something to be spent. Men of course cannot take this simplified explanation. Money is far too important to their ego. And so money is the cause of more trouble between men and women than anything else, including sex. And quite naturally men resent, or tend to deprecate, the woman who manages money as well as they do—or better.

I have a friend who looks like a fragile pampered female, but who was one of the really incisive powers in a brokerage house before she married her husband. Now a widow, she supports her lavish country home and even more lavish travels by quietly playing the market; a disgruntled suitor once accused her of sitting in her upper New York State home running barefoot through her money. She does not expect to marry again, although she is only in early middle age, because she thinks men resent her attitude toward money—or want her to take care of herself and them, too. An independent soul, she cringes at the thought of hiding behind a man in financial matters and does her own income tax, as well as her own stock transactions, as a matter of course. She remembers, with some chagrin but more pride, that she once rejected a proposal of marriage from a man by saying, "Why, Marvin, you can't even do your own income tax."

There are women like her who understand money and consequently are not afraid of it. As time goes on, I suspect there will be more and more women brokers and vice presidents and treasurers. But that does not mean that the problem of money will be banished between women and the men they love, or like. On the contrary. As long as they can, men will hold onto the purse strings. That is why so many widows who know nothing about their husbands' affairs are left panic-stricken and bewildered when they die, and so many divorcees find it a whip with which they are still being punished for preferring their freedom. Men joke about their "hard-earned money" and about their wives "throwing it around," but they are not really joking. No matter how enlightened they may be about everything else connected with marriage, they deliberately keep their hands on money, do not let their wives know the extent of their holdings (sometimes even what they earn), and prefer to dole it out on a system of rewards and punishments.

When a man goes out to dinner with a woman, he picks up the check—or diminishes himself by letting her slip him her billfold in advance. To the American husband, money is potency and masculinity. When he marries a woman he supports her, or at least he manages the finances; one man I know who is married to a successful actress says that the fact she earns more money now than he does is not a problem because "she has no idea how to handle it." When children are born, the husband is the boss, the court of last appeal because he pays the bills. And it is a point of male pride to feel that, when he dies, he will leave a neat little nest egg of money for his wife and children to go on living in the style to which he has accustomed them.

Despite this male mystique, most of the money in the United States is in the hands of women. They own 40 per cent of the real estate and control 65 per cent of the nation's private wealth. But they are only in temporary possession, usually in the later years of life, for the money has come to them from husbands, occasionally fathers, and will be passed on to children. And they are in control only technically, because the banks and trusts that manage the money are run by men.

Women resist knowing about money not because they are stupid, or because the money-understanding cog was left out of the female brain, but because it is psychologically important to the male to handle finances, to be the boss. I have discovered this is one of the important reasons why many successful businesswomen stay single; they see married friends being led around and bullied by the husband who needs to use money as a whip, and they decide they prefer to balance their own budgets.

A brilliant and independent widow married an artist who moved into her house and, because he earned far less than she did, she continued to pay all the bills. Then she lost a large sum of money and he had to take everything over. She said to me, "He's much more of a man now—sexually and every other way."

One of my acquaintances, before her marriage, was manager of a company and took care of its finances. Now, except for a small personal allowance for lunches and taxis and the beauty parlor, she has charge accounts for everything, and her husband pays the bills. Once a month, they have what she calls a "night of horror" when she presents the bills and her husband checks them over, item by item. She says, "Perhaps I should have established my right to be a human being over money before we were married, but it never occurred to me. He always seemed so generous—he still is, in many ways—that I never dreamed it would be like this."

Another woman is married to a man of inherited wealth who has built a modest fortune into a great one. In financial circles, he is considered a genius. His wife's evaluation of his talent is something else again. Although they have several homes, with staffs of servants, all the maintenance is paid at his office. She has an allowance for personal use so small that: "I have to think twice before I pay fifty dollars for a dress. Once in a while, for a special occasion, he will tell me to get a new evening gown, or a cocktail dress. He'll pay for it—and then I will find he has deducted the amount from my regular allowance the next month. Yet on my birthday, he gave me a diamond bracelet and took me and two dozen close friends to London, first class, all expenses paid, everything on him. It was a surprise. I got tight on the plane and cried and told him I would rather have had the money. He was hurt and astonished. I was ashamed and apologized. But it's true."

Perhaps there was a time when men honestly believed women could not handle money. Times have changed. Even in countries like Japan, where the status of women does not approach that of the United States, men in lower income brackets hand over their paychecks unopened to their wives, and the ladies decide what the men can spend and dole it out to them. But as soon as these men begin to earn more money, or are given bonuses, they pocket extra cash for themselves or take over the entire lot. This same situation holds true in our country, with rare exceptions. It is the men in the upper- and middle-income brackets who insist on keeping the purse strings. And the women, although they rebel secretly and complain among themselves, accept such domination. Even today, in this so-called age of liberated women, I know wives of rich men who keep their own secret little caches of money, for emergencies, that they have saved out of their allowances, to give them a feeling of security.

Few women divorce their husbands because they refuse to let them be partners in money matters; we have been conditioned too long to accept this and to make the best of it. In fact, sometimes a woman will not find out how stupid her husband was about money until after he has died—or until they are divorced for another reason.

Five years after the divorce, a Louisiana divorcee with two children under twelve is still trying to get her affairs in order because: "I thought the man should take care of the bills, that the house and children were my domain. The result was that he put us into a terrible financial state. He went into business for himself, ended up with a huge inventory and then managed to keep going by not filing an income tax for two years. I never knew, until he finally ran out on us, how bad things were. I got a job and spent the year while the divorce was becoming final catching up on bills. I am still paying the government twenty dollars a month, all I can afford, on those unfiled income taxes. I don't know how I could have sat back and let all this take place. Yet I suppose I'd do it again. I wouldn't be married to a man I could dominate, I'd want him to take charge."

But once divorced, no matter what the reason, the woman who has asked for her freedom finds her husband still trying to punish or reward her (in most cases it is punishment) through money. The attitude can be deliberate, or it can be unconscious.

I know a man who divorced his wife twenty years ago to marry his secretary. At the time he gave his wife $75 a week alimony, the same sum his secretary had been earning, and on which she had been able to live. There was a clause in the divorce agreement to the effect that if his salary ever went down, he could reduce the alimony, but not one word was said about raising it if his salary increased. Now, twenty years later, she finds $75 a week very slim pickings and she has tried to get the sum increased. Although he is a high-salaried executive, he has refused—but he butters his ego and puts a little on her daily bread by sending her "presents" of money from time to time.

A thirty-one-year-old divorcee left her husband because he was constantly having affairs with girls he would pick up. She told me, "I always hated asking Joe for money, but I suspect he liked doling it out. Now he knows he can hurt me through finances and uses them as a device to keep me in line. He is very careless, which drives me wild. Once when his check was late, I had to stop payment on the checks I'd mailed. Another time, his check bounced; so then, of course, all of mine did, too. He really has plenty of money. This is a way of showing me he is still boss."

A woman in Evanston, Illinois, a divorcee with three children, was so miserable married to an alcoholic that she took no money for herself, and very little for child support, when she divorced him. Now she is working and living with her parents, struggling to make ends meet, while he has remarried and seems to enjoy annoying her by giving the children expensive gifts of things that she has refused them. When I saw Marie T., there was a motorcycle in the driveway which her ex-husband had given her fourteen-year-old son for his birthday; she had turned the boy down when he requested it not only because of its cost but also because she felt he was too young. She said to me "I want you to give women who are getting divorced one bit of advice—take all the money you possibly can out of him, while you are still in litigation. Don't be noble, and don't feel sorry for him. He's going to hate you anyway even if he pays you only a token. And don't try to be considerate because afterward he will use money to humiliate you in front of the children."

Hard and cynical? Perhaps. But the lady in question was giving other women the benefit of the one thing she has learned from her husband—that money is not only money. Many a woman scorned hits back at her divorced husband with the one weapon she knows will hurt most—money, *his* money.

A Southern belle I encountered married a dull, rich man only because he was available and she felt she was getting too old to be single. It was never a love marriage on her part, even though she had three children. When he started playing around, she divorced him, extracting large alimony. But she still cannot seem to manage to keep out of debt. Once in a while, when creditors press too hard, she puts the bills in a big envelope and sends them to him. And he pays. Her friends figure it is his way of keeping in touch with her, and her way of punishing him for being rich, but not dazzling.

Melina Mercouri, the Greek actress, said, "If you take a European woman's husband, she has nothing. But if you take an American woman's husband, you make the wife rich."

There are some women who, even if they cannot afford it, are so glad to be rid of their husbands that they refuse alimony. I have also known proud self-supporting gals who scorned it; one said to me, "It is far more honorable to be a kept woman than take cash from an ex-husband for past favors." I have also met the martyr type, who, even if she cannot afford the gesture, refuses to touch a cent of her husband's money. (Secretly, I suspect, she hopes to bring him back by showing how noble and selfless she is.) But these women are exceptions. The average woman scorned will bleed her husband dry. Grabbing all of the money she can get is an instinctive, catlike form of revenge. A banker told me that many men do not know their wives are leaving them until they find a check has bounced and they discover that the little woman has cleaned out the joint account. Taking his money is the most vindictive way she can think of to break the news. And bleeding him dry in alimony and child support gives her the satisfaction of knowing he and the other woman are going to have to pinch pennies. Legislation is pending on a bill designed to give divorced fathers more leeway in reporting the money they give their ex-wives for child support—primarily because the mother frequently declines at tax times to provide the father with the necessary information so he can take a deserved deduction.

I know of one divorced wife who has reduced her husband to living in a cold-water flat, although he earns $20,000 a year. The two older boys are at expensive prep schools. The youngest is an invalid and she regularly tries to get more money out of his father for the opinions of more specialists, threatening him, "You're so tight you'll let your son die for lack of medical attention."

A malicious woman often will press financial demands, hoping her husband will not be able to marry again, and will return on his knees to her. Many divorced men are not good marriage prospects simply because they are so tied up financially. And sometimes a woman who is still in love with her ex-husband, or who thinks she is, will use money as a way of inconveniencing him or of simply seeing him. It is not at all uncommon, for example, for an ex-wife to let insurance lapse, or mortgage payments, so that she has an excuse to call her ex-husband and beg for help. If the man has not remarried, he may be touched by her helplessness, and even go back to the poor muddled little thing. If he has remarried, he often finds these calls a source of discord between him and Wife Number Two—which is, of course, what the first wife had in mind all the time.

I know of one miserable woman who, although her husband has been happily remarried for seven years, has not remarried because it means giving up her alimony, which she still takes to punish him, although she has a large income of her own. Not long ago, her ex-husband and his second wife decided to take a year off and live in Italy. The day before they were to sail, he received a notice that she was taking him to court, on the pretext that she was worried about whether she would get her alimony while he was out of the country. The suit was thrown out by the judge, but not before she had managed to inconvenience the couple by delaying their sailing.

An obstetrician in Tennessee finally divorced his wife because her obsessive jealousy was ruining his practice and his life. She was able to extract an enormous financial settlement from him, and she still makes his life miserable by getting into money scrapes, coming to his office with his ten-year-old daughter dressed in dirty rags, and demanding that he bail her out.

Hard as it is to believe, it is not uncommon for angry women to abuse their own children in an attempt to punish their husbands with that deadly weapon, money.

One divorced man living in Paris, barely able to keep himself because he pays so much in child support, told me that when his children arrived for their annual visit last summer they were dressed so badly, in clothes they had outgrown, that the first thing he had to do was take them shopping for new outfits. Another knows in advance that his children will have holes in everything, including their teeth, when they arrive for their holidays with him. According to his story (I have learned, when dealing with embittered divorced people, that there are usually two sides) his wife has remarried and is using the $18,000 a year he pays for child support to indulge her new husband in luxuries.

Divorcees, playing their own game of tug-of-war with male money, say they envy widows. Yet, simply because of the male mystique, money is often more of a worry than a comfort to widows. Some, free for the first time of having to ask for money to pay bills, grab the cash and buy clothes "as though they were going to stop making them" and invest in around-the-world cruises, deluxe. But too many widows, in their ignorance about money, and frightened at having to cope without their husbands, are terrified they will spend too much, once the wage earners have disappeared.

A widow is fortunate if she has someone knowledgeable about

finances whom she can trust—a family lawyer, a banker, a broker who sees beyond his immediate profits. Relatives, no matter how well-meaning, can be essentially as stupid as she is and, under the pretext of helping her, get her deeper into messes. Despite all the fanfare, many men do not understand money, either. But they are always flattered when they are asked for advice. And about the worst mistake a widow can make is to turn to the husband of a good woman friend, or the male half of a couple she and her husband knew well.

At first, the wife cannot say anything—who could be so cruel as to object to her husband's helping a poor little widow? But complications can develop fast, and wives, being female, have concealed weapons. In Los Angeles, I knew two women who had been roommates in college. They were married within a year of each other, were in each other's wedding parties, and settled down to raise their kids in the same suburb. Then Alicia's husband died suddenly of a heart attack.

Her best friend, Jean, was a rock. So was George, Jean's husband. They took the children. Alicia was urged to go away for a rest and, while she was gone, George went over her affairs with the family lawyer. When he found out that there really was not enough for Alicia and the children to get along, he found a job for Alicia in his own organization and Jean persuaded Alicia's widowed aunt to move into Jean's house and take care of the children. Alicia went around telling friends she would have killed herself if it had not been for Jean—and George.

Alicia had been a widow less than a year when I had lunch with Jean. A simple inquiry about Alicia turned Jean rigid. Then the dam broke. Jean said Alicia was always about. Every weekend she either came to their house or invited them to hers . . . to discuss her affairs. She was tired of having her underfoot.

"It will be over when the estate is settled," I suggested.

"Like hell it will," Jean said. "It will be over before that. I've told George either he gets a transfer to another city or I leave him and take the kids. I'm tired of being treated like his other wife. She pays a lawyer to look after her business—she can damned well use him."

There is an old cliché that every woman falls in love with her obstetrician; when the nervous father-to-be is falling apart, she needs someone strong to lean on. It is much more dangerous for a woman alone to start leaning on the wide shoulders of a married male friend, because it can become a habit. And she may find herself cut off not only from his wife but from all of their mutual friends. With lawyers, even those who have been long-time friends, the relation is different. Like obstetricians, the lawyers have been through all this before, they have the impersonal professional touch, and they have many other clients. They also know from experience when it is time to nudge the lady out on her own and insist that she learn to handle or supervise the handling of her own money.

I met a woman in Connecticut who found the loss of her husband considerably cushioned by the professional attentions of her lawyer, an attractive bachelor some fifteen years younger than she was. She did not take a job which was offered her because she was so busy taking care of "her affairs," which consisted of fixing delightful little dinners for him when he called on her with papers to sign. A year later, after the estate was settled, it was a different story. I met her by chance in a New York brokerage office.

"I'm handling my own money," she told me. "God, when I go over my bills and discover how much that vulture of a lawyer was making out of me, I could die."

Some widows have been victimized by unscrupulous lawyers— as well as by brokers and financial "experts." I have been told that some of the men who attend the mature singles parties are married brokers, trying to drum up business. On the whole, however, the world is not waiting like a hungry wolf, licking its jowls, to feast off the woman alone, widow or divorcee. There are indigent young men who go on cruises with the deliberate intention of meeting women alone with money. I have also heard of men who try to borrow money from widows on short acquaintance. But these are easy to spot—and reject.

At first, most widows must accept the help they get from professionals in good faith—or switch to someone else. Unless a woman is basically a fool, she will know before long whether she is being taken, whether it is by a lawyer or a would-be suitor.

Widows have the right to protest fees to the court if they believe they are excessive. A widow also has the right to go slowly, ask questions, and find out what is going on about her husband's will, and the estate, and why. If you feel your lawyer—or anyone else who is serving you—is being impatient, unsympathetic, or evasive, it is only common sense to leave him. I long since got over being tender about the feelings of professional men when I discovered how many doctors move around among their colleagues, consulting one and then another if they are not satisfied.

Some women prefer not to know about their financial affairs. But the majority of women can, and should, find out where they stand and what is being done with their money. Courses for women in money management are available at universities and night schools. Brokerage houses also give free lectures which a woman can attend without obligation where she can learn her ABC's. And, once interested, she can learn a great deal from the daily newspaper, even if she is not ready for the *Wall Street Journal*. Even if a woman thinks she has no interest in finance, gradually, by osmosis, she finds herself picking up information. For one thing, she no longer has to be coy. The relation between her and her adviser is a professional one and he is there to answer questions. If some of the questions are stupid, there is no call to feel embarrassed. I remember I once apologized to a French teacher for asking a stupid question. His answer was, "No question which is asked is ever stupid. It is only the ones you are afraid to ask, for fear of looking foolish."

No matter how confused and ridiculous you feel, remember you are not the first. I talked to one woman who lost her checkbook shortly after her husband died; she was wild with anxiety because she thought that anyone who found it could write checks until the money was all gone—and it took several days before she got up courage to tell her lawyer what had happened. There are women who do not know how to write checks, who do not know the difference between a checking and a savings account, between paying rent and making payments on a mortgage. I heard of one woman who was so upset when she heard that the bank used money she deposited that she drew it all out, prepared to keep it in the modern equivalent of the old sugar bowl. Another widow— brilliant in her own field of fabric design—grabbed her son and fled to Mexico because she thought her husband's relatives were trying to get custody of her son. Finally her lawyer had to fly down there to convince her that the husband's relatives, quite justifiably suspicious of the mother's knowledge of finance, simply wanted custody of the money he had left for his son, so that his mother would not throw it away foolishly.

From observation, I have reached the conclusion that it is therapeutic for the woman left suddenly alone to spend money on herself. There's an old tale about canaries which to me seems apropos: "When a canary loses her mate, she will often droop and die of a broken heart. The only hope of saving her life is to immerse the disconsolate widow in water. The occupation, always interesting to the female mind, of rearranging her plumage so diverts her thoughts that the once inconsolate bird recovers from melancholy and joins once more in feathery society."

It is also healthy for her to indulge herself a little, to take a trip she has always dreamed of (although it may not be as great as she had hoped), to stay on in a house even if she really cannot afford it. The trip, even if it is a disappointment, puts her in surroundings which are not constant reminders of her loss. And sometimes she finds ways and reasons to keep a beloved house, although at first it seemed impractical. I know of a widow whose four married children tried to move their mother out of the big hilltop house she had built when the family was all together. She begged for time . . . during which she sold the acreage around it, not only supplying her with money to run the big place, but giving her neighbors so she would not be alone.

There are some women who will go on spending and spending until the money is gone. These women are usually lavishing gifts on other people instead of on themselves, and they do need some form of curb, for they are actually trying to buy affection because they feel inadequate, unworthy of love. Sometimes they hit bot-

tom, and have to be supported. Sometimes they have to go to
work—therapy, because it gives them a sense of worth. Often they
remarry—the giving nature has a strong attraction for men—although the first thing the new husbands have to do is to place the
ladies on strict budgets.

More often a widow, once her husband is dead and there is no
regular paycheck coming in, goes into a panic and is afraid to
spend money for anything. An estate lawyer told me of a widow
with vast holdings who gave up her membership to a museum (a
matter of some $18 a year) because she felt, with her husband
gone, she could no longer afford such luxuries.

Nobody wants to come down in the world. Worry about where
the next dollar is coming from is debilitating, and a certain
amount of security gives a woman dignity, relief from pain and
anxiety. I know of a doctor's wife who, left with very little except
his insurance, was smart (or lucky) enough to double it in the
stock market. Her two sons are now both doctors, married, with
families of their own. The widow lives in a one-room apartment
in a slum area, pinching every penny, for she is determined to
leave the exact amount of the original insurance to her children
when she dies.

Some children, some relatives, are greedy. There are people in
the world who think only of money, and what they can get out of
others. Such people do not deserve a second thought. A widowed
teacher I know, who has more fun on the tiny income her husband left her than anyone I have ever known, told me, "I think
of myself as a survivor on a desert island. I don't have everything
I want, or need. But, by invention, I can manage to supply my
wants, and I am determined to enjoy everything more for that
reason. Each day is a challenge; I take it as it comes and don't
worry about tomorrow. Money is meant to be used. Saving money
for your children—or holding it out to relatives as a bait to make
them take care of you—demeans you and them. Whatever I have
—my health, my friends, my assets—are here at hand, to be enjoyed. I'm not completely foolish. I have a bit of bread and cocoa-
nut tucked away for a rainy day. But I don't brood about it.

What if tomorrow never comes? I've had today and I haven't wasted an instant of it."

Contrast her with another woman, who really does not have any money worries but thinks she has. A widow, once a musical comedy star, she is living in a Park Avenue apartment which rents for at least $450 a month. The place is filthy; she won't spend money for a maid. She has three fur coats, but never wears them. She never goes out, except to shop for sandwiches and milk. Her clothes are dirty and she uses safety pins instead of combs or hairpins to hold up her hair. Until recently, her friends knew she was not in poverty because she got regular checks from her lawyer. But her lawyer has died in the past year, and she refuses to tell anyone where her money is, how she pays for the apartment, or where she cashes checks, if she does get checks. It is even surprising that a few old friends continue to worry about her, because she, once a smashing beauty, presents such an unappetizing picture.

She is, of course, akin to the hoarders who live in abject poverty and leave trunks of furs and costly jewels when they die. Terror of spending money can be pathological, but many women left alone start down that path simply out of fear and ignorance. Thornton Wilder writes in *The Ides of March,* "Now isn't a large part of fear the memory of past fright and of past predicament? Caesar . . . identifies the possession and accumulation of money with weakness . . . and fright."

Many young people today are rebelling against the materialistic society of their parents; they feel they need to be free of money to feel free. We older people realize that a little money gives us a cushion. However, unless money is regarded as a means to an end, not an end, it can be an obsessive burden. Money cannot guarantee happiness; some of the most miserable women alone I talked with were the richest, with big houses, and cars, and children whom they indulged.

I know of a very rich woman, a widow, who is deliberately persecuting herself, living abroad in a country she hates, to avoid paying United States taxes. She is despised by her neighbors there because she pinches pennies on every hand, and gets lip service from her son and daughter-in-law only because they are waiting to spend her money . . . which keeps piling up, because she has devoted her life to its care and feeding.

I said earlier that women are essentially realists about money, that they believe it should be spent. I still feel that statement is true. And when we panic, or hoard, or save unrealistically for our children or our old age in a nursing home, we are simply hiding our heads in the sand, acting out of old male-conditioned fright. There is at least one small satisfaction we can hang onto, when we see ourselves being ridiculously frugal, cutting unnecessary corners. Men alone tend to be much worse. There are bachelors who are rich by any standards who never pay back any of the hospitality they accept, or send flowers, simply because they are frightened of an unloved old age.

Once money owns you, you are lost. But when you know where you stand financially, and can figure out how much you need to live the kind of life you really want, half the battle is over. You may have to cut corners; but you can do it realistically, without moaning. More likely, if you decide what you want, you will find experts who will find ways to help you achieve it.

Every money problem is individual, and the solution for one woman may be poison for another. A woman who tries to manipulate without studying the picture can defeat her own purpose. An estate lawyer gave me the example of one of his clients who went to a broker and asked him to rearrange her portfolio so she would have more income. He did this—without either of them realizing that this gave her some $40,000 in capital gains on which she would have to pay income tax, giving her less net income than she had had originally.

There are few blanket rules. The only one on which the experts all agree is that a widow must first decide what she wants, and then arrange her holdings so that she is able to function as well as possible within practical limits. But everything must come into consideration—her age, her temperament, her tastes. A nervous woman, for example, can have peace of mind only if her investments are very conservative. An impetuous woman must recognize that tendency in herself and depend upon her adviser to keep her in check.

We all know the change in attitude we have when traveling and spending foreign money—it does not seem real, it is just a way of getting what we want, food, drink, hotel rooms, things which give us pleasure. There is no mystery about money. The rudiments can be learned in an afternoon, if you want to be knowledgeable. Afterward, if you wish, you can go deeper into the gold standards, and inflation, and stock and bonds. A prominent New York woman broker told me: "Once a woman gets over the bugaboo about not understanding money, she makes a very good investor. She tends to be more reasonable and logical than a man."

And a New York lawyer, who handles estates, added: "There is nothing sacred about capital. If a woman wants something within reason, there is no cause to feel guilty because she isn't passing on her husband's hard-earned cash intact to her children. Money is meant to buy things. After all, we aren't going to live forever and it's one thing we can't take with us."

8 THE WOMAN ALONE, EN ROUTE

Travel really made the difference. Once I found out that I could go alone, and take care of myself, I no longer cared so much about what my friends at home were doing.

CHICAGO DIVORCEE

I don't mind traveling alone so long as I have people to look up in the places I am going. Sometimes I will even change my itinerary when I have names of people who sound interesting.

DETROIT WIDOW

I traveled with a group from Texas, by train and then boat. When we reached Honolulu, I liked it so well I decided to stay for a while. I regret that now. I missed my friends on the tour, and the new acquaintances. There weren't many men, but there were a lot of jolly women and we went places together.

HOUSTON WIDOW

There is only one way to travel, and that is alone. You'll be lonesome, once in a while, and wonder what you are doing in some out-of-the-way place, miserable. Then you move on, fast. Alone, you can keep flexible, stay if you are having a good time, get out if you aren't.

NEW YORK DIVORCEE

Travel happens to be one of the few things a woman can do better alone. She can decide when and where she wants to go, and set out when it is convenient, instead of waiting for someone else. If she has little money, she can discover the adventure of going economy class, where you often meet the most interesting people and age is less of a barrier than it is in first class. If she does not have to pinch pennies she can use her money to go to offbeat places, instead of plunking it down on luxury cruises and expensive resorts full of other rich widows and divorcees. If she likes a place, or a person, she can change her plans on the spot, and linger. If she is having a miserable time, she can move on. As never before in her life, she is flexible, and with sophistication and experience comes the courage to do things and go places which seemed impossible when she was younger.

A widow, traveling alone for the first time in her life, went down to dinner in the dining room of her hotel, and found she was the only unescorted female. Feeling unloved and unwanted, her impulse was to turn tail and have dinner sent up to her in bed. But pride made her stick it out. And it paid off. The next day, an attractive man stopped her in the lobby to say, "Are you an American? We saw you dining alone last night and admired you so much. No one but an American could carry that off with such poise and grace. Would you join us for dinner tonight?"

You never know when a pleasant experience, or a little adventure, is around the corner. Often when you feel most depressed, something nice happens—if you continue to go out instead of brooding in your room. A widow from Minneapolis, traveling from France to Spain on a train, found herself fumbling desperately at the border because she could not speak Spanish. A group of charming Spanish people came to her aid, became fast friends, took her over, and showed her Spain.

Travel is an ace in the hole for the woman alone. It gives her something to look forward to, nice memories to tuck away, and friends in far places. A widow in North Carolina, with children grown and moved away, was left with a farm to manage when her husband died. She felt both lonesome and conspicuous; if a man came to help her, there would be gossip in the little nearby town about him and "the widder Thomas." She had never traveled, much less alone, but one Christmas she took a bus to New York to visit one of her sons. It was a revelation to her. She made a whole new set of friends, with whom she corresponded the rest of the winter. Life no longer was so confining. Now she visits all her children, including one in California, with increasing frequency, always taking the bus. Sometimes she stops off to see people she has met on previous trips, otherwise she stays comfortably and safely and inexpensively in YWCA's.

"My neighbors think I'm crazy," she said to me, smiling. "Do you know? I couldn't care less. I'm having a wonderful time."

Travel not only gives you a vacation from your own surroundings and old friends, it gives them a vacation from you. In the Orient, a street hawker walked alongside a busload of tourists, cajoling, "Buy something pretty to give to all those friends who will be meeting you when you get back home." We do not have the custom of gathering in big groups to greet or say goodbye to a traveler, as they do in the Far East. (The woman alone must get used to managing by herself and looking as though she didn't mind a bit, even if she does.) But it is fun to gather little gifts for other people to tuck in your suitcase as you go alone, to show people back home you were thinking of them. Often something that costs a few cents in a foreign place looks quite charming back home.

You do not need to be beautiful, or young, to acquire friends along the way. Usually just the fact that you are alone makes you interesting. A redheaded New York secretary, a divorcee, told me that even when she is returning from a trip she is already planning what to do on her next vacation. She travels economy and, instead of spending her time in expensive places like Paris and London, goes to places where accommodations and food are cheaper and she is, in her way, a kind of celebrity. Once, when she left a town to continue her trip on a bus, virtually the whole populace came to wave goodbye to her. She already speaks enough French and Italian to get by, and this winter she is study-ing Russian; she has read that any American is an object of inter-est in Russia and she wants to see for herself—by herself.

I met a Nebraska widow, head of a large savings and loan asso-ciation, who has no language skills, is in her sixties and admits it, and who each year goes to some place a bit more remote than the year before—Africa, India, Russia. Usually she goes alone. Occa-sionally she joins congenial friends, fascinated with travel like herself, whom she has met on previous trips. She has bumped into wars and tribal celebrations; she has occasionally been scared but not enough to keep her from going on. And her experiences, espe-cially when she tells them back in Lincoln, are hilarious.

It takes courage to start out alone, even if you are joining a group tour. It is much easier to go with another female, so you have someone to talk to if things go wrong, a friendly face across the dinner table in a strange town. I can only say, from the expe-rience of many women, don't. You may be good friends when you start, but the chances are you will hate each other before the trip is over, especially if you are economizing and sharing a double room. (I know two women who managed to sustain a lifelong friendship by switching to separate rooms midway on a trip.) You will be missing opportunities for meeting people because you and your shadow are always together. You will be limited, hampered by the tastes and personal habits of another female. And you will be less interesting to strangers.

When I was first alone, another widow suggested I join her and still another widow on a freighter trip around the world. If a kindly fate had not intervened, I would have made a ghastly mis-take. For one thing, if there is anything worse than a pair of wid-ows traveling together, it is a trio; one of you is always on the outside, looking in. For another, we would have been cooped up for an interminable time on a small boat with a handful of other people; many freighters take only eight to twelve passengers. There is nothing to do except sit, sleep, and eat, and no guaran-tee what the other passengers will be like. I heard, for example, of two ladies, really dedicated bridge players, who took a freighter to Europe. The other ten passengers were all nuns, leaving the frustrated bridge friends to playing double solitaire and honeymoon bridge, a fate (to them) worse than death.

A divorcee who makes a business of traveling by freighter because she is not in any rush and can do it so cheaply, has this advice: "Try to go by one of the lines which takes around fifty passengers, you're almost sure to find someone congenial in that number. Don't sign up for a long cruise without finding out something about the other passengers. Take plenty of reading matter. Don't expect to make time with the officers; some won't do more than nod in your direction and regard passengers as the most objectionable kind of cargo. And, above all, don't travel with another woman friend. If you don't want to push her overboard, she'll push you."

There is a great deal of snobbery about tours and cruises. Just the idea of joining an organized tour is enough to throw some women—and their friends—into shock. I can say from experience it is all nonsense. Of course there are times when you look like a bunch of sheep waddling after their leader. But going with a group has definite advantages. Everything is arranged for you in advance—tickets, baggage, transfer, hotel rooms, sight-seeing. You do not have to speak a foreign language or know how to handle foreign currency. You see things, which is far better than staying home feeling sorry for yourself. And you have built-in companions.

Don't go expecting to meet your mate, or to find a lover. There may be only women on the tour, with a smattering of married couples. A single woman from another city may be a bridge to another kind of life for you; she may even have a bachelor brother. And a woman from Detroit told me that the couples she meets on tours often invite her to visit them afterward, and make more effort to find eligible bachelors for her than her old friends.

A widow who took her second cruise alone (her first was with a woman friend and she learned her lesson) told me that she made a point of going to bed early, especially at first, and getting up early, to enjoy a good breakfast, and walking the deck with the few attractive bachelors on board. She had a wonderful time because, "Actually, I had no competition. Most of the women were much older, or were traveling in pairs, permanently attached. The only other woman alone who might have been competition sat up dancing and drinking while we were crossing the Atlantic —and was so worn out that when she tried to do the sight-seeing with us, she got sick and was a dropout."

There is never any problem getting acquainted when you travel with a group, particularly if you start by yourself. But a cruise director told me that it is wisest for a woman to go slow, and not get swallowed up with pushy people who really do not interest her. And it is far better for a woman to go to bed early than sit wistfully by the dance floor, drinking too much and being conspicuously available. "In the evening, select the smallest, most intimate bar on the ship and drop in there casually for a drink—or a beer, or a coke—before you dress for dinner. If you fall into conversation with a male passenger, and he invites you to have a drink later, okay. Otherwise, after you put on your dinner dress, go right to your table—and slip off to bed when the meal is over *unless* someone urges you to dance. There is nothing gloomier than sitting around all dressed up and no place to go."

On a quick trip to Europe, or a brief cruise, the very fact that time is short makes it easy for intimacies to develop. On a long ocean voyage, or a tour, you get to know people so well you break up into factions and begin to quarrel among yourselves, like a big unhappy family. But you cannot be lonely.

This is hard to believe unless you have tried it. I know any number of bright, high-salaried, attractive single women who stay home because they are afraid to go alone and too proud to join organized groups. In fact, one of them, a pretty executive of a large corporation, confessed, "Every secretary in my office has been to Europe at least once. I've never been out of the United States. I won't go alone, I wouldn't dream of going with another woman, and I loathe groups."

I went on a trip to South America with a group of eighteen and not only had a good time but continue to see half a dozen of the people I met. But it is best to be a little selective about the groups you join.

I know a talented artist in Evanston, Illinois, who travels with groups by preference, although she has many devoted relatives and married friends who try to persuade her to take trips with them. It is her way of escape from the atmosphere she breathes the rest of the year. But she makes a point of never going with a group from her own community, because she deliberately seeks a change of pace, she wants to meet people with a different outlook. Consequently, she joins groups from Georgia, from California, from Iowa, from London. And she now has friends, a surprising number of them men, from all over the world. When she travels with new groups, she often crosses paths with friends from previous trips. She, who has never married, laughs about the men she meets. "One said he was attracted to me because I wore the same kind of shoes his dead wife always liked."

But a good friend of hers took me aside to say, "Jane is much more relaxed and happier than she was ten years ago, before she started to take off on these trips. I wouldn't even be surprised to see her get married one of these days."

My friend the cruise director, who has worked both on small ships and ocean liners, feels a short trip is a good way for a woman to start traveling alone. A long one, particularly if the people are not too congenial, may discourage her before she has learned to project herself and mix with all kinds. She also believes a woman alone will benefit from traveling off-season, if she wants to meet men and have a good time; some business firms offer cruises as a reward to employees, and unattached males go alone. If, for economy reasons, a woman shares a cabin with another woman, it is a good idea to keep your relation friendly but not intimate. Two women tied together tend to stand aloof and not participate in planned social events. Also, in case of seasickness, a female roommate should be left strictly to the care of the stewardess. "There is no point," said my knowing friend, "of being a martyr and staying in to help. The sick one won't appreciate it. I've seen cases when the invalid revived and practically loathed the roommate who had insisted on sitting by her bed, holding her hand."

Offbeat cruises, or trips, often offer amazingly rich rewards—if you are offbeat in the same way as the other tour members. For example, I was told by a widower that cruises offered in yachting magazines often have single men, boat-owners. Educational tours, which include language study as well as sightseeing, sometimes attract male professional types.

Travel agencies should know of other special interest tours that might be unusual enough to attract solitary males. But I would not advise the yachting magazine cruise, for example, if you are the seasick type. Or if boats bore you. Because you just might find yourself without a bachelor to interest you, thrown back on your own just to enjoy the sea and scenery. Even riskier, it seems to me, would be a trip that appeals to athletic types if you are an indoor girl.

The American Forestry Association, 919 17th St., N.W., Washington, D.C., 20006, sponsors summer wilderness trips in national parks and forests. Horseback, hiking, and canoe trips of about ten days' duration usually cost under $300 from point of origin and would be ten days of heaven—or hell—depending on how you take to the open spaces. There are other kinds of specialized trips; recently one advertised in the *New York Times* Sunday travel section offered an all-inclusive excursion to view the America's cup races, five days for $265. Experts tell me that any trip that has a sports angle, from sailing to deep-sea fishing, is more apt to attract men, often single men. Sporting magazines, as well as travel sections of newspapers and travel magazines, often feature these.

But if you are not the athletic type, you might fancy one of the various "singles tours." These are organizations that run trips and cruises all over the world, at a variety of prices, aimed deliberately at the single man and woman. They do not promise an equal number of men and women on each trip, so don't count on being paired off immediately, but the emphasis is on parties, dancing, night clubs, as well as sight-seeing.

I have a friend whose husband hates to travel. When he is away on a long business trip in the United States, she takes off alone on group tours and has a wonderful time. True, she is not under the same kind of pressure as a woman alone, who invariably is asked when she gets home, "Did you meet anybody interesting?" She goes to see things, which is exactly why the woman alone is supposed to be traveling, too. And, even when you are with a group, you are under no compulsion to do everything en masse. If you feel in need of privacy, leave the rest and go off on your own. Or, better still, if you have invitations from friends of friends in the countries you are visiting, accept them, even if it means skipping a scheduled sight-seeing trip you have already paid for. You can always go back and visit a place; people are more interesting.

In anything, the first time is the hardest. And, unless you make plans carefully, you can be miserable alone in a lot of countries. Even the best-laid plans can go astray. An experienced friend, once a widow and twice a divorcee, told me seriously, "A lot of these dames pretend they like traveling alone. Believe me, it isn't always so great." (But now she has a husband who travels a lot and takes her with him.) I also heard of a widow of three months who went alone on the round-the-world trip she and her husband had planned before his death, and wept for three months solid, on mixed sleeping cars in Russia and at St. Peter's in Rome. In addition, if you have not traveled much previously, or if you have had a husband who took care of tickets, tipping, and arrangements, you simply may not have the guts to start out alone; you need some kind of support. Most important of all, if you are new at being alone, and a bit shaken up over a recent loss, you are not in very good shape to cope with anything, much less mechanics of foreign travel.

I find many of the ladies who write so blissfully about the joys of going solo have never been married. They are used to managing themselves and money. They have jobs; some of them have traveled alone on business. And they have never known the solid comfort of going places and seeing things in a relaxed atmosphere with a congenial man. They write wittily about experiences with male guides. Or recommend that you go down to the hotel bar in a tight-fitting, low-cut dress to meet new friends.

I met any number of charming ladies who thought nothing of going into hotel bars in strange cities, where they would not dream of going alone back home. A dean of admissions from a Midwestern university says she often meets up with groups of young people in foreign bars, who immediately incorporate her.

An extremely sophisticated Australian woman writer was amazed that I should even question the idea of a woman alone traveling going into a bar: "It's much better than sitting around a lobby looking wistful."

However, some of us just do not have the courage to go into bars unescorted. As for guides, I met an impetuous divorcee who, on her first trip alone, became engaged to her Italian guide because she thought he must be brilliant, to speak such good Italian when hers was so miserable. But, whether you are chicken or hawk, you have to do a good deal more planning for a trip than you do when you are with a man.

I know married couples who are impetuous travelers. They take planes on impulse, arrive in foreign countries without reservations, and invariably have fascinating experiences finding hotels and restaurants. Once in a while, accidents will propel a woman alone into marvelous adventures. But, especially at first, it is a good plan to have plane and hotel reservations well mapped out in advance, whether you make them yourself or go through a travel agent. Even then, there can be slips; I remember a late-at-night session at a hotel in Cambodia where I arrived and found they had no record of my reservation. After we had gone through the lists for the past month, and I was close to tears, I asked, "What are you going to do with me? I'm all alone." And the courteous answer came: "Oh, Madame, we have plenty of rooms, I just wanted to show you we didn't have your reservation."

It is also a good plan—practically vital, I would say—to have names of friends-of-friends in the cities you plan to visit, whether at home or abroad. A divorcee I met on my South American trip told me, "Ask everyone you know for names. One of my most interesting friends in Japan came to me through an introduction by my hairdresser."

Of course, there are stumbling blocks here, too. After you collect a notebook full of names of friends-of-friends, will you have the nerve to use them? At dinner one night in Honolulu, my muumuu'd hostess turned to me and said, "Last month, my husband and I had thirty-five calls from women alone visiting in

Honolulu, all of whom expected me to rush down and show them the sights. Some of them were sent by virtual strangers, people I had met only once. Others were from distant relatives. I often didn't have a clue as to whether the caller was my children's age, our age, or my mother's age. I try to make an effort to at least take the woman to lunch. But there aren't enough days in the week to see them all. And we do have a private life."

In some places—Honolulu, New York, Paris, and London are not among them—the arrival of a visitor is a source of stimulation and pleasure. Experienced women-alone travelers warn me that you have to use judgment, and tact: ask friends for names, to be sure, but, as one traveled divorcee put it, "Don't use these names unless you are really stuck, or know you have something in common with the people, really something to offer them. Pulling a name out of the hat and calling is in the same league with asking the American Embassy for help. It may be necessary in time of trouble; otherwise, skip it.

"On the other hand, if you can get your friends to write a letter to the people in the city you're visiting, and mail it well in advance, in time to get an answer, you are in luck. You won't necessarily be met—although it happens sometimes—but you will usually find a letter or a bunch of flowers at the hotel, an excuse for you to telephone and say thank you, and invite the sender to lunch.

"Also, if you have the name of someone whom you would like to meet, whether or not your mutual friend has sent a letter telling him about you, it is always proper for you to extend an invitation. For lunch, if it is a woman; for tea or a drink, if it is a man. In this way, you won't be imposing too much on the time of your victim, and you will give him or her a chance to look you over, at no expense. Also, make the date specific. Don't just say, 'Come and have a drink some afternoon.' And mention the date of your departure from the city early in the conversation. If the victim seems reluctant, or unsure about his schedule, give him your name and room number at your hotel and sign off—pleasantly and quickly. If he calls back, fine—but be sure to pay the check the first time you see him. If you don't hear from him, congratulate yourself that you haven't been a nuisance. And don't take rejection to heart for he (or she) doesn't know how charming you are, the friend who suggested you call maybe *persona non grata,* or you may have arrived at an inconvenient time, when the couple were divorcing or the children were all down with bubonic plague."

The worst time of the day for a woman alone is the evening, the close of the day when other people are meeting friends for dinner or drinks. Even if you have made your plans well, there will be nights like this. You can retire to your room, call room service and have dinner sent up, and write postcards. This is all right once in a while—your first night in a strange place when you are tired, for example—but as a steady diet it is both depressing and dull.

The best advice I received on how to cope with evenings came from a trio of sophisticated ladies who are on the staff of *The Reader's Digest* in Asia, and who travel alone frequently on business. They agreed that it is not a bad idea for a woman to eat alone in her room her first night in a new place, particularly if she is not looking her best and needs a night's sleep.

But the next day, she should inspect the hotel and decide which dining room will be the most comfortable. They feel it is understandable if the woman alone will pick a coffee shop, or something equally unpretentious. But it is not being adventurous. She should not eat only in the main dining room of the hotel, she must enjoy other restaurants, even floor shows she wants to see.

The technique here is to call in advance, give your name *and* the name of the city you are from, and request a table for one. Your identification with a foreign city means you are traveling, and hints that you are someone of importance in that city. If a woman alone is not welcome, you will receive that information over the telephone, not in person. "And sometimes you may be surprised to discover that you will be given special attention."

One of the three, a divorcee, told me that, on a trip to Honolulu, when she requested a table for a particular show she wanted to see at her hotel, she was given the best one at ringside, and as the evening went on, she was joined there by other friendly people.

A young unmarried lady, a Chinese, whom I shall call Miss W., then related the story of the high point of her travels alone. She has worked for several American magazines and gone around the world, alone. One evening she was having dinner alone in an Oriental hotel that had divided the top floor into two parts—one for the dinner crowd, another a night club. As she was eating her dessert, she heard music from the night club area and called the waiter to ask what kind of a show it would be. He looked embarrassed. "Not for ladies, madame." She repeated her request and he confessed that it was a nude show."

She said, "Book me a table. I'll have my coffee and brandy in there."

And so she did. If she had been Caucasian, this might have created some stir, but for an Asian in an Asian country, it took positive daring. I can only say, go thou and do likewise.

Being slim and lively, Miss W. has also had her shares of passes from men. But even if you are neither, there may be moments when independence can be misunderstood. I have a friend who refuses to travel alone in latin countries because of an experience she had with a man in Mexico. They had been properly introduced by mutual friends. Even so, he parked his car in front of a motel she had heard was notorious, gathered her up in his arms, and carried her forcibly into a room. She is not sure how or why she finally got out without being raped. She only thinks now, "Latin men are different."

In South America, a room waiter tried to embrace me when I had buzzed him to order breakfast. I managed to shove him out—he was not in very good condition physically—but afterward he continued to follow me down the hall murmuring, "Bellissima, bellissima." I was reluctant to report him because the whole incident made me feel like such a fool. I simply did not eat any meal, including breakfast, in my room after that. Ladies who lived in South America told me I was silly not to have complained. I guess I was afraid I would look like another neurotic female if I did.

For I shall never forget overhearing the driver of a chartered bus talking to two others about a woman on one of his conducted tours. "Do you know what she wanted? When the rest of the bunch was eating lunch, she wanted me to come up to her room for a drink and you-know-what. And she was an *old* bag." Also, from a Tourist Bureau representative, I heard the tale of the lady on the cruise ship who complained because the woman she had drawn as a roommate smoked, drank, and stayed up after midnight. Then one night the roommate felt tired and decided to go to bed around nine. The cabin was bolted and the haughty lady came to the door holding up a bath towel in front of her and said, "Give us another half hour, will you, darling?"

A divorcee told me she always travels first class in planes to ward off the jerks. When she returned from a trip to Turkey, she called to say, "I met the worst jerk of my life on the way out—in first class yet. He was quite presentable when I got on, and I thought to myself, you're a lucky girl. Then he bolted a lot of liquor on top of what he must have already been drinking and began to fumble around my legs. I didn't like the idea of me, a mature woman, appealing to a young stewardess for help. So I adopted the pose of passive resistance. At last he fell asleep and when he woke up, he hardly looked at me."

Most of the women I interviewed prefer to travel tourist, and not only because it is cheaper. A widow who went to Australia last year told me, "On the trip out, I took first class, because I was so tired. The people I met were large families traveling together, or dull businessmen. I came back tourist and there were all sorts of interesting people—and we all felt informal, and changed places once in a while. I had my most fun with a group of students."

Tourist or first class, a woman alone will occasionally run into a bore—or a mess. Drunks are bad news anywhere. But a complaint to the steward or stewardess in a plane, or to the driver of a bus, or to the conductor on a train, usually can get you transferred to another seat. As for the professional pass-makers, there are various techniques. A sophisticated divorcee, who is also a beauty, told me that laughter is a good weapon. "And, if that doesn't work, try staring at his feet, or his tie. It will make him so nervous he'll move away from you."

She adds, "There is nothing wrong about making friends with a pleasant stranger, and letting him take you to dinner. But it's a good idea to watch your drinking—and his. And don't go to his hotel for a meal, if you can help it. One night I was having dinner with a man in a revolving restaurant on top of a hotel—his hotel, as it turned out. On the way down in the elevator, he punched the twelfth floor. I didn't like to make a fuss, as there were other people in the car, when he stood aside to let me out. Then I asked where we were going. He said he had to get something in his room. I said, 'I'll wait for you here.' He took my arm and tried to push me along. I simply smiled and told him, 'If you don't let me alone, I'll run up and down the corridors screaming that my husband has gone berserk and needs a doctor. Now take me down and put me into a taxi.' He did—and I had no further trouble with him."

Miss W., my attractive Chinese friend, told me that one night she got rid of a persistent young American officer by arguing about Vietnam—"He got so mad he wanted to kill me, not go to bed with me." A divorcee in Mexico told me she shed a bore who was dogging her footsteps at a hotel by saying, "Can't you see you're ruining my vacation?" He was hurt, of course—but he left her alone after that.

The consensus of opinion is that it is better to sense a difficult situation and sidestep before it becomes crucial. But you can also be taken by surprise. So it is the better part of judgment to keep out of dark streets and little restaurants "only natives know." And when in doubt, take a taxi home—alone.

A widow who works in a travel agency gave me her ten rules for women traveling alone which I quote below:

1. Talk to strangers, everywhere. If rebuffed, move on to the next one.

2. Don't write postcards in public. It marks you as a bore.

3. Don't travel with another woman. If you get stuck, don't sit with her at meals or on sightseeing buses.

4. Travel with a married couple if you're asked. But don't hang around their necks like an albatross. Take side trips alone. Give them privacy.

5. If a man offers to carry your bag, let him.

6. Visit friends, if urged. But don't overstay. Set a departure date and stick to it, even if they want you to stay on.

7. Pick up checks. Even with men. Then they won't expect to be paid off in bed.

8. Dress for dinner carefully, even if you're a mess the rest of the day. This is especially important if you are dining alone.

9. Don't be an ugly female American. Instead of demanding your rights loudly, speak softly and be pathetic. This works especially well in foreign countries.

10. Write prompt thank-you notes—on post cards, if must be. But don't address them in hotel lobbies, restaurants, or bars.

9 SEX AND THE WOMAN ALONE

If I were a real cute little trick, I wouldn't be surprised at having passes made at me. But I'm a big woman. I think sometimes if I rolled over on one of the little ones, I'd squash him.

DETROIT DIVORCEE

Worst of all is this terrible fumbling and pawing you get from every man who takes you out—and some who don't want to spend a dime on you, who just want to drop by at their convenience. It's like being back in adolescence again, not wanting to insult the ones who are eligible, yet not wanting to get the reputation of being promiscuous. And you can't pretend you're a lily-white virgin the way you did when you were young. I don't know what the answers are. I wish to God I did.

HONOLULU DIVORCEE

You get so that if a man doesn't make a pass by the third or fourth date, you think he is homosexual.

NEW YORK DIVORCEE

In Europe there is a much more permissive attitude about sex than there is here. For example, I have a feeling my neighbors are shocked when they see men leaving my house early in the morning. If the men were married, I would feel guilty. But these men are unattached—I am unattached—whose business is it?

MASSACHUSETTS DIVORCEE

I have more to offer than a girl half my age—after all, I can cook, I know how to keep house and make a man comfortable. I know I can satisfy a man in bed. But men these days want youth, for a young wife builds up a man's ego, makes him feel young again. It may even keep him more active sexually, for who wants to look at a woman's body after she is forty and has had three children? But I am wondering how those marriages will wear, especially if there isn't a lot of money. Or am I just being bitchy?

WIDOWED CALIFORNIA SCHOOLTEACHER

I miss the companionship of a man. Even more, I miss the kind of companionship you have after sex. That's why a casual affair isn't enough for me. I want all the trimmings, all the 'gingerbread,' as one man told me. We had a glorious weekend in Atlantic City, of all places. Then he didn't call me again for three months.

DIVORCED NEW JERSEY MOTHER

D<small>R</small>. Robert Harper, director of counseling clinics at Ohio State and Merrill Palmer Institute in Detroit, wrote, "Most of the people who write about sex fall at the reactionary-conservative end of the continuum. They have been conditioned to think and feel in accordance to what has been presented to them as the moral verities. . . . They are also afraid to let friends and the community know what they think, although they are privately liberal."

Sex can consist of many different kinds of urges. It can be motivated by revenge—on an ex-husband, on society, on those "goddam smug wives," on fate. It can be a desire to reaffirm your attractiveness. It can be a device to hold a man, or to lure him into matrimony.

I doubt if anyone today, including the experts, is sure where the sexual revolution is leading us. Perhaps, in another fifty years, there will not be marriage as we know it now, or family patterns.

Meanwhile, we can only guess. And ask questions. Women have told me that they would not "lower their standards." I am not quite sure what they mean because the major problem a woman who finds herself alone faces is that her entire world, and her standards, have been shattered. She is more or less unwelcome and unprotected, in a society that has no place for her and no rules. She has to make her own.

Some men are as confused as we are. For example, what about the man who does not make a pass on the first date? Is he a gentleman or a homosexual? Or, after she has said no and giggled, what is the next step? Try to get beneath the surface of panic or look for another woman? Men have their problems with those hell-bent-for-husbands girls. And the ones at cocktail parties who come up to a man and say, "I'm leaving. Do you want to take me home and go to bed?"

There is also that natural female built-in duplicity. A divorcee —a beautiful divorcee—admitted that she has a widower she would like to keep as a handy escort, although he repels her physically. So, whenever he puts his arm around her, she sits stiffly and begins talking about his late wife. Another dimpled lady, a widow who admits to many tricks, says she uses tears when a man will not stop when she tells him to: "No man finds it possible to rape a weeping female." A divorcee told me that, when annoyed, she gets revenge on her lover by sleeping with another man; but she pretends to him that she is lily-pure faithful.

We use men, sometimes as much as they use us, sometimes more. We use them to bail us out of debt—but complain if a man tries to borrow money from us. We use them to take us places we hesitate to go alone, and then we are lousy company. We make big eyes at them in public—and fun of them privately. We read their love letters to other women, and laugh.

A woman told me about going to the apartment of a psychiatrist for "cocktails." He met her at the door naked, playing a violin. I do not know what happened there, but she told the story all over town, and it got back to his patients. Did she care? "Not a damn," she said cheerfully.

Now what about you—who are not cruel, devious, or indifferent? The only answer I can give, after many late-night talks with women who are equally perplexed, is that when you have your balance, remember: you don't have to do anything you don't want to.

Perhaps to a man this sounds silly. But women have used sex as a device for so many years that the issue has become muddied. Now I think most women alone are able to face the fact that sex has not always been pleasant or satisfactory for them in marriage, but that they have suppressed complaints out of fear of offending their husbands—or an antiquated notion of modesty.

The advantage of being free and alone is that you do not have to do anything for effect, or to please a man, or to save his feelings. You can be honest with him, and with yourself. Perhaps a woman with a low sex drive would be better off not married—why not face it? And perhaps a woman with strong sex urges is happier with a variety of sexual partners than with one husband.

On the other hand, you have no time for regrets and recriminations. If you have made a mistake, done something that you regret but that cannot be undone, consider it an experiment that taught you a valuable lesson, and then forget it.

Most important—cultivate discretion. Men and women both told me that women tend to talk too much about their sex lives. A bright young woman who lived happily as a divorcee for many years before she remarried—also happily—told me: "Cultivate the air of being a woman of mystery. Leave early at a dinner party, but don't say where you are going. If a mutual friend, usually a married woman, pries a bit about your social life, put her off. Resist the temptation to ask advice *from anybody*. The minute you give a friend a clue, a name, she will be asking, have you heard from X lately? Don't even give married women full reports on the men they have produced for you. If you've said no, they will abuse you for being too choosy. If you've said yes, they are apt to turn a bit jealous on you.

"For if nothing is going on in your life, you don't want people to know and feel sorry for you. If, on the other hand, you have something going, you're better off if nobody knows except that one person."

SEX AND

THE ELIGIBLE MAN

It's the first date, arranged by mutual friends. He calls for her and she gives him a drink. Then they go to dinner. She has been divorced six weeks, separated for a year, and is just starting to date. He has been divorced nearly a year. Their conversation is mostly about divorce, children, loneliness. After dinner, he hails a cab and says, "Shall we go to your place or mine?"

Louise knows, because she has been on a few other dates, that if she doesn't go to bed with him, she won't hear from him again; why should he call her, when there are so many women alone who are available? If she does, he might. Or he might not.

Sue is a widow, with a twelve-year-old daughter. Her husband, who died of cancer after three expensive operations, left her a small income which she has to supplement by working. She would like very much to get married again. A widower in the same building has a son about the age of her daughter. Through the children, they meet. He invites her to a dance at the country club. All the other couples are married. On the way home, he suggests they stop at a motel on the outskirts of the town, because they can not go to his apartment or hers, on account of the children. He is a nice man, she would like to continue seeing him. She is attracted to him physically. But the idea of going to a motel revolts her.

Clara is a widow, forty-nine years old. Her husband, a much older man, has been dead for seven years. An attractive man of sixty, divorced, financially solvent, is glad to have a more or less permanent affair with her but he does not want to get married. His excuse is that he has had one bad failure and does not want to be tied down again, because he thinks he might behave badly if he were. She feels she is at the age when security is vital, emotionally more than financially. As their arguments grow sharper, their sexual life deteriorates. Finally she "punishes" him by going away on a cruise to the Mediterranean. When she returns, she discovers he has been making love to a thirty-five-year-old divorcee. But he says he is willing to return to the original arrangement if she is . . . that there was "nothing except sex" in it with the divorcee.

A Texas widow told me she is utterly confused. After being alone for five years, she became interested in a divorced man and went to bed with him, as a matter of course. ("We were mature and in love.") But when marriage was mentioned, he began dragging his feet. After six months, she gave him an ultimatum—marriage or she would break off. They broke off and he married another woman, a divorcee in his office.

Recently, her sister-in-law arranged a blind date for her with a lawyer from New York, a widower. While she was out in the kitchen mixing them a drink, he came out and kissed her. Before the drink was finished, he had thrown her down on the couch and was on top of her saying, "I know you want it as much as I do." She slapped his face and told him to get out. Later, her sister-in-law chided her, "X just announced his engagement. You didn't handle him right."

When a woman alone goes on her first dates, she discovers that with eligible men, sex is on an "of course" basis—unless the man is otherwise fully occupied, is overage and a bit unsure of himself, or does not want to get married. The only question is whether intercourse is regarded as a gonadal exercise or surrounded with a little aura of romance and courtship. Even then, old-world courtship can last just so long without the man declaring himself one way or another—and the first declaration is rarely an old-fashioned proposal of marriage. ("Unless, of course," one pretty widow of forty-three told me, "the man is so unattractive that he knows from experience no woman will fall into his arms because of mad passion.")

Some women, after a flurry of dating, will give up the whole thing. I have had very attractive still-youngish women tell me that they do not miss sex. (Either, "Thank goodness, I have a low sex drive," or, "You get used to going without.") But others tell me that they will sleep with two or three men without feeling in the least promiscuous. ("What is promiscuity anyway? Just a Puritan guilt feeling.") A charming cultured woman told me, "If a nice man wants very much to go to bed with me, why not? If I enjoy it, fine. If I don't, I can always say no when he asks me again."

This woman is from Europe and perhaps is more liberated than some of us. But she admits that she has not yet been emotionally involved with any man with whom she has had intercourse and that the affairs have been of short duration. Another divorcee, who has since remarried, said quite casually that, "Of course I went to bed with a man if I liked him—sometimes it was great, sometimes not." Yet she added, a bit ruefully, that it was quite different when you found yourself becoming more than incidentally interested in a man:

"It's a perpetual problem, sex. When you first say yes, you don't plan to get involved. You say to yourself you can be just as casual as any man, take it or leave it. But something happens. It may become a matter of pride, or dependence on him, or perhaps some mysterious built-in Pavlovian reaction to the intimacy of regular sex with a man. You begin to care, and then you suffer.

"Your life becomes one long vigil, waiting for the telephone to ring. Or you get in such a nasty state you call him, and you suspect, from the offhand way he talks, he has a girl with him. You begin to hear her heels tapping around the room, see him putting his hand over the mouthpiece and gesturing to her to light a cigarette. Finally, you can't stand it, you break off. You are relieved, free and independent. The telephone is no longer a monster. Yet you know deep down the whole thing is going to be repeated and, in a way, you want it to be."

It seems that men are much luckier. The need, it appears, is much simpler and more direct. Sex is an end in itself. (A delightful old Irish lady told me, "The man goes off with his hands in his pockets afterward, whistling, leaving us to break our hearts.") They are not burdened with the whole nest of complicated emotions which sex seems to bring on in women—or at least, women who were raised in the old American tradition of mixing sex with love and wedding rings and babies.

I sat at dinner in the Midwest with six women, ranging in age from thirty to fifty-five. When the talk switched—as it inevitably does at a certain time of night—to men and sex, one of them said, "A middle-aged girl, if she does fall, is just as bad as a teenager, and more hurt when she loses him. I remember a singles party where one of the men announced his engagement to a young divorcee. The other girl who had been dating him burst into tears and kept weeping in corners all evening. We tried to make her stop, or go home, but she had no shame. She wanted to cut herself to little bits watching him."

The young generation today is supposed to be much braver and brighter about sex. They make a great point about frankness and freedom. Various contraceptive methods, including "the pill," have supposedly liberated the female because she no longer needs to fear pregnancy. The strange part of this is that girls still continue to have babies out of wedlock. The only difference from my generation is that they are not disgraced in their contemporaries' eyes, merely "unlucky." And, of course, the boys are not under nearly as much pressure to marry the girls. For one thing, since freedom is the order of the day, how does he know the baby is his? For another, he didn't rape her; she was as eager for sex as he was. And for still another, why in hell didn't she take precautions?

A gynecologist told me that few young girls who are not married take "the pill" with any decree of regularity, even when they are having regular sex. "They pop a pill in their mouths just before going on a date," he said. "They know better, but they're careless. Or maybe more romantic than they pretend. Safe sex isn't as exciting as when there is a danger of getting caught."

As for the woman who has been married, or hasn't but is in the age bracket of the widow and divorcee, the problem of sex is much more complicated. We are supposed to know our way around, to be equipped with "the pill," the diaphragm, what have you. Obviously, we cannot be virgins; even women who have never married are regarded as very strange indeed if they have not had experience, but if so, the pitch here is, "Honey, you don't know what you're missing. Come on, you're a big girl now." We should not be coy. Yet at heart we are as silly and confused as adolescents. A young widow told me, "I stiffen when a man puts his arm around me. I'm more scared than when I was fifteen." A divorcee told me, "My sister had a dinner two weeks ago for her son, who is going to get married. I left early. My brother-in-law wouldn't let me go without kissing me goodbye. Then all the men lined up and wanted to kiss me. I felt like a whore."

A San Francisco divorcee said, "I understand with the young people, if a girl isn't attracted by a boy, she tells him so bluntly. Or she says she is frigid. I went on the basis of telling the truth, saying I'd had such a messy sexual life with my husband I didn't want sex with anybody, I wanted companionship. Wouldn't you think some men would have felt the same way? Obviously not. Even the ones who admit they have orgastic impairment as a result of the way their wives have acted, go after the girls who make it clear they are absolutely available. I think it's a sad state of affairs, to remove all the romance from sex, but my friends tell me this is it, this is the way things are and are going to be. So I might as well get with it, if I don't want to sit alone the rest of my life."

At a Parents Without Partners meeting in Detroit last fall, I heard a psychiatrist ("I am one of you, I am divorced.") talk in favor of courtship, "that neglected art." Afterward, many of the people who attended the meeting gathered at a local bar. I tried to talk to some of the men about courtship. One laughed at me; why bother courting when the women chase you? A divorced banker said he believed a man should not have sex without some emotional involvement, which entails (he said) courtship. A man who had been divorced six years (and was notorious in the group for always making a beeline for the pretty new members) agreed. But he added, "You come around to that gradually. At first, whether you're divorced or widowed, all you want is sex and you couldn't care less who gives it to you, so long as she isn't repulsive."

The women tried to be equally casual. One said, "I don't go to bed, and men know it. Not moral scruples. It's just—why should I take on a man who has worse problems than I have?"

Another said: "The first time I went to bed with a man after my divorce, it was a big emotional deal for me. He left saying I was terrific and he'd call me next day. Do you know when he actually got around to telephoning? Two weeks later—and he asked me for a date that night. He couldn't understand why I was hurt. Now I've learned better."

A New York widow, a real honey-colored charmer, told me a story about her experience with the new cool attitude about sex. "I just couldn't go to bed casually, on a first date. If I had, I would have felt dirty, cheap. But I had been noticing a young man in my building, and we'd had several nice conversations. One evening when I was coming home from work, he asked me to come up and have a beer. It was a soft spring night. He put Mozart on the record player, just like an old movie. Even his approach was sweet. He told me how much he had admired me, and when we finally made love, it was natural and wonderful. I thought he'd call the next day. But he didn't—or the next. When I finally met him on the stairs about ten days later, I looked right through him and said, 'Hi, Henry.' His name is John. I never dated him again. It was a one-night stand. I was so ashamed I got out of the building as fast as I could. Now I'm living without sex, and devoting myself to work. I won't ever get married simply because I can't be casual."

A PWP member in Chicago told me, "We had a speaker who told us it was all right to have intercourse with a man after the third or fourth date. The men all hooted, they expect it on the first. Of course you can say no. But then you never see them again."

A pretty widow with three young children added, "You can stall the older men. They keep coming back because they want to be seen out with a younger woman, pretending they're making out with her. But the ones my age don't even bother to work up to it. They ask you to go to bed the way they ask you if you want a beer. If you say no, okay. It's off to someone else. There's no damned romance any more. My husband and I had fights, but he really made love to me, he told me I was beautiful."

The "sexual revolution," which started with the teenagers, is confusing even the doctors and psychiatrists. Psychiatrist Max Levin of New York wrote in a *New England Journal of Medicine* article: "The pressures that confront the adolescent girl are confusing to her, and she needs help in order to keep her feet on the ground. Speaking as physicians and not as religious teachers, we must help her to see that premarital intercourse is risky, not merely on moral grounds, and not merely because of the danger of pregnancy, but because it threatens her emotional well-being."

Dr. Ralph R. Greenson, clinical professor of psychiatry, University of California, Los Angeles, School of Medicine, said in the magazine *Today's Health:* "In both boys and girls, sexual intimacy often precedes romantic love. They get to know each other sexually before they become close emotionally or intellectually. . . . This public sexuality does not lead to real sexual satisfaction, but on the contrary, indicates some degree of orgastic impotence. Quick and easy bodily intimacy and familiarity makes for promiscuity and 'organ pleasures,' but not for a rich orgastic experience . . . consequently we so frequently find love without passion and sex without emotional involvement."

But a Kentucky doctor wrote to the editor of the *New England Journal of Medicine* after reading Dr. Levin's article, "I enjoyed Dr. Levin's sermon. However, since it was obviously delivered to the Society for the Suppression of Vice sometime in the 1890s, why did you wait so long to publish it?"

And, according to *Medical World News,* this comment epitomizes the viewpoint of many leading sex educators, that "sexual activity, in itself, is not a source of emotional difficulty for adolescents." Dr. Edward T. Tyler, associate clinical professor of medicine and obstetrics and gynecology at UCLA, says that only a limited number of teenagers come to him with sexual problems, and, of these, most are interested primarily in information about contraceptives. Dr. George E. Beckerman of Santa Monica believes that "experimentation" is a better word than "promiscuity" to describe current teenage behavior and adds, "Teenagers are better off going through this experimental revolution than if we had continued with our hypocritical code of ethics."

This confusion, and the bewilderment of my generation and environs, prompted me to talk to three young New York girls, just out of college, who are living sardined together in a one-bedroom apartment on the upper East Side, the chic place to be if you are young and single.

A long-legged blond peach of a girl stared at me in astonishment. "Passes? Oh, you can always handle them. It depends on your attitude."

There was a moment of deep silence—from me. Then it turned out I was speaking another language. Passes come from absolute strangers you meet in bars or restaurants. When it is a question of someone whom you have met before or who has taken you to dinner and bought you a few drinks, then it is legitimate procedure, something we agreed to call an "approach."

"If you want to, okay. If he doesn't appeal to you, tell him so."

"But what if you would like to see him a few more times before you decide whether to say yes or no?"

The girls studied the question. A tiny girl with long dark hair and big, dark, carefully rimmed eyes finally answered, "You make a gag about it. You say something about your zippers being locked."

The blonde added, "Of course, it's no problem with three of us in a one-bedroom apartment. Even if you're alone, a roommate might pop in any second. Weekends are, of course, trickier. If he knows darned well your roommates are all away . . ."

"What about going to his place?"

"Usually they have roommates, too. Unless he is older, and making enough to live by himself. Then you don't get away with kidding."

"What happens?"

The redhead who had spoken last ran a comb through her hair. "Then you never see him again. Unless you say yes."

Later I talked with two girls, one a freshman at a coeducational college, another just back from two years in Africa with the Peace Corps. The coed said, "There's a saying around school. 'If it moves, caress it.' The girls don't rely on the pill. The boys all carry their own contraceptives."

"What do you do about a pass?" I was relieved to know that they understood what I mean, perhaps from listening to their old square mothers.

The coed said, "If you can anticipate him, and keep laughing, okay. Make it sort of a game."

The Peace Corps volunteer shook her head. "That's okay for kids. Teasing is half the fun. It's different with us. One night I had my first date with a volunteer from another region. I liked him a lot and would have enjoyed seeing him again. When he made a pass, I tried to be funny about it. Maybe he had been in Africa too long, or maybe he didn't have a sense of humor. But I didn't see him again."

Some young women are not "promiscuous." Even so, they tend to talk this new sex language, while they are quietly protected by roommates or their own freshness. Others are self-reliant and lovely enough to dictate when and if they want sex, and will only accept it on a more or less permanent basis—when they are considering marriage. Others hold out; although their contemporaries look upon these with some suspicion. I was told that some girls will be completely proper at home, where they are known, but go off on flings traveling in strange towns. But the young girl, with all the innate allurements of youth, has a definite advantage over the women-alone set.

For one thing, most of us are missing sex ourselves. We even know the symptoms of irritation and depression which come with lack of sex. Some of us have learned, the hard way, that most married men, and some married women, regard sex so lightly that they almost constantly have an affair going. We also want dates, and we soon find out, if we have not already heard it from other women alone, that no heterosexual man, married or single, will date you regularly unless sex is part of the arrangement.

A pretty friend of mine said, "A man may take you out for coffee, or an occasional movie, just because you're an old friend and he likes you. But he isn't going to take you to big parties, or even to fancy places to eat, unless he is also taking you to bed. That is something you have to realize in advance, and make your own adjustments."

A widow in Minneapolis, who rents the checkroom concession in a large restaurant patronized by men at noon, has collected a few carefully selected beaus out of her acquaintances there. She told me, "Of course I get passes, but I say, 'This little chick doesn't go in the house, she stays out in the yard.' I don't have trouble." I met other women alone, particularly in the Midwest, who say they date, or keep a retinue of three or four escorts, without having intercourse. In some cases, particularly when the man is an old friend, or the husband of a woman friend who has died, a woman alone does not even have to fend off passes. ("I suspect he's sleeping with a young woman," a widow told me. "I couldn't care less, so long as he doesn't bother me. We belong to the same bridge club, we often are invited to dinner parties together, and it's pleasant on both sides.") I know a beautiful woman who has been a widow for three years who says, "I don't go to bed" (What's more, I believe her!) and who has a string of lovelorn suitors wanting to marry her. The catch here is that she is under fifty, possessed of a comfortable income, has a wide assortment of friends and adoring relatives—and that she does more for her escorts, from the standpoint of offering hospitality, than they do. She gives frequent big sitdown dinners, she entertains small groups in expensive restaurants (where she is so well known that the check is never brought to the table) and she gives theater parties in which she includes an escort and another couple.

Returning hospitality is the key to a continuing relation with a man which never goes beyond friendship and a mutual pleasure in each other's company. It is the way sophisticated woman operate—those who do not want to remarry but do like to have men as escorts and companions.

However, what if you do want to remarry?

Sex is not the only reason men get married a second time. There are practical considerations of households to run, meals to get, children (or grandchildren) to think of. Some men need companionship, particularly of women, and are unable to live alone. But only a rare man of any age does not have sex on his mind when he marries again, even if he marries primarily for money or security. Nor can I believe, with the sexual revolution in full cry, that he will take what my grandmother used to refer to as a "pig in a poke." And, according to the French author, Camus, "The body's judgment is as good as the mind's." ("Better, perhaps," says author Jessamyn West in her book, *Love is Not What You Think*, "in a matter in which the body is to be so intimately involved.")

In California, I talked with a widow who seemed to have everything it takes to attract men. She has a good sense of humor, she dresses well, and she is extremely bright socially and in her own career. Yet, although she has a number of men friends—while I was in her apartment, the telephone rang constantly—she has been a widow for eight years.

She said, "Of course I've had affairs. But they were love affairs, not just the casual sexual experiments. Sometimes I didn't want to marry the man, after we were intimate. Other times, I knew he wasn't interested in marrying me, so I accepted what fun we could have together and tried not to suffer.

"Then one evening, just as I was about to leave a big birthday celebration of a dear elderly gentleman, an attractive man came into the room. It was just like the song—our eyes met across a crowded room and we clicked. So I sat down again. As soon as he had greeted the gentleman whose birthday we were honoring, he came right to me and asked if he could take me home. For a week, we went out every night. He told me he had been divorced twice, but it didn't matter. I was head-over-heels, crazy about him. It was like being eighteen again. But I wouldn't let him go all the way. I didn't want him to think of me as just another affair. I wanted to get married.

"The upshot was that I lost him. He married another woman. Perhaps it was because she was a big society figure. Or perhaps it was because she went to bed with him instead of holding out. How can I tell?"

There are no black-and-white answers to sex and the woman alone. Psychiatrists say that women in middle years are more promiscuous than young girls, that young girls at least think they are in love each time. I am not surprised. Nor am I shocked . . . not any more. Early in my interviews, I was taken aback when a seventy-year-old woman dimpled and told me, "I was such an innocent when my husband died that I didn't know men came in different sizes." I was also a bit astonished when a *grande dame* confided that her sister's widower always kissed her goodnight, "But there isn't any sex in it."

Some women attach less importance to sex than others. And some rush into sexual affairs when they are first alone as a way to forget, a form of emotional drug. Oddly enough, it is not always the most passionate woman who goes on a binge of promiscuity. It is often the one who has felt sexually frustrated or suppressed, even the woman who wonders if she is frigid, who runs recklessly from man to man.

Sometimes children will deter a woman. It is almost impossible to have any kind of sexual relation without children catching on, no matter how young they are. There are women who shrug this off, figuring that children in this enlightened age should take a variety of sleep-in uncles in stride. One divorcee told me she makes a point of sending the current uncle into the living room toward daybreak, so that the children will find him on the couch there when they waken. She says she does not think the older ones are much fooled but "I'm not really concerned. Sex is natural and I want them to grow up realizing it's much better for me to have a lover than to turn into an old wrinkled prune."

Other women, no matter how relaxed their personal attitude toward sex, are unwilling to have lovers at home because of their children. One of the most personally liberated young divorcees grumbled because her full-time lover does not offer to split the cost of a baby-sitter when she visits him at his house and has to leave her little girl. Another, who has a live-in maid, says that no matter what the hour, she leaves her lover's bed and goes home, so that her daughter finds her alone in bed each morning. Perhaps this is hypocrisy. I talked with teenagers who spoke regretfully of the fact that their mothers had given up all sexual relations "for the sake of the children" and now feel they are too old.

But I also talked with the mother of a boy who begged her, soon after his father died, never to "lower her standards." He was a freshman in college at the time, and although he is now married, she has obeyed him.

Nor is it just as simple as saying yes or no. Women tell me they make up their minds to relax and be permissive: "What have I to lose?" Then they lose their nerve, either turning formal and icy or hiding behind giggles and girlish protests, repulsive enough in the young, horrible in the no-longer-twenty set.

A divorcee who came to New York to recuperate from an unpleasant divorce told me she had a blind date, arranged by the folks at home, the night before she was to start her job as a receptionist in an advertising agency. He took her to dinner and the theater which, she says, in light of what she knows now, should have been the tip off. ("Nobody expects to spend that much money on a girl without getting into her bed.") But when he began making love to her in the cab on the way home, all she could do was giggle. He folded his arms across his chest and said, "I've seen more mature behavior in my twelve-year-old daughter." Without another word, he opened the cab door for her to get out at her apartment and she stumbled over his feet.

She never expected to see him again. But she did. When she reported for work the next morning, she discovered he was one of her bosses.

Sometimes on dateless evenings the ladies alone mutter to each other about the lack of quality in their dates. Sometimes a woman alone will get so tired of being pawed or bored, or both, that she decides it is far better to sit home with a good book. But invariably, after a while, she decides "to go back to the dregs and start over," as a New York divorcee puts it. This means getting on the telephone and extending invitations to the men you have already scratched as impossible . . . including, of course, those who are of an age so advanced that you look like a young chick to them.

This problem of the aging date poses, of itself, certain complications. A charming widow in Chicago had been going out on occasion with a man who was closer to eighty than he was ready to admit. He was a perfect gentleman; the only problem was that liquor went to his head faster than in his salad days: "One night he had his usual two martinis before dinner, and then because it was my birthday, ordered wine. He was all right so long as we were sitting down but he began to lurch as soon as we got out of the restaurant. I left him hanging on to a lamppost while I tried to flag down a cab. But none of them would stop. Finally I realized they thought I was some kind of a babe on the make, trying to roll a drunk."

These gentlemen of the old school are not as difficult to handle as the young eager-beavers. You can, I am told, keep them at a safe distance by using the old standby, "I am not ready to become emotionally involved." A crisply efficient Midwestern lady told me, "When a man gets that settled-in look, I simply stand up and thank him for a nice evening—or for coming to eat my cooking, if I've had him to dinner. There is nothing for him to do but go." But a lady whose real estate transactions exceeded several million last year said, "I doubt if some of my dates would be able to follow through if I said yes. But they feel they should make passes, otherwise you'll mark them as too old. They pretend to be hurt when they are rejected. I'll bet most of them are secretly relieved."

On the other hand, for many gentlemen alone, particularly widowers, time is running out. They lack patience. If marriage is what they have in mind, they do not want to shop around cautiously, pinching and testing; they snatch the first reasonably attractive lady who is available. If all they want is someone to take to dinner, you cannot blame them for wanting the young and attractive. As for something more permanent, we have to recognize that inside every old man is a young and ardent lover struggling to get out. You can't hate them for trying. In a way, it is a sign there is life there yet. One of them complained to me recently that a widow, a friend of his own age, told him she had a houseguest coming to town, adding, "You get another old geezer and we'll all four go out." Can you blame him for being annoyed?

I have a private theory that, when we start the dating game the second time around, we also automatically revert to adolescent behavior. An upstate New York widow told me, "I was really pleased when I sat next to a man at a college reunion dinner, and he asked for my telephone number. I was even more pleased when he called and made a date. That night, I was sure he wouldn't come. I hardly knew how to make conversation, I was so shy. Then, about our third date, he began making passes. I had to stiffen—he was actually repulsive. It was the same awful chill I used to have when I was a teenager. Yet I didn't want to push him away rudely and tell him to keep his nasty hands off me, because I wanted to go out. I wanted my telephone to ring. Isn't it pathetic?"

A divorcee said, "I am attracted by a man—until I see he is interested in me. Then I decide he's a jerk. One told me I needed psychiatric treatment and maybe he's right."

A Wyoming widow, the mother of four and still in her thirties, said, "I always go out once, even if I don't like a man. I remember my mother used to tell me, when I was in my teens, 'He might have a nice friend.' But then I find myself acting like a child, getting cross, insulting him, having headaches when he comes to see me. I even send my kids to the telephone if he calls, to say Mommy isn't home. You'd think I'd have maturity enough to handle it tactfully, but I haven't."

A pretty divorcee in New York said wearily, "I can't tell you the number of times I go out to dinner, giving little sly glances at my watch to see how soon I can say I have to get home, because of the baby-sitter. Yet I have to keep going out, for my own morale. Even if I loathe the guy. Because otherwise I go and lie on my unmade bed and read a book or watch TV."

Does it hurt a man's feelings when you tell him you do not want to sleep with him, as the younger girls do? Or does it increase his interest, challenge him? Or will he drop you and hurry on to someone who will? What will he think of you if you say yes?

Would it bother him if he thought you slept around as freely as he does—or would like to? If the sex is good, would he want to marry you—or will he play for a while and then go on to someone less easy? Or can you manage to go out indefinitely and still hold a man off with a minimum of fondling?

These are the problems a woman alone faces when she is back on the dating circuit, after a lapse of years. And they are problems because there are no rules for us. The wife of a divorce lawyer said to me, in her wisdom and experience, "A mature woman doesn't have to live by the rules of young people. She does not have to kiss a man if she doesn't like him. I am sure a mature respectable man appreciates that. Older people don't have that hectic curiosity about sex which drives our young people today."

Maybe she is right. But many women alone—and men in the same fix—have been knocked off pedestals and are utterly confused, more unsure than any young people could be. Nor do we lack curiosity about sex. Lots of us are more innocent than our children.

It may be that a man who is seriously interested in a woman respects her "standards" when she says no. It also may be that even if he is only dating her, he will stay around far longer than if the friendship develops into an affair. But the women who say they do not bed down also say that they set up their defenses in advance—just to avoid embarrassment or misunderstanding. Children in the house, or a live-in maid, are excuses any decent man will understand. A residence club may mark you as a square, but it keeps men downstairs, away from your bedroom. Roommates, mothers, aunties, nieces, and grown children are all efficient chaperones. Or a family hotel may do the trick. I know one woman in New York who fights off the wolves by living in the depths of Brooklyn; her dates are quite willing to put her on the subway instead of paying for a cab ride all the way out to her apartment and back. And she is still such good company and so pleasant to look at, that they enjoy buying her dinner occasionally.

Mainly, however, the woman alone must know what she wants. Then she can make her attitude loud and clear. And if she decides no to sex, the men who continue to take her out will do it simply because they enjoy her company (men can get lonesome, too) and because she, in her mature wisdom, returns hospitality, an eye for an eye, a tooth for a tooth.

"There's no such thing as an old-fashioned date," a California divorcee of ten years' experience alone told me. "Some men will take you out because you are safe and don't want to get married. These are usually men who have a large variety of women, and you take your turn. You are also expected to reciprocate, provide them with a home-cooked meal occasionally, which is all right. But if you want to get married, these men are not for you. You must enter the open fray and cope with the gents who want to bed down, sooner or later. And whether you say no or yes, you must be prepared for a pretty rapid turnover in gents. Eventually you may be down to one old friend, faithful dog Tray, and also eventually, some girls just give up and marry him."

In the early stages, divorcees cling to divorced men—in spite of the many problems they have between them. "We have more in common," I was told. A Connecticut divorcee under thirty said, "I took off my wedding ring and went back to school. But I was just too damned bored with the boys who wanted to date me. They were callow. Marriage, even a bad one, gives you experience." A young Chicago divorcee said, "I went out with a widower one night. He spent the whole evening telling me how great his dead wife had been. When he kissed me and indicated he'd like to come in and spend the night, he needed a woman, I said, 'You told me all about your wife. You didn't ask a damned thing about me. I'm just a thing and I certainly am not going to comfort you just because I'm handy.'"

Just being divorced is not a basis for long-term rapport, but it helps in the beginning. If a divorced man is cursed with impotency problems, a divorced woman will be generous and understanding, having dealt with a "son of a bitch" herself. But when both have been badly maimed and are seeking help, the results can be confusing. A divorcee in Connecticut, in love with a man who has recently also divorced, reported, "We can only see each other three times a week. He goes to his analyst on Thursday and

isits his kids Sunday. I go to my analyst on Monday, and to
group therapy on Wednesday. Then I drive my little girl into
New York to her analyst on Saturday. That leaves Tuesday, Friday and Saturday—and often I'm so tired after my long Saturday
we have a fight."

Occasionally, a man and woman who knew each other when
they were married to other people, will find wedded bliss. This
makes everyone happy, including the concerned and sometimes
guilt-ridden children of the pair involved. Their discovery of
each other may even be romantic. But the cards are stacked
against this happening.

A widower in Wisconsin said, "When Mabel died, the widows
in the neighborhood were very attentive. They kept inviting me
to dinner, and we'd sit and talk about the old days, what Mabel
and George used to do when they were alive. It was all right for a
while but it certainly wasn't very exciting and, as my lawyer said,
I had at least ten good years left in me, and why didn't I enjoy
them? The finish came when a widow suggested we spend Memo-
rial Day together—we'd put flowers on her husband's grave, and
then we'd put flowers on Mabel's grave, and then we'd go to her
house and she'd make roast chicken the way her husband had
liked it. I said I was busy. I went right out that same night and
joined the yacht club, a younger crowd, and began to take out
women who had never met Mabel. I married one of them, too."

Most people who have been married feel freer if they date, or at
least begin dating, with new people, out of the pattern of their
past lives. For one thing, there is the pleasure of discovery of a
fresh personality in yourself, as well as in a stranger. For another,
sex has more promise. A Detroit suburban divorcee said, "Going
out with the few widowers I know is too reminiscent of necking
episodes in cars at country club dances. I can't imagine marrying
an old duck who made the same passes at me fifteen years ago
even if he is serious—which I doubt."

For most women alone, sex is seldom really casual. It may be
exploratory, and she may decide the man is not for her. But she is
seeking. Her objective, which society approves, is to remarry.
Sometimes an affair prepares her for marriage with someone else.

More often, she has to face the heartbreak of having an affair with a man and conditioning him to the idea of remarriage—only to have him chase after a fresh face. "That is part of the risk," a Florida divorcee told me. "Once a man who has been divorced, or even widowed, discovers his sexual potential, he wants a new liaison. He forgets that when the novelty wears off, it may not be so great with the new wife. I have a man who keeps telephoning me, trying to come back, he and his young wife aren't sexually adjusted. I think he realizes now what I did for him. But it's too late. I don't want to break up his marriage. Even if I did, I wouldn't trust him."

A widow from Long Island, who has since remarried, told me, "Thank goodness I held out, for I remarried a man from my own community and I would have hated now to have the kind of reputation some women alone have around here. I had opportunities, of course, for I was quite young and pretty, and that in itself was a help. There was always someone new coming around, after others had stopped calling me because I wouldn't sleep with them. But I'm not sure it is so easy with women who are over forty. Maybe they can't hold out—or else they just sign off and give up dates."

Eventually, of course, there comes a time when the sex-and-dating game palls. If a woman does not remarry after five or six years, she stops struggling and settles for no sex, the companionship of escorts who abide by those rules, or the company of couples and other women alone. Sometimes this is defeat, and she feels bitter. But sometimes it means that her time is just too valuable to waste on the available jerks, and she is more content on her own without them.

Meanwhile, there is the alternative that has to be considered whether you accept it or not: sex with married men.

SEX AND
THE MARRIED MAN

A FRIEND in the Midwest wrote me, "I've learned not to dwell on past mistakes. But the other night I made a lulu and I think I should tell you about it for the record. I'd had a pleasant evening with an old friend and her husband. He was having difficulty with an old back injury, which made it necessary for him to lie flat on the couch, on a heating pad. When I got up to leave, like a sap I leaned over and kissed him goodnight.

"All the way upstairs when I was collecting my coat in the bedroom, I could feel the ice forming on the wife. By the time I had reached the front door, she was a solid block and I dashed out into the night, knowing I'd not get another invitation from her for a long time. Yet the injustice burns me up. Her husband had always kissed me goodnight, and there had been no comment. It was when I made the gesture and it was obvious that he liked it. . . ."

A divorcee in Lincoln, Nebraska, said to me thoughtfully, "Men are very gentle and unsure. They should be treated like very dear people. Women are tougher, harder, meaner. The male in sex life needs to feel he can perform. Lots of divorced men are castrated. Some bitch woman's fault, because their wives did things like cleaning house all day so they'd be too tired to go to bed with their husbands. I'm not at all surprised that married men look to widows and divorcees for comfort and encouragement."

And a pretty redheaded divorcee in Minneapolis said, "I'm just trying to do a job, raise three sons without a father. One of the men in our church, who has two girls, used to take my boys to baseball games, and father-and-son dinners. Once in a while, when he'd bring them home, we'd have a drink together. But that's all. The other night at a church dinner, his wife deliberately cut me when I spoke to her. Later, the husband wrote me he was afraid he couldn't take the boys out any more, she was objecting. It burns me up. For it hurts my sons."

A woman who moved to London after the death of her husband told me, "I rented a house in a hive of married couples, mostly for the sake of my children. And they did include me. Then one night the husband of a friend who was in America invited me to go to a masquerade party in the neighborhood. I'd been invited too, so it was nice having an escort. There had been quite a bit to drink so when we got home, he asked if I'd make him a cup of coffee.

"In the kitchen he began making passes. My children were asleep upstairs but the maid was in the bedroom next to the kitchen. He agreed to go in the living room and wait until I brought him the coffee. I found him asleep there, or pretending to be asleep. He refused to wake up, no matter what I did. I had visions of his being there in the morning when the children woke. So I went in the kitchen and got a milk bottle full of cold water and poured it over his head. He woke up and ran off. But the next morning, the children came and told me, 'Mummy, there's a man sleeping in a car in front of the house.' I looked and it was he.

"I dressed and went out and told him to get going. He muttered something about coffee but I walked in the house without answering. But of course, the neighbors all saw him, and of course they reported. Now I'm the scarlet woman."

A divorcee in a Midwestern suburb told me that she found the ladies at the PTA were criticizing her for wearing a low-cut dress to a Christmas party. "From that time on," she said, "things went downhill fast. I'd bought the dress because I felt so drab, so depressed. And it wasn't that revealing. But some of the husbands went out of their way to be nice, saying they were glad I'd given up the old dark mourning clothes I wore at first. Before then, the wives were always good about including my kids when they went on outings, and I would take the kids off their hands on Saturday, figuring to give them more time with husbands. After that, they deliberately excluded me and the kids, and didn't even let them come over on Saturday. I finally gave up and moved back to the city. Here I don't stick out like a sore thumb."

Another woman alone sent me a column in a newspaper which read, "Dear So-and-So, The other night my husband took me and a widow in the neighborhood out to dinner. He helped her off with her coat before he took mine, and steered the conversation so that she did most of the talking. When I reached home, I blew up. He was astonished. He said he was just being polite. I said, 'How about being polite to me for a change?' "

One of the real shocks which occurs when you are no longer a wife is the changed attitude of other women: the wives. No matter how little interested you are in other women's husbands, you are immediately suspect. No matter how little a particular husband is interested in you, you notice that his wife makes a point of cutting off communication before anything can happen between you. Perhaps this is, in a way, a compliment. Or perhaps—and I lean to this view, and I do know wives who do not react with such jealousy—it is simply an indication of weakness on the point of the wife, of insecurity and fright.

Just the same, it can be inconvenient and it can be plain insulting.

During a recent evening, I watched husbands gravitate toward a widow who was wearing a very short white dress. The most distinguished guest there, a physician, sat next to her after dinner and managed to let his hand fall on her exposed knees whenever he made a point in the conversation. His wife, a heavy woman, took him home early. On the way home in the cab we shared, the widow said, "I hate wives."

Suddenly, I remembered an evening several years ago when my husband and I were being entertained at the home of the late Maggie Eittinger, the famous Hollywood publicist, the cousin of Louella Parsons. Among the guests was Betty Hutton, the actress, who was at the time divorced. Out of the blue, or so it seemed to me, she turned and snarled, "I hate you goddam smug married women."

I also remember the Christmas Eve when we went to a tree-trimming party at the home of old friends. The husband had brought home his secretary, who was from out of town and had "no place to go on Christmas Eve and wanted to be with little children." If the secretary had been old and ugly, or even never-married, she might have been tolerated. She was cute, blonde, and a recent divorcee. The wife tried to ignore her at first, then she began making nasty cracks at the girl and her husband. The husband, who had already had quite a bit to drink, had more and fell into the Christmas tree. The wife stormed into the bedroom and slammed the door, saying she would not come out until "that woman" was gone. At that point, we left, taking the secretary with us, and dropped her at Grand Central Station so she could get the subway to Flushing.

I did not feel sorry for her then. Not even the picture of the girl alone on a subway near midnight before Christmas moved me. I thought she had a hell of a lot of nerve, turning up on Christmas Eve at a home where she had never before met the wife. Now I wonder about a lot of things. I wonder if my husband might not have taken her out to Flushing in the cab if I had not been there looking down my big nose; not because she was cute, but because she was alone and it was Christmas Eve. I also wondered if the girl might have suspected she would not be too welcome, but was so lonely she had jumped at the chance to be with people.

Nearly every woman alone has at least one story to tell about the changed attitude of other women after she is alone. Sometimes she learns the facts of life the hard way, in a series of swift, nasty blows from women who used to be her best friends.

A divorcee in Honolulu with two children told me that, when she was married, she and her husband used to take the children to a beach club every Sunday. At first, when her divorce was fresh, she continued the custom, thankful that it helped fill lonely weekends. Gradually, however, she found she was no longer included in the groups that gathered at each other's houses in the evening after swimming, for cocktails or potluck dinners. And more gradually, she began to feel more welcome with the other single women than with the married.

"Perhaps I was oversensitive," she admitted. "Just the same.

when I arrived at the beach with the kids, I got the idea the wives were looking at each other thinking, here she is again. Our conversations weren't the same; I just wasn't included in the gossip and jokes, who got drunk at the club, who made a pass. The wives just don't trust you any more. No matter how carefully you avoid their husbands, or any hint of being flirtatious, you're an outsider."

The women who have never married are amused when I mention this. They have found out a long time ago, through experiences with married ex-roommates, or wives of office colleagues, that an attractive single woman must walk a very straight and narrow line when she is with married couples. No matter how little interested you are in particular husbands, or husbands in general, when you are alone you have joined the list of suspects. Unless you are ugly and fat (and sometimes not even then) you discover that the attitude of wives around you has changed— sometimes subtly, sometimes not so subtly.

A divorcee from Boston said, "You have to stop thinking as a wife, do a reversal. Behavior which is perfectly okay, even cute, in a married woman suddenly becomes brazen in a divorcee—and, to some extent, in a widow. No matter how discreet you are, you are a potential predatory menace. Yet all the time you're being cast in the role of Wicked Witch of the West, you are a repository for the kind of complaints about husbands you wouldn't have heard when you were married. I don't get it."

A pretty widow in a fashionable suburb of Minneapolis agreed with this. "Women practically yank their husbands off the sidewalk when I walk past. Yet these same women come and pound on my door, saying they'll kill themselves if I don't let them in, they have to talk to me. When I do, against my better judgment, they will tell me the most repulsive and intimate horrors about their husbands, things I don't want to hear."

"Because you're alone, you're fair game," a divorcee in Chicago said. "A woman I always thought was a model wife, happy as a lark with five bright kids, broke down and had hysterics in my living room because her husband never made love to her any more. She said she couldn't tell anybody else, but she felt she could trust me. But when I got a job and went in on the same train with her husband in the morning, she began making sure he didn't get on the car with me."

I have no way of knowing how many of the wrongs inflicted on women alone—particularly women newly alone—are imaginary and how many are good, honest reporting. I do suspect that many wives are jealous on two counts: one, because married men do find the woman alone a challenge, and two, because they envy us our freedom. It is hard for them to imagine themselves in our shoes, yet the notion both repels and titillates them.

For example. It is difficult for almost any wife to believe that the approaches a new widow or divorcee gets from married men are not invited—or imagined. ("You can't tell me that the wolves are waiting in the bushes ready to pounce on a woman before her husband's ashes are cold," the neighbor of a widow told me.) Yet often the wolves in question are the husbands of the ladies who are so unsympathetic. I refuse to speculate on whether this is cause or effect. All I know is that these passes do happen. And that they come from the least expected sources.

A young woman whose husband was killed in Vietnam had a telephone call almost immediately from her husband's uncle, telling her to get packed, he was taking her to Europe the next week. She said she would call his wife and get her advice on what clothes they might need. He answered, "Honey, Aunt Maggie ain't going with us and your clothes won't matter. I'm going to keep you in bed most of the time."

Advances from husbands of best friends and neighbors may seem horrifying, but they are far from uncommon. I am also sure that they would not be so prevalent if they were not accepted occasionally. Sex can be a refuge. It provides not only the comfort of being held close physically, but also the consolation that your life as a woman is not ended, that men, or a man, still finds you attractive and exciting. Perhaps no man deliberately sets out to prey on women in shock. Perhaps the sight of a woman suffering, alone, really stirs him and he honestly feels he is doing her a favor by making love to her.

A widow told me that her husband's best friend came to her

shortly after her husband died and said, "If it would help, I would like to make love to you." She thanked him, said no (his wife was also her best friend), but was genuinely touched by his offer.

Perhaps some men, having discovered that women are touched, and grateful, develop a pattern. I suspect some do this innocently and warmly at first, later simply because it is a proven technique. It could be there are cases where the man involved does not know the approach is going to happen himself until the opportunity presents itself.

I must add that in all the stories I heard—and I have heard many—the men invariably were married. This is not coincidence, I believe. The single man, bachelor, divorcé or widower, is too wary to get mixed up with ladies who might take him seriously. He waits a bit. In the first place, no eligible man needs or wants to take advantage of a woman in a crisis of this sort. He prefers to have more fun, less trauma. In the second, these men are in a vulnerable position themselves, for the inexperienced ladies still do not know the rules of the dating-sex games.

The married men, if I may be a bit cynical, can offer unadorned sex, comfort. Their very protection is that they have wives and children. They are merely offering their *services*. ("One showed me pictures of his kids with one hand," a widow told me, "and fumbled with my garters with the other.") The lines they produce are often so corny they sound embarrassing in print: "We are both mature people" . . . "It hurts nobody and it will help you" . . . "I've loved you for so long, if only I were free, but we wouldn't do anything to hurt my wife, would we?"

These men step in fast, probably because they know the woman is off balance. I have found in my researches that they also tend to bow out fast, before the relation becomes a full-fledged affair and the lady in question becomes less appreciative and more demanding.

When a woman is newly alone, and still feeling as she did when she was a wife, her first reaction is usually indignation. But it is not long before she finds a certain amount of satisfaction, even comfort, in the fact that she is still attractive to men. And she also, being human, cannot help feeling a small amount of triumph. Because women alone often get the impression that wives are flaunting husbands—and regular sex—in their faces.

A widow told me, "One couple, who had been talking about divorce as long as I can remember, invited me to dinner shortly after Don died. The woman could hardly keep her hands off her husband." A divorcee, spending the night in her sister's guest room, told me, "I couldn't sleep all night. Every time I dozed off, they woke me with the bed creaking, and her whooping about what a great orgasm she was having."

Women alone in general—including unmarried girls—feel sex is used as a punishing club by wives. In some cases, this may be true. However, I suspect that new widows and divorcees are in a very delicate position and normal behavior and activity may seem abnormal, even vicious. I also suspect that our deprivation and our grief act as sexual stimulants to the wives in question; they feel the need of reassurance from husbands. To another married woman, the sounds of sex in the next room can be cause for amusement. For women newly alone, the effects are anything but amusing.

There is therapy for a miserable, lonely woman in a love affair. Perhaps ideally, the man should be as free as she is. But sometimes the solid comfort of knowing the man is married, and unavailable, lends an air of make-believe to a romance.

An upstate New York divorcee, who travels in a group of young single women, told me, "You don't want to make decisions, but you want to be treated as a woman, to function as a woman. This is where an affair with a nice, decent—and I'm not kidding when I say decent, some of them who play around are a lot more honorable then their whining wives—married man can be a Godsend. He won't talk; he doesn't want to be hurt any more than you do. He won't make scenes. And he will be generous in bed and out. In my group of friends, there is a hell of a lot less travail in affairs with married men than with those who twist the knife in the wound because they are available, and know it."

Even when there is no hope of marriage, the interest of a man does much to bring a woman back to reality. This seems to be particularly true after a painful divorce, when the quarrels and conflicts have already made a woman feel undesirable. Having a man admire and desire her, even temporarily, can restore her confidence.

A woman who divorced an alcoholic husband because he was becoming dangerous to her children, told me, "It had been a love match. I really still yearned for him and missed him. For six months, I cried at the drop of a hat. In the office, someone would be whistling one of our songs, and I'd rush to the washroom and dissolve. I had lost so much weight that even my children said I looked terrible. I was sure nobody would ever look at me again and stopped caring about my appearance. Then John came along.

"It wasn't all the sex. Although wanting him sexually, and having him want me, made me feel alive again. It was the attention. Every morning he'd call at work to know how I was. He sent me flowers—roses, after the first time we made love. I felt like a young girl again. I knew he had a wife and two nearly-grown sons. He never said a word against his wife. He just said he loved me.

"I never considered a permanent relation. What was wonderful was that someone cared what I did, how I felt, if I bought a new dress, or had my hair done. It didn't hurt when he told me he was being transferred to another city, it didn't make me miserable when he said his wife had never liked New York and was glad to be going back to the Midwest. I wished him all happiness when he left, felt a few pangs, but mostly gratitude. Now when he comes to town, we see each other like old friends, but not as lovers."

A widow in San Francisco told me, "I met Ron through business, when I was writing copy for his firm. I had just gone back to work after my husband's death, and Ron took me out a few times for a drink. It was a long time before he asked me to dinner, and then it was casual, lighthearted.

"I knew he was married. I also knew damned well that when you accepted a dinner date from a married man, you couldn't act coy if he made a pass. But I was low, low, low. It was better than going home and looking at the seconal bottle and thinking how easy it would be to take an overdose. The first night he kissed me I told him no, I wasn't a homewrecker.

"The next week, he took me out to dinner and said he didn' want his home wrecked, either, he was fond of his wife and chil dren, but he was in love with me. Just hearing him tell me that, listening to him describe me as glamorous and seductive, made me feel like a real woman. Our love affair was like that, all the way. Maybe it was better because both of us knew there was no chance of its developing into a humdrum marriage. At any rate, the beginning of the end came when he changed jobs. He had less time for me and, in my spare time, I met a widower. I began dating him and then a bachelor in my office. As soon as Ron found out I was doing all right, he vanished. But I still remember him with tenderness."

Not every married man is a Ron. Some are crass, ugly. Some, even if they don't get anyplace with a pass, try to make it impossi ble for you to meet eligible men, as one young divorcee put it, "like a dog in the manger." Still others, rejected, spread lies. A Washington woman who went to bed with a married man once, and found the whole business repulsive and against her nature, told me that he went around whispering to her friends that she was a nymphomaniac.

In my experience, I have found women alone on the whole reluctant to embark on affairs with married men. "There is too much danger of its becoming a habit," a Boston divorcee told me darkly. "You get trapped, you don't work at meeting other peo ple." A schoolteacher from Ohio said, "I'm still thinking of how I would have felt if my husband had taken a mistress. You just can't play around with married men in this society without feel ing soiled." Other women, usually the younger divorcees, regard guilt about sex as an old-fashioned notion and have little or no patience with the jealous sit-at-home wives. A vivid dark-haired divorcee from a rather gay suburb in Westchester told me: "I'm fed up with your so-called available bachelors—they're spoiled, they're selfish, they're cheap. Married men are much nicer. The only problem, and it is a problem, is that you have to keep it all on a light, undemanding level. Start getting serious and bitchy and he'll run home to Mama—or to another woman alone."

Perhaps one day, when we approach the "bright new world" of honest and uncluttered sex that the men in the Think Tanks tell us is on the way, marriage will be different, and women alone will feel perfectly free to have sex with any attractive man who comes along, married or not. But right now, there are practical complications which involve furtiveness, secrecy.

A married man prefers afternoon dates to evenings. Even if he gets away to take you out to dinner occasionally, it will be to obscure bistros rather than good restaurants—unless his wife is particularly understanding or resigned. Even then, he is seldom available for weekends, leaving you with long sterile periods when you can consider cutting your throat. And if he does break down and whisk you away for a trip, a woman usually finds herself at some obscure traveling man's hotel in Bethlehem, Pennsylvania —or at a resort out of season.

Of course, if you are young, sexy, beautiful, and conniving, you may get him to leave his wife. I heard of one three-time divorcee, who grew richer each time, who made it a point to tantalize a man sexually, allowing him every liberty except the ultimate consummation—until he told his wife he wanted a divorce. I have also had other multi-divorcees tell me that the only fertile hunting ground is among married men. They may be right. But most of us, lovable and amiable as we are, do not qualify as jet-set *femmes fatales.*

The early passes from married men, which come while a woman is still muddled and groping, may open her eyes, but they seldom matter. Even if she succumbs, her salvation lies in the fact that nothing, including the experience, seems real afterward. The affairs that are entered into after a while, simply as affairs, may or may not be satisfactory, mostly depending upon her own attitude. If she feels guilt before, during, or afterward, she is not a good candidate for any affair, especially one with a married man. Because, to justify her conduct, she will tell herself she is in love. And very soon she finds justification for this love, and its future, by deciding the wife is a bitch.

A secretary whom I interviewed, a divorcee, has become hope-lessly involved with her boss, a toy manufacturer, while they are struggling to keep him from going into bankruptcy. She told me, "And his wife sits out there on Long Island wearing two mink coats."

"At once?" I asked.

But she was beyond humor. She said, "He works late at night, doing things like wrapping bundles. She calls up and says dinner will be ruined if he doesn't come home right away. Sometimes he leaves and—"

"You finish the bundles," I said.

She nodded. This time her eyes filled with tears. "I'm in love with him. I can't help it."

There are times when the life of a woman alone seems glamor-ous to our married women friends. And, not wanting to disillu-sion them, we do not explain that our social lives are not that fascinating. But often we do go out more than we ever did when we were married; we make a point of planning our social lives in advance just because we do not want to get caught with low dull periods. We probably need more clothes than we did as wives, so we buy them, without having to ask approval. We can be as ex-treme as we like; unless there is a steady man lurking in the back-ground, no one complains if our skirts are too short or our neck-lines too revealing. We get impatient and bored with the talk about the care and feeding and foibles of husbands, a subject which used to be a source of much interest. We also get a bit impatient with some of the habits and demands of the ladies themselves. After all, when you are on the other side of the fence, the perspective is very different.

A divorcee with three children told me, "My noon hours are spent shopping for my boss's wife. If I need anything for myself or my children, I have to wait until Thursday night when the stores are open. Her excuse is that she is too busy with her community affairs to get to town. She should try being father and mother and breadwinner for three kids—and coping with a neurotic ex-husband."

An unmarried executive who spends most of her time with married men is frankly disgusted with most of their wives. She said, "They act as if work were a private club where men go to have fun. If a man has to work late or go out of town on a weekend, they scream as though he were doing something wrong. And, incidentally, some of the men get damned sick of the wifely nonsense and look elsewhere for understanding. And, believe me, they can get it in an office."

Of course, there is more temptation in an office than in a home setting. An attractive man is thrown with women whose job it is to please him. Of course many of the girls are young, unmarried. But these ambitious youngsters will accept lunch, a drink or two, seldom more; they are looking to get married and do not want to waste time. Women alone, or unmarried women who are past the very-young classification, are the ones who are available. They are better company than the youngsters, they usually have their own apartments and they are, as Benjamin Franklin once noted, more appreciative.

I sat in the other night at a conference of enlightened and outspoken young married women. I expected them to be infinitely more liberal about extramarital sex than my generation. To my surprise, they were not. Most of them agreed that, if there were no children, the wife should walk out. But once there are babies, the wife is trapped and cannot afford to make scenes. So she, in the classic tradition, should look the other way, pretend she knows nothing, and wait until it "all blows over." One bold soul suggested that perhaps a wife should have her own little fling, in revenge. She was voted down. That was no way to hold a home together. It would only give him excuse for more adventures.

Very seldom does the woman alone consider breaking up a marriage, by the same set of rules; she has "scruples." She lets him talk about his children, and is endlessly patient and understanding about his office problems. She eventually knows more about his wife than she wants to, and not all of it is bad. As time goes on—and it can go on without anything "blowing over"—the mistress tends to be identified with the wife. And she can become so much a part of the familiar picture that if a man does decide to divorce his wife, he never thinks of his faithful mistress—he wants someone new and fresh.

A divorcee who is trapped in this situation told me, "You always know what you are doing. If not, there are any number of other women alone who will tell you. But once you get involved, there is no way out, unless you're doing it for kicks. If you really love him, you're stuck. You give more and get less than his wife. Yet when society is handing out boots in the pants for being a wicked woman, you're the one who wins the jackpot."

As it is with everything else, the innocent and naïve woman alone is the one who gets trapped, and suffers. I am not being moral. I have watched too many of them weep, and curse, and weep again. For we are not as tough as the wives think, no matter what we do. Nor is our freedom that glamorous.

In Minneapolis, I met a young widow whose husband had died in the crash of a private plane. To recuperate, she took her children and went back to the college town where she had been born, to visit her parents. She told me: "At first, the girls were terribly sympathetic. Then, after a while, I began to notice something else. When I'd talk about the future and my uncertainties, they would get impatient. Finally, one of them, my best friend in college, blurted out, 'What I'd give to be in your shoes—a whole new life in front of you. All I have is the same old stuff—PTA, kids, boring office parties, bridge tournaments, and my husband looking at you as though you're the angel on the Christmas tree!'"

Sometimes everything would seem almost funny—if it weren't so ridiculous. Sitting on what we consider the sidelines of life, a not completely unprejudiced audience, we watch wives who are jealous of everything: their husband's job, the "fun" he has at the office, the women he meets, the exciting lives we lead, "getting away with something, having goodness knows what exciting adventures." Those of us who work come under greatest suspicion. But, working or not, we women alone are the heavies. An analyst told me that in his practice of many years he had encountered only one woman who was alone and not resented by wives. She as a divorcee who came from an extremely social old Dutch family. Her social prestige was great, which was important to wives; much more important, however, was the fact that she was not interested in men from her own class, only the ones who did hard physical labor.

So what are the answers?

Certainly nothing is loud or clear, or black and white. A doctor told me about the experience of one of his patients, a widow in her early forties. She lived in a small town that is centered around a medical clinic, and the few bachelors she met were patients there. She was an attractive woman and the doctors' wives saw to it that, when such men were included in dinners, she would be the extra woman.

He said, "She came to me for a checkup and asked if she should have intercourse before marriage with a man from Maine who had returned for a checkup. I answered it was up to her; but as they were both mature, I saw no reason for scruples.

"She didn't marry the man. It was nearly a year before I found out why. The eligible bachelor, although he tried several times, could not make love to her. In her frustration and anguish, she fled to a nearby city. There she met one of the married doctors, alone in town for a conference. They had dinner and she went to bed with him. The physical relation was marvelous, better than she had ever had with her husband. She said to me, 'I have orgasm after orgasm. He says it's the same with him. We know we should stop seeing each other but we can't. I'm not jealous of his wife. I don't want to break up his marriage. What should we do?' "

"I don't know how to answer that one," the doctor told her.

10 REMARRIAGE

It's possible to fall in love at fifty, sixty, seventy and I've seen it. That's why I won't compromise and marry for companionship or convenience.

NEW YORK WIDOWER

Second marriages are much better. You don't get carried away with the business of sex and marry for that alone. You also have more to give, for you've learned from your mistakes. And you're more tolerant. At least, I am.

BOSTON DIVORCEE, REMARRIED

Remarry as soon as possible. Otherwise you will get too set in your ways.

CALIFORNIA DIVORCEE, REMARRIED

Women marry men—but men marry houses. I've seen it happen again and again.

MINNEAPOLIS DIVORCEE

I'm not going to remarry and become an old man's nurse. I cared for a dying husband for six months, but that was different—I had his young years, too. I wouldn't go through that hell again.

HONOLULU WIDOW

O NCE the first impact of grief or anger or humiliation—depending on how you lost your husband—is over, the normal feminine instinct is to remedy the situation. Few women admit they are looking actively for a replacement. They sit around saying, "I will never marry again," while their brains click like computers whenever an unattached male is mentioned. A blind date with someone described as a broker sets them to reading the *Wall Street Journal* and unconsciously preparing to introduce the future husband to rich widows. One evening with a rich homosexual as a dinner partner has them abstractly wondering if sex is so important after all.

Other ladies are more frankly on the manhunt. They are the ones who pester acquaintances to produce unattached men. At parties, they are single-minded; no one except the available bachelor gets their attention. The desperation of these women can seem undignified to the rest of us who are also alone. But, in a secret way, we admire their guts. What no one on the outside can realize is that whether we weep, flirt, or keep a stiff upper lip, we are acting almost unconsciously.

For we suffer from that old feeling of female inferiority—we feel we are nothing unless we have managed to get our man. Even the widow or divorcee who is popular and has several beaus of indeterminate age and attraction chasing her, isn't satisfied; she worries about tomorrow. Will they all vanish? Wouldn't it be better to pick the least unattractive and settle down before it is too late? Besides, we ex-marrieds are used to living with a man, running our households with him as a focus, or an excuse, used to having him come home at night, used to spending weekends, holidays, vacations with him. Habit is so strong that we cannot imagine spending the rest of our lives alone. And we also want to climb back into the safe haven of the couple society: "Other women have remarried; so can I."

Some women do not even stop to show what is considered by the world as a decent show of grief. They rush out to grab another man before the funeral flowers are wilted. A young woman whose husband was killed in Vietnam, leaving her with an infant daughter, told me, "I began to date right away. I put my ring on the other hand. I didn't exactly neglect my baby, but I left him with my mother, assuring myself it was okay because I was out to get a new daddy for him. In my mind, I was behaving rationally, but I shocked a lot of people including my late husband's parents. I know now I was in a daze. All I wanted was a husband and I would have married almost any man who asked me."

Nor is it only young women who begin thinking immediately in terms of a replacement. It's an old cliché that people who have been happily married tend to remarry again soon. So this raises false hopes in many a widow. "I'm not ready to be put on the shelf with the rest of the old ladies," a sixty-year-old in California told me. "I love my grandchildren, but I don't want to baby-sit and play bridge with other women the rest of my life. I don't feel like an old lady. My children would be shocked to hear me say this, but I miss sex."

Divorcees feel under pressure to justify themselves, whether the divorce was their idea or not. A woman in Wyoming, whose divorce had just become final, said, "I see no future for myself unless I remarry. When my two older kids go out on dates, they look back at me, cleaning up the kitchen or watching TV alone. Sometimes the boy will say, 'Are you okay, Mom?' I can't have them feeling sorry for me, or guilty because they are out having fun. I know I take my sexual frustrations out on them, too. But I won't cheapen myself or hurt them by having affairs."

Some brave women tell all their friends how lonesome they are, how much they want husbands. Presumably this is to disarm wives, and have them alerted to look for men who are eligible, freshly widowed, or recently divorced. However, some of us cannot help feeling that discretion is the better part of valor. We still cling to the old idea that men like to do the chasing, and that over-eagerness will scare them away. We also feel diffident, unsure of our charms, wondering if we can attract men any more. And, if a woman is over forty, she has to face the fact that men her age or a little older prefer young women.

I know of one widower who married his daughter's college roommate. Many of the women I interviewed told me that their stepmothers are younger than they are. Often it gives a widower pleasure—and a feeling of being young again—if his second wife starts a second family, presenting him with children younger than his own grandchildren.

One of the most attractive women I have ever known, who had a career of smashing hearts before she married, is now sixty-four and a widow. When I asked her about remarriage she said sadly, "I'm too old."

Yet a widower of sixty-four regards himself as prime husband material. He seldom waits more than a year to remarry, if that. All you need to do is watch the newspapers and you will read of men of seventy and eighty remarrying women younger than their late wives; often, if the man is prominent enough, he is able to attract a young secretary, or a divorcee or widow in her early thirties. You cannot blame a man of that age for taking a younger woman if he can get her; it is good for his ego and could prolong his life, although there are different points of view about that. Nor can you fault him for being in a bit of a hurry. A Westchester, New York, rabbi told me he is often asked to hurry up the unveiling of a dead wife's stone, which marks the end of the traditional eleven months of mourning for the Jews, so that the widower can remarry.

The devotion a man felt for the dead wife has seldom anything to do with the case. A friend of mine told me that one of the most grief-stricken widowers she ever encountered was a sixty-six-year-old professor of philosophy at a Midwestern college; he talked about his loss constantly, declaring his life was barren. To console himself, he took a trip to Africa and promptly married the young woman who was a guide.

A man who has had a devoted, attentive wife misses being pampered and cared for. Without her he is at loose ends, unable to complete the simplest household chore. But many a woman, without a man to care for, is equally desperate. The difference lies in the law of supply and demand. The daughter of a Vermont widower told me, "He was out every night. Immediately after my mother died, all the women alone started to rush him. He was like a debutante. If we wanted a quiet night at home, we'd have to close the garage doors, eat in the kitchen, and not answer the telephone. He finally married a woman who had been a widow eight years. She told me, 'I went after him, Irma. Nice men like your dad are hard to find. I knew he was at loose ends after your mother died and some woman would get him. So I just arranged to be the one.' "

The problem, as almost any woman alone will tell you, is that women are the surviving sex. In the United States today, at age eighteen and over, women outnumber men by nearly 4 million. Widows outnumber widowers about four to one—9 million widows and only 2.25 million widowers. For the 2.2 million current divorcees or separated women, there are 1.6 million men in the same situation.

In all phases of life, from conception on, the female is stronger and more likely to survive than the male. Because most wives are also younger than their husbands, the odds are high that the great majority of them will spend the final period of their life cycle as widows . . . if they don't divorce. *The National Underwriter* estimates that if the trend continues, there will be ten million widows in the United States by the end of 1975.

Some fast marriages are marvelously happy. I know a widow with two young children who married six months after her husband's death, and found a delightful man who thinks she is wonderful and treats her children as his own. Love at first sight is possible even, I am told, at a mature age. But second marriages are more trouble-prone than first; even the very young who attempt them have emotional tag-ends which can interfere. And many a person, unstable in grief, leaps "out of the frying pan into the fire." Sometimes the choice is so unwise that the liaison explodes before it is hardly off the ground. A woman in Portland, Oregon, described her uncle's marriage:

"Almost as soon as Uncle Ed became a widower, the widow next door began showering him with attention, baking him bread, helping him shop, even cooking the food when he gave little dinner parties. He got to depend on her. The next thing we knew, he had sold his house, they were married, and he moved in with her. About six weeks later, my husband had a call from Uncle Ed. He had fled the house, leaving his clothes behind him in his haste. He wouldn't even go back for them himself, he made my husband do it."

Visiting in Vermont, I also heard the saga of the one attractive single man in town, a widower of about fifty-five. After his wife died of cancer, he went to California for the winter. There he met an Arizona widow, rich and handsome. Being New England-thrifty, he liked the idea that she had her own money and was not marrying him for security. She was also a great deal freer and more open than the women alone in his home town. So he married her and took her back to Vermont.

Her breezy Western ways were criticized by his friends. She wore her diamonds openly, instead of playing them down, as was considered proper among his Vermont acquaintances. His dead wife's clothes were still hanging in the cedar closets. When she objected, he suggested she send them to the local thrift shop and arrange for a tax deduction. She grew bored with the local entertainment—hunt teas, church bazaars, an occasional musicale or museum opening in Boston. One day when he was in his office, she left on the noon train. Alerted, her husband watched the taxi containing her and her jewels go down the main street. But he did not try to stop her. That night he packed up everything she owned (including, I was told, broken combs and half-used bottles of medicine) and sent them to her—collect.

This, I'm afraid, is cold comfort to unmarried ladies on the sidelines, for these once-burned gentlemen seldom care to repeat the experiment once they escape. What does cause concern is its effect on the already rather dim chances of a healthy, attractive woman in her middle years to remarry. Prospects for a woman's remarriage also tend to vary inversely with the number of young children she has, unless she finds a man with an equally large brood who is bedazzled enough to want to have his own home-style kindergarten. For by the time the children are grown and out of the hair of prospective suitors, the lady is not in the age bracket to make a man feel like playing leapfrog again.

As of 1964, there were 2,968,000 women over thirty in the United States and 3,458,000 single men. This sounds promising, and even hints that there might be some marriageable bachelor here for the divorcees and widows. But, according to a Los Angeles psychiatrist who is an authority on homosexuality, the number of male homosexuals in the United States ranges from 2 to 4 million. Even if some of these men are married or divorced or under thirty, the estimate cannot help but destroy any hopes which flutter in the hearts of women alone. It even explains why women shy away from marrying confirmed bachelors.

I have heard single men complain mildly that they are under pressure from families and other married women to marry. Of course these bachelors are invited to parties as escorts for unattached women. But the pressure on these desirable (socially) males to remarry is nothing compared to that which women put on themselves. For, even after a woman takes stock of the situation and decides she does not want to marry any of the men who want her, or that she is really better off living alone than making the compromise marriages she sees taking place among her friends, she feels like a social misfit. A widow told me, "The fact that my husband was an enormously attractive man, who could have married any number of girls but chose me, doesn't seem to matter. I've been single for six years now. Even his relatives are beginning to wonder if there isn't something odd about me."

A widow in Iowa told me, "I was good old Grandma to everyone, including the milkman. Just because I wouldn't go out with the decrepit old men in town that people tried to match up with me, they decided I was over the hill. Then I met a man in a camera store when I was shopping in Chicago. We liked each other and I began making trips to Chicago to see him. Nobody suspected a thing—they thought I was too old for romance. Even my own children didn't know what was up until I gave a big party at the country club to introduce my fiance. It was naughty of me. But I got a kick out of showing them there was life in the old girl yet."

Some women never reconcile themselves to living alone, never give up hoping to meet Mr. Right. I suppose, in a way, this is good—a sign that a woman still has young ideas. But it seems to me a bit pathetic to go on chasing an impossible dream. It is one

hing to fall in love again; it is quite another to go on hoping for
n illogical happy ending. I think it is far more sensible, and
attractive, to bend your mind toward more realistic ambitions.

Any happy marriage depends to a great extent on luck, plus an
normous amount of adjustment on both sides, particularly on
he part of the woman. I found a number of divorcees who admit-
ed that they refused to adjust to first husbands—yet are repeating the same mistake with men they are dating now. One told me,
'I took my fiance to a cocktail party during Christmas at the
home of an older woman, a widow. I've never seen Harry like
that—he was scurrying around helping her open the door and
serve drinks. After we left, I asked him why he never did that at
my house. He said, 'She needed help. You never do.' My first
husband always said I was too damned self-sufficient. Am I making the same mistake with Harry?"

There are women who never have had and never will have the
capacity or desire or duplicity—call it what you like—to subordi-
nate themselves to a man. Or they will do it in business, and even
on casual social occasions, but when they become emotionally involved, they insist on having equal rights. A woman who tried
living with a man before marriage told me, "I discovered all sorts
of things I wouldn't have known if we hadn't made a trial run.
He hogged the bathroom; I was consistently late to the office.
When I complained, he asked why I didn't get up early and get
through before he was ready. He liked a hot bedroom—I loathe
it. He raised hell because I always have a cigarette after the lights
are out, it calms me and puts me to sleep. We agreed on all the
major things, but it was the little things that broke us down.
We'd decided on a three-months trial. After a month, I knew it
was no good, but I stuck it for seven weeks. Then one night he
told me I was trying to diminish his ego by arguing with him. I
packed up and left at midnight. I've never seen him since—thank
God. But also thank God, we found out we were mismatched before marriage."

We all know women who have adjusted to living alone far better than they would to marriage, or to remarriage. They are the
ones who are short on compromise or who have grown so used to

being alone that they are what is referred to as "set in their ways." I see nothing wrong in this; more power to the ladies, who are invariably good company. The problem is that so many of them simply cannot or do not face the fact that they are what they are. They keep hoping for miracles.

A vivacious blonde divorcee who crushed her weak first husband to a spineless pulp, stopped in the middle of her Saturday shopping to tell me, "I'm sick and tired of the whole routine of dating. I long to have it all behind me, to have someone I can count on when I want to go out, to be able to stay home if I'm tired, to be able to take off these damned false eyelashes and relax. Do you suppose I'll ever find a husband? I'm not so bad-looking, am I?"

The answer, if I had dared to tell her, was yes and no. Yes, she is very good-looking and no, she will not find a husband because all she wants is a built-in escort or a fireside companion, something like a dog but less nuisance.

When women alone talk wistfully about remarrying, they remind me of the young girls who have wedding dresses all picked out, but haven't found the groom. They forget marriage is not an end in itself but a beginning. And beginning again at a mature age can be very difficult. Unless both parties concerned bring to remarriage understanding and wisdom gained from experience, the results can be disastrous. All of us have been exposed to second marriages that limp along in such low gear that we return, with a long sigh of relief, to our single beds. Selfishness which wrecked a first marriage—or in some cases helped in destroying a first wife—seldom improves with age. On the contrary.

Recently, I met a couple from Arizona at a dinner party, a second marriage for both, after previous divorces. The wife, a girlhood friend of the hostess, was shaking with nerves. When her husband pointed to an ash tray, she jumped. At dinner, she dithered over the roast, making sure his portion was rare enough. She hardly ate a bite herself. After dinner, she went to the kitchen to make his coffee herself.

The hostess took me aside to say, "Mildred divorced her first husband because he was a bore. Ed seemed everything different—urbane, charming, sure of himself. The very fact that he was so demanding was attractive. What Mil didn't realize was that he was absolutely, completely spoiled and cared nothing for anyone except himself. So long as she caters to him, their marriage goes along smoothly. But in the process, she has lost all her charm and most of her personality. She's turned into a vegetable."

American husbands are reportedly permissive; they have been criticized for this abroad and at home. Even so, as a man grows older, particularly as he approaches the grim age of retirement, he develops quirks and habits that make menopause symptoms look mild. A wife of long standing often decides she can't take it; many women turn the tables and go out looking for work when their husbands retire, preferring the tyranny of routine jobs to the tyranny of home, housework, and the constant husband. A second wife often finds herself in a much more difficult position. She not only has to cope with a husband who has retired, she finds herself competing with a dead wife or—infinitely worse if a man has always been indulged—the tender memory of a dead mother. If there is a possessive daughter involved, she faces not only a rival, but a younger, and often prettier, girl who automatically hates the intruder.

It should be easier to compete with a divorced wife—no matter whether she has rejected the husband or he has been the one who wanted change. So strange are the vagaries of human nature that this is not always the case. Divorcees talked to me with some humor about their replacements. A woman in California, who has not remarried and still lives in the same small town as her ex-husband and his new wife said: "On Christmas, when the children were visiting him, he showed a lot of our old home movies and kept saying, in front of his bride, to the children, 'Doesn't Mommy look pretty there?' When we were married, he used to say I was always pestering him about taking care of himself, acting too maternal. Now he will call me up at night—and I suspect she is standing right there—to say, 'Remember that awful ache I used to get in my shoulders? Well, it's back. I wish you could tell Anne how you used to massage it. Or could you give me the phone number of a nurse or somebody who would know the trick?' ''

A man may grow to loathe his wife during a trying divorce. They may snipe at each other over the children. But time dulls resentments. Just as a husband—or wife—may forget his or her dead spouse's faults, so may a divorced wife begin to seem less trying in retrospect.

A man of considerable wealth divorced a grasping, ambitious wife and married his secretary. The new wife was a pleasant change from the first in every way. But, having been privy to his business, she also knew what an outrageously large settlement the first wife had obtained, and she resented the arrangement more and more as time went on and as she was called on to make "sacrifices" because of Number 1. On a trip to Europe, they happened to be near the town in the south of France where Number 1 was staying. He insisted on driving over and was annoyed when Number 2 refused to go with him to call on Number 1. They had a row that night which left bitter memories, for he now resents any criticism of Number 1 as an indirect criticism of his taste and judgment.

In a small town in California, the executive of a large firm divorced his wife and married a widow who was working in the corporation. The ex-wife continued to live in town, with the children, and has succeeded in making Louise F.'s life miserable. She persecuted her with calls at the office until the general manager "suggested" Louise F. quit and become a housewife. Now at home, she still gets calls from the first Mrs. F. and insults from the children. She wants to have a baby herself but Mr. F. says they cannot afford one. Yet wherever Louise goes—to the country club, the market, or the beauty shop—she sees the first Mrs. F. spending money freely and mocking her. And when she complains to her husband, he grins and says, "Shut up. You've got me, haven't you?"

Some women are so unhappy alone that they will settle for any husband. One who was getting ready for remarriage told me, "I may be miserable but at least I won't be miserable alone." Sometimes things work out better than expected; usually, worse. Marriage for security, on either side, is almost the worst mistake a man or woman can make. A Massachusetts widow with two young children who married a rich alcoholic—in the old days he would have been called the town drunk—said to me, "I'm to blame. Lou was between divorces and I let him think I loved him, that I wouldn't mind taking care of him. It's a life of horror for me and the children. If I had known what it would mean, I would have scrubbed floors happily."

In talking to women who have remarried, one phrase keeps repeating itself, "It isn't the same but——"

As I probed further, I discovered that most of these women had married mainly for convenience, had been pushed into it by friends, relatives, even their own children. In one case, the widower's children were tired of catering to his whims, as their mother had always done, and dumped their father into the waiting arms of the widow next door who was having a hard time getting along financially. At her age, she was no better able to adjust than his children, but so far she is trying to make the best of what she knows is a bad arrangement.

In another case, a Midwestern widow with a considerable fortune met an attractive younger man in the hospital, where they were both patients. Although she was aware that the comforts she could offer him were influencing his affections, she was sure they could be happy. Not until after their marriage did she discover that he was a homosexual, and had a regular sweetheart whom he intended to support with his wife's money. She divorced him immediately and is a broken, embittered woman.

Occasionally, marriages of convenience never take place. In Chicago, a widower with three small children was engaged to the widow next door who had cared for his youngsters, along with her own, while his wife was dying of cancer. Shortly before the wedding, the new bride-to-be discovered she had suspicious lumps in her neck, and her doctor wanted her to go to a cancer specialist. Without waiting for the results, the widower broke the engagement. He said, "I can't go through that again."

That old phrase, "in sickness and in health, until death us do part" rings very hollow in a marriage of convenience. I know of one man, a widower, who was so genuinely in love with a widow, a friend of his ex-wife's, that he disappeared when he found out he had cancer, and she never heard from him again until his brother brought a letter written to her before his death. I have also discovered, in talks with men, that some of the nicest have decided never to remarry simply because they don't want to burden a strange woman, however sympathetic, with the ailments that inevitably accompany aging. More often, a person who has gone through the death of a spouse will shy away from marrying anyone in poor health.

A Connecticut women told me, "I have a man of sixty-five who would like to marry me. I like everything about him except his age. He's always been in good health, but one of these days, by the law of averages, something will hit him. I still have nightmares about my husband's last illness. I simply don't have the courage or strength to go through such a thing again." Another, who does a great deal of hospital volunteer work, said, "I'm getting so I'm a great little diagnostician. One look at a man and I can tell you whether it's kidney trouble or heart disease. And believe me, I stop dating a guy right away if I suspect something is wrong. I've had the bedside bit."

Are these people cynical? Or merely realistic? And are second marriages, as I have been told over and over again, "different," less romantic, based on mutual convenience rather than love?

Some of them are, of course. Some of them break up fast, for in such a marriage the man or woman does not have any desire to try to compromise and wants to cut losses as fast as possible. In other cases, where a woman is financially dependent, she will try to struggle through, and refuse to admit her mistake. And in still other cases, where a woman has been duped, or where she boasted a bit too much beforehand, she is ashamed to admit her mistake, and goes on suffering.

But a second marriage can be better than a first, if both parties are mature. The man or woman who has learned something from a mistake, or a loss, has more to give to a second marriage. The whole approach is different, wiser, more reasonable, less selfish, more tolerant.

A divorcee in a small city became pregnant about a year after her husband deserted her. The father was a prominent married man. She chose not to name him or accept any money from him. She had the baby out of wedlock and kept her, although she was widely criticized. "I found out who my friends were." Among her friends was a divorced man whom she had known professionally, because he sold printing to her firm. They had never dated before, but he made a point of taking her out during her pregnancy, and afterward. When the baby was two years old, they were married and he adopted the child. They are now so happy that she made a point of asking to see me, so that her story could be included here.

A married couple I know, both previously widowed, combined two sets of home furnishings in one apartment. Afterward, she said, "Isn't it lucky our tastes are so similar?" His answer was, "We wouldn't have gotten this far if they hadn't been." Later, when I admired a bag she was carrying, and heard he had given it to her when he was courting her, he said, "Correction. I am still courting her."

I know of a marriage where a divorcee waited half a dozen years for a widower, until his youngest daughter left home to marry. The girl had been so attached to her father that the wise older woman refused to try to compete. Friends warned her she might lose the man. She didn't. Now not only are she and her husband extremely happy—the daughter, with children of her own, is now closer to her stepmother than she is to her father.

A woman writer married a man who is an intense golfer. It was a love match, but friends wondered how she was going to adjust. The first year, she waited around the country club pool for him. She acquired more tan than she thought was becoming and grew tired hearing the complaints of the other golf widows. Now she has rented a small apartment near the country club where she spends weekends writing and reading.

A widow of a number of years married a recent widower and moved to another city with him. In his house, she found that the housekeeper kept fresh flowers in front of the various pictures of the dead wife, which were scattered all over the house. Although

her husband had been dead for many years, and his memory no
longer tugged at her, she made a point of mentioning his name
often, coupling it with the name of her husband's dead wife. On
their first anniversary, she gave a party and said to the assembled
room, "I'm sure Frances and Bill are looking down on all of us
tonight, blessing our happiness." Not long after that, friends noticed that the pictures of Frances quietly disappeared from the
house.

A divorcee who has made a great success of her marriage to a
divorced man (who admits his thoughtlessness was basically responsible for his divorce) told me, "You should have interests in
common. But you also should have private areas, and respect privacy in your husband. Perhaps the word that is most important is
respect. If I hadn't respected Don's mind and his integrity, I
might have bogged down on minor things like his temper and
impatience."

Essentially, it is the woman who is eager to give, who is happiest when she is most needed, who makes the ideal second wife. I
know such a woman who is the fourth wife of a man whose three
other marriages ended in divorce. The reason this one is succeed-
ing—and it is, brilliantly, to many people's amazement—is that
she demands so little and wants to do so much for him that he, in
exchange, has made a serious effort to correct the personality
quirks and failings his other wives thought were intolerable.

Perhaps love the second time around is no longer the wonderful intense pain and joy it is when you are young. But it does
happen with all the strength of youthful love, even if the passion
is not quite so intense. And it can hit at an advanced age . . . or
shall I say, an age which seems advanced to other people.

A widower I know has a charming woman friend who wants to
marry him; she has everything to offer, a lovely home, gracious
manners, and beauty. But he hesitates because, although he likes
her very much, he is not in love with her . . . and "What if I
should fall in love after we were married?"

Sometimes, true love begins with liking. Interests in common,
similar backgrounds, mutual respect all help in making a marriage succeed. And a sensible marriage, based on mutual conven-

ence, can and has sometimes developed into romance. But you can't count on this.

I know a woman close to eighty, who recently turned down a proposal of marriage from a widower of seventy-three who lived next door to her. She said, "He wanted somebody to cook for him, and watch television with him. Why should I settle for that, at my age? The time to be sensible is when you are young. I'm old enough to demand love—or nothing."

A doctor whose patients are women said, "Whenever a woman comes in and asks if she should marry so-and-so, I immediately say no. If she has to ask me, she's not enough in love to get married. Nor should she listen to her children or her relatives or her friends. She is the one who is getting married. To hell with what the rest think."

I have seen real love matches, remarriages at seventy, seventy-five. In Chicago, one of the most difficult lawyers in town, an embittered divorcé for twenty years, bloomed into a devoted husband and charming man after he married a widow two years his senior. At seventy, the doctor I quoted above remarried a widow, his long-time patient whose children and grandchildren he had delivered; affection over the years ripened into love.

And just remember that old truism: beauty and love are in the eye of the beholder. A pretty divorcee, whom I met in the course of writing this book, used to stop by on Sunday evenings to report on her weekends. Mostly, she would say gloomily, "I'm sick of the pot-bellied old men my friends trot out for me. Don't you think I deserve something better?" Or, "I'm not going to remarry. The young ones don't want me, and I'm not going to spend my declining years nursing an old dodderer."

One night she flew in, announcing that she was engaged. She'd met *the* man—fascinating, handsome, bright, charming, et al. She could hardly wait to show him off to me.

When she did, he looked to me like just another pot-bellied old man. He also has chronic asthma and she already is trying to get him to stop smoking.

11 THE WICKED STEPCHILDREN

Children give you a feeling of continuity. But they can also ruin you and themselves, if you let them cling too closely. A woman alone must make sure her children are exposed to other families, and plenty of friends their own age.

MINNEAPOLIS DIVORCEE

My daughter said she would kill herself if I remarried. I refused the man and he married someone else. Now we are both sorry. At least, I know I am and I think she is.

CONNECTICUT WIDOW

My son is getting married to a very nice girl. I try to like her but I can't. I say to myself it's because I know they are sleeping together, that it isn't proper. Secretly, I know I am jealous. My daughter suspects that, too. The other night she suggested I try to find a man of my own. After the wedding, I'm going to pack up and move to another part of the country and to hell with them both. But think of the years I've wasted.

CALIFORNIA TEACHER

I'd been divorced for ten years before I found the man I wanted to marry. It was just great—until his daughter found out about it. She carried on so that I broke the engagement. I know I could never compete with her.

NEW YORK DIVORCEE

Rachel H., a beautiful precocious child, was eleven when her father died of a heart attack in a small boat in New Orleans' gulf. She felt guilty because he had asked her to accompany him on the fishing trip and she had overslept. Hiding her sorrow and chagrin under frantic activity, she told everyone that her mother did not like her, but preferred her sixteen-year-old brother.

Her mother found it necessary to go to work as a secretary. When Rachel was fourteen, Mrs. H. became engaged to a bachelor from New York, for whom she had worked when he was in town. Her son was delighted. But Rachel said, "If you marry and disgrace my father's memory, I will do everything in my power to make you miserable."

The boy tried to argue with his sister, "In a few years when you're ready to get married yourself, you'll be delighted to have Mom off your hands." Rachel, however, refused to be cajoled into approval. And she was shocked when her mother went ahead with the wedding, saying, "Rachel, as a minor child, you have to move to New York with me. Because this will be our home, and I want you to have friends of your own age there, you will go to a private school there for a year, which your stepfather will pay for. If, at the end of that time, you still do not approve of him or my marriage, we will send you away to school."

From September until April, Rachel maintained her war of nerves. She refused to speak to her stepfather and spent a great deal of time alone in her room. Because dinner hours were so difficult with her present, her mother served Rachel her dinner at 6 o'clock and the girl went into her room and closed the door when her stepfather came home around 6:30.

He was a patient man . . . "an angel," his wife says. He did not try to bribe, scold, or coax Rachel to mend her ways. By April, they decided nothing would change her attitude, so her mother said to her, "I can see this won't work. You've won your point. Pick the boarding school you want and you can finish the term there. You can go to summer school, too. You can even spend vacations with your friends, if you like."

Rachel was startled out of her surliness. She protested, "I don't want to quit in the middle of the term. Besides, I like my school."

"Then," her mother said, "you shape up. Start speaking to your stepfather. You can begin when we all eat dinner together tonight."

Rachel, faced with what she recognized as an ultimatum, tried. Afterward, her mother realized that Rachel had already changed her mind about her stepfather but did not know how to say she had been wrong. Although she is now close to her stepfather, and invited him up alone to her college on Father's Day, she has never been able to apologize for her attitude. Being stubborn (like her mother) the nearest she has ever come to it was when her brother eloped with a girl the family did not know and Rachel went to her mother to say, "Don't decide too quickly you won't like her. Or say anything harsh to Bud. It's very hard to live with your past errors and statements."

For the last twenty-odd years, we have been living in a child-oriented culture. Parents feel guilt no matter what their children do—witness the attitude of the mothers and fathers whose children have joined the hippies and are on drugs. But when you are a stepparent, trying your best to please and win a child, particularly a child who is in the teens, you can hardly do anything right. This is difficult enough when the previous parent is dead, for the natural tendency of any boy or girl is to glorify his mother or father, endow him with all virtues and no flaws. But when the parents have been divorced, when they are already worried about what they have done to their children, or when one of them is using a child or children as a club against the other, the stepparent has an almost impossible task. Particularly if she is a woman.

The wicked stepmother of Cinderella legend is no more. Instead, we have the children ruling the household, relegating the stepmother to a position in the household of an outsider with few rights. The divorced man, living in terror for fear his ex-wife will alienate the affections of his children, goes to all sorts of lengths to conciliate them. If he remarries, the stepmother is supposed to play along with his attitude. A stepmother, trapped in such a situation with a man she loved deeply, told me, "Ralph goes without a new car he needs in his business so that his sons can attend camp. Yet when we went up—on the train, incidentally, the car wouldn't take the trip—to see them one weekend they were positively rude. He didn't say a word, just went around being sweet and gentle, and gave them each a ten dollar bill when we left. Afterward, he begged me to be patient. I guess I'll have to. I'm not angry because of myself, I'm annoyed because they are so mean to Ralph."

Many a divorced wife is jealous of the woman her husband marries—even if she did not want him herself—and manages to destroy her with the children, so that the role of stepmother is automatically impossible. I know one remarried divorcee who, unable to have children of her own, waits eagerly each year for the arrival of her husband's children, hoping it will be better. It never is, because as the boy grows older he resents his father increasingly for leaving him and his mother, and the girl consciously uses her lovely developing body to fascinate her father and make her stepmother feel a thousand years old. This past summer, she wore a brief bikini to the dinner table, and when her father suggested that she put on a jacket, she batted her eyes at him, saying, "You don't mind really, do you? We're just family here, except for your wife."

Even when a divorced wife does not have custody of the children, or seldom sees them, her influence still remains in the house, and a stepmother finds her stepchildren measure her against the impossible standards of a "real" mother. A Chicago widow told me that she felt more like a slave than a wife.

Mrs. T., childless, married a divorced man with three children, aged ten, twelve, and fifteen. Their mother is in a sanitarium, a hopeless alcoholic. At the end of the day, after working hard at her job of furniture salesperson in a big store, Mrs. J. comes home and cooks dinner and cleans up afterward. No one offers to help her. The children often do not make their own beds, and their rooms are cluttered with dirty clothes and broken playthings and games. On her day off and Sunday, she tries to make a little order out of chaos. When she finally suggested that the children help her, they answered that they never were expected to do housework when their real mother was at home. The fact that their mother did not work, while their stepmother feels she has to, in order to supplement the income, is of no concern to the children. Their father says he hates to force the issue for fear they will turn against him. He has suggested that she quit and take over the house. She told me, "Frankly, I'm afraid to. If the marriage doesn't work—and I'm not at all sure it will—I want to be able to have my good job. In fact, the job is important to me now. At home, I feel like a servant and an outsider. Here in the store, I'm liked as a person and I belong."

I have seen stepfathers trapped in similar positions, powerless because the children of another marriage are in their houses but not technically under their control. The mother of a twenty-year-old boy who has flunked out of three colleges said to me, "I wish his stepfather would be more understanding of Jimmy's problems." As an outsider, watching Jimmy sitting around all day reading or eating, and borrowing the family car to go out at night, I can understand his stepfather's impatience. This past summer, when Jimmy was making plans for a camping trip to Canada, his stepfather said, "Having a vacation from your vacation, Jim?" The boy's mother was angry and horrified.

But a man, simply because of his sex, is never as diminished or walked over by stepchildren as is a stepmother. Even when there is liking and affection between them, she is used as a whipping girl if the children want something from the father. Because they usually live with the mother, and are visiting their father only occasionally, the stepmother cannot try the kind of daily discipline she might attempt if they were in the house all the time. And, unless she wants trouble, she has to sit by and watch her husband spoil them—often ignoring her and her own children.

Martha D., a redheaded divorcee of forty-one with a little girl, married a prominent Los Angeles attorney. His three boys, by a previous marriage, lived with their mother, who had also remarried. Martha anticipated no problems. To her anguish, the boys, all in their teens, resented her and took their revenge on her ten-year-old daughter, Peggy. She finally sent Peggy away to school in order to protect her, and tried to win the boys over in her absence.

It didn't work. Whenever she and her husband planned a trip, or even a weekend outing, the boys found an excuse to take him away on an excursion which excluded her. At Christmas, when Peggy was home and Martha had planned parties for her, the boys insisted that their father take them to Sun Valley for skiing. Martha rebelled and spent Christmas with Peggy. Her husband came back for New Year's and they had the worst quarrel of their married life, during which he insisted that the boys had to have priority in his life because he had hurt them by allowing their mother to divorce him.

"It's not love they feel for their father," Martha told me. "The only affection they feel is for his money. The mother gave up her share of his estate when she remarried and the boys are determined they are going to get every penny due them, which is why they resent me and Peggy. I can't win against them, and their father refuses to see what is going on. Now it's just a matter of when I leave him, not if. I'm determined now to see that Peggy and I get some kind of a settlement, to make up for the pain and anguish we both have suffered."

Many widows and widowers remarry for the sake of the children. In the case of motherless boys and girls, this is infinitely preferable to having them raised by grandparents or housekeepers or maiden aunts. The children appreciate this, in their hearts. But they often test a stepfather, to see how far they can go. And they particularly resent the presence of another person taking the place of a beloved mother in the house, and in the bed of their father. I know the case of a man who lost his mother when he was six years old. Although his stepmother raised him as her own, and, if anything, favored him over her own children, he resented her all his life, even after he was a grown man, with children of his own.

Mothers favor sons and fathers are more indulgent toward daughters. This is a natural way of life and does not cause real conflict if the parent of the other sex is not jealous or overpossessive. But death imposes emphasis on natural tendencies and normal reactions can become neurotic. In the case I just mentioned the man's attitude toward his stepmother was definitely neurotic and he continued to yearn for the lost mother when he was in his fifties. In the same way, a girl misses a dead father and turns against her mother if she wants to remarry. Or, if the mother dies, the little girl's attachment to her father becomes more intense, obsessive.

Sometimes the little girl feels it is both her right and duty to take her mother's place with her father—and, unless he is very wise, she may never give it up. I was introduced to one of this tyrannized breed, a widower, one night at a dinner party. Three times during the evening, twice during cocktails, once at dinner, he was called to the telephone. At ten o'clock he excused himself, explaining that his daughter was not feeling well and he wanted to get home. Afterward, my hostess said that this happened whenever he was invited to dinner and the daughter was not included. And when the poor man, whose wife has been dead five years, takes a woman to dinner, he has to lie to his daughter and swear to secrecy anyone who sees him.

Occasionally a widower recognizes that such devotion is bad for the girl, as well as uncomfortable for him, and chooses to remarry against her objections. This can work out eventually for the good of everyone. But it is a brave woman who walks into this kind of a situation with her eyes open. And if she does not have her eyes wide open, she is in for the kind of hell that only a young woman can impose on an older one.

I know one lovely sixteen-year-old girl who threatened to kill herself when her father remarried. I admit he was not very grown-up about the remarriage—he and a twenty-four-year-old girl in his office eloped to Mexico and came home and presented sixteen-year-old Lucy with a *fait accompli*. At first, Lucy was sweet and docile—disturbingly docile. She played on them both, using her wiles on her new stepmother to get extravagant masses of new clothes, then demanding that her father take her out to night-clubs and the theater to "show her off." The stepmother made a poor third most of the time. Even so, a few nights before Christmas, when her father and stepmother were attending a party where Lucy had not been invited, she went into her bedroom and slashed her stepmother's fur coats and evening gowns to ribbons with a razor blade. Just before they were due to come home, she cut her own wrists with the same razor blade, by then dulled and fairly innocuous.

Right now, she is back living with her grandmother and going to an analyst. Although her grades are excellent, she has refused to finish school and is working on her father to provide her with an apartment, a maid, and a big dog. Just what her next demands will be is anybody's guess. But the sophisticated betting is that the new stepmother will not be able to compete.

One day when I was at my doctor's, waiting for a checkup, a nervous young girl was pacing the floor, lighting cigarettes and stamping them out, and pestering the receptionist, demanding to know why the doctor would not see her right away. Later I found out what was the matter.

Linda D.'s mother died of cancer when Linda was thirteen. The parents were divorced, and Linda's father had remarried. After her mother's death, Linda had to live with her father and her new stepmother. The new Mrs. D., a sensible woman with two older girls, did everything possible to make Linda feel at home, excused her rudeness and lack of consideration for many months, attributing it to grief. But finally, after an outburst in which she announced she hated her stepmother, her father sent Linda away to school, that limbo for children of broken homes.

This was a luxurious, expensive school. Linda had her own room and her own horse. Three months later, the authorities sent her back home because they felt she was unstable. She had spent one whole day standing in the window of her bedroom threatening to jump. The family doctor recommended analysis. At the moment, she is having daily sessions—again at great expense—and making life a living hell for the family. No one knows what is going to happen but her father will not desert her, even if it means losing his current wife. He has, perhaps foolishly (the doctor who told me this story thinks so), made this promise to Linda.

Some men and women are sufficiently cowed by their children so that they give up any idea of remarriage. And some have such a close relation with their children—usually with emphasis on the child of the opposite sex—that outsiders quite wisely stay clear of involvement. On the other hand, many divorced or widowed women devote the rest of their lives to children out of a sense of guilt that comes, we can only surmise, from their feeling of having been responsible for the death of the other parent. Or they think they cannot give their children to another father to be disciplined, they want to hang onto the reins themselves. Or they are weak enough to listen when their daughters beg them not to remarry, forgetting that the day will come when these demanding children will grow up and want to leave home.

A widow I interviewed confessed that as a girl she had prevented her mother, forty-five when she was left alone, from remarrying. The two traveled all over the world together and, whenever a gentleman was interested in her mother, little Adele found something about him to ridicule. The now-contrite Adele said to me, "Children can be inspired devils. I knew my mother well enough to pick little characteristics in a man which, if built up, would annoy her. Then, of course, I married and went to live in Europe. I saw mother once or twice a year, the rest of the time she was alone. She never resented me, or mentioned what I had done. And I didn't realize it fully until recently."

A girl of thirteen, devastated by her father's death, made her mother swear on her father's coffin that she would never remarry. At the time, the mother, just as grief-stricken, found the vow easy to make. Five years later, when a charming gentleman, a professor from a nearby law school, was courting the mother, her daughter sternly reminded her of that promise. The mother, with the support of her husband's relatives and the minister of their church, decided that she must remarry. The daughter, although she is married now, with children of her own, has never forgiven her mother and still refers to her stepfather as "Professor X."

A Minneapolis widow devoted herself to a fourteen-year-old son after the death of her husband. For a long time she did not go out socially unless her son was included—even in an otherwise adult party. Her husband's partner, Bert H., fell into the habit of taking the boy to ball games, and occasionally Mrs. C. was invited to go along. As time went on, he became a regular Sunday visitor, a substitute father for the boy more than a date for her. For Bert H. realized it was important to have the boy like him before he talked about marriage to the mother. When the boy was accepted at Harvard in the beginning of his senior year of high school, Bert H. felt he could propose. He was accepted and the marriage planned for the following June, so that the three of them could go to Europe, and leave the boy in the East in September. But as soon as the boy discovered the plan, he decided he did not want to go to Harvard, that he wanted to live at home and attend the University of Minnesota.

Here stories differ. Mrs. C. told me that Bert refused to marry her unless she got rid of her son, and that his attitude toward the boy changed so drastically that she broke the engagement—"He was asking me to choose between my son and him." Bert H. says sadly that the boy needed to go away to school, to free himself from his dependence on his mother, and that he had tried to tell the mother it was for the boy's ultimate good. He said to me, "I suppose my attitude did change. I was disgusted with the kid. I told him it was time he grew up and stood on his own feet. And I also knew one other thing. I wasn't going to move into that house and be a tame crow, number three in the pecking order."

Under the circumstances, I am convinced he did the only possible thing. If the child in question had been a girl, perhaps the story would have been different. I heard of one case where a son of a widowed mother wanted to live at home and go to college, instead of trying to get into a school some distance away, and his mother's brother persuaded him that she needed to be on her own. Mothers, especially when they are single parents, find it difficult to be strong and positive about setting children free. To them, such a step symbolizes rejection.

In the Midwest, I heard a story that is not uncommon today, about a teenage girl running away from home. The factor which made it more poignant was that Susan's father had died when she was fifteen. Her grief was so intense that the doctor suggested her mother sleep with the girl in her own bed. After three months the girl announced she would be all right alone, adding bitterly,

"Why did it have to be Daddy who died? Why couldn't it be you?"

Mrs. J. tried everything—being permissive, then enforcing rules, finally sending the child to her sister's for a month. Nothing worked. When there were rules, the girl broke them. Without rules, she behaved so outrageously her mother feared she might harm herself. For a year, the struggle between them went on, with tension increasing. Curiously enough, Susan's school marks were still good, and she engaged in all kinds of school activities, drama club, athletics, and the like.

Two weeks before high-school graduation she ran away, taking nothing with her except eight dollars—no clothes except those she had on, not even a bobby pin. She was discovered waiting on tables at a hotel in Aspen, trying to save money to go on to California and join a boy from home who was working in a drive-in and trying to become a jazz musician. She refused help from her mother and said she did not want to see her. Six months later, she wrote her mother a card, giving her a California address.

Exhausted and thin, Mrs. J. took this for an invitation. She flew out to California and spent a week there, inviting her daughter and her boyfriend out to dinner and feeding them properly, and seeing that Susan had a medical checkup and started some needed dental work. The girl had worked at a variety of jobs, mostly clerking, but never stayed long any place—first, because of her appearance (she was wearing jeans and long dirty hair) and second, because she lacked discipline.

The mother herself came close to a breakdown when she returned home. During this period, the doctor who had been taking care of her, a divorcee with grown children, proposed. Although Susan was invited to the wedding, she refused. Six months later, she consented to come home if her mother would send a check. Despite the size of the check—which was to include clothes—she got off the plane in her dirty jeans, a leather jacket, and bare feet. Over her arm was a long orange dress, unhemmed and fringed. Her mother burst into tears. Her new stepfather took one look and said that if she wanted to stay with them, she would bathe immediately, cut her hair, and go down that afternoon and buy a ress. Otherwise, she could wait at the airport and take the next lane out.

To his surprise, Susan agreed to the rehabilitation program. During the two weeks she spent in her home town, she began to dress much like other girls her age there, and when she went shopping, she would bring her parcels home for her stepfather's approval. Although she went back to Los Angeles, she is no longer planning to marry the boy she went out there to join, and she is talking about going to college in the fall. Her mother says nothing, leaving the discipline and suggestions to the new stepfather. She says she is still too afraid of hurting and alienating her child. The stepfather says he is sure Susan wanted discipline and guidance or she would not have agreed to come home in the first place, adding, "Anyway, I'm not the type to stand aside. She either has to take it from me, or let me alone."

There are an estimated 2,150,000 broken-marriage families in the United States today with children under eighteen. In most cases, mothers are heads of families, whether the marriage was dissolved by divorce, legal separation, or death. (In divorce today, it is only under severe provocation that custody of children is given to fathers. When a marriage is broken by death, the wife stands a 2 to 1 chance of being the survivor.)

For a woman alone, young children are a reason for living. Older children, even those who are married with families of their own, give a sense of continuity, a feeling of never being without ties. (Daughters-in-law sometimes discover how tightly a son can be tied to a mother who is alone. One said to me acidly, "A man may divorce his wife but never his mother.") Yet whenever I talk to a woman alone who cannot carry on a conversation without dragging in some mention of a son or daughter—particularly a son—I want to shake her. Daughters can and do escape, only causing the mother a temporary hurt. But a son trapped in her loving embrace can have his life ruined.

When a man dies, or leaves his family, and the eldest child in the single-parent family is a boy, a loving mother may consciously or unconsciously promote him to the position of head of the household, long before he has the maturity or desire to take on responsibilities. Yet, because it is a compliment, and because it flatters his ego to see his mother depending on him, he takes over. The result is a man with a prefabricated family: a mother who has no need to remarry and younger brothers and sisters who continue to lean on him the rest of their lives.

A talented set designer of thirty-five is employed in New York but commutes to New Haven every day, where he lives with his mother and unmarried sister in the house left to them by his dead father. At fourteen, Jim became the "man" in the family. His sister, now twenty-six, never had a steady beau or a job. She and Mom wait up for Jim at whatever hour he may return, and always have a hot meal for him. He turned down a good job in California recently because his mother did not want to go so far from home. Co-workers think he is a homosexual; I doubt if he strays ever that far from his mom and sister.

A professor at a Midwestern university is teaching summer school this year in order to send his sister and four nieces to Europe. His father died when he was in college, leaving him a mother, a sister, and a house with a mortgage. He has been tied to all three ever since. His mother was a chronic invalid. His sister, a neurotic with great talent, has never been able to keep a job or a husband for long. The mother is now dead, but he continues to support his sister and assume responsibility for his nieces. When the girls are not in trouble with boys or school, his sister is undergoing another of her crises. He has no money to spend on other women, barely enough to support himself. He is not a homosexual, but the few women who have been in love with him have not been strong enough to buck his responsibilities.

The sad part is that no mother wants her son to be a misfit. Often the son she victimizes is her favorite. She "sacrifices" herself for him. Long past boyhood she waits on him, irons his shirts, cooks his favorite dishes, saves the biggest piece of pie for him. Recently, I met a widow who was shopping for her annual trip abroad. She told me, "One month of the year, I am a woman. The rest of the time I am a mother." When I asked the age of her son, she said, "He's twenty-nine. And he still needs his mama."

Every single parent thinks he or she puts the children's happiness before his or her own. The problem is, good intentions are often misplaced. A young mother, afraid of neglecting her children, refuses to become involved with men. By the time her children are ready to leave home, she has lost any desire (and, sometimes, chance) to find a husband, and she is used to being alone and having her own way. If along the way she has developed interests of her own, if she has a career in business or public service, the transition may be smooth. If, however, she has spent her life caring for her children, she may continue to hang around their necks the rest of her life, a guilty load.

A Wisconsin divorcee who had refused several proposals because she did not want to relinquish the complete supervision of her two sons, now teenagers, told me, "My father says the boys are eating me alive. I don't care. They are better behaved and get better grades than any of their contemporaries." A Denver widow, left with three young children, said, "Once I came close to remarriage. The man had two sons just the age of mine. It all seemed ideal. But one night, after we had all spent the day together, I realized I just didn't feel anything for his sons, and there was no reason he should care about my children. I felt I just couldn't risk giving him control over them. So I called the whole thing off."

Any remarriage of parents with children under eighteen has double problems. Sometimes a marriage that would have survived without children will blow up because of them. But if such a marriage can succeed, all parties concerned, including the children, benefit. Occasionally the arrival of an infant, a new baby for the whole family, helps pull the group together. Other times, the constant effort to adjust helps everyone involved to new maturity. But there will be problems. Parenthood in itself is not either easy or predictable; children from normal homes often are worse headaches than those from broken families. Mothers and daughters quarrel, draw apart during the period of adolescence. Sons rebel against the domination of fathers. And when a stepmother or stepfather is involved, there is focus and added fuel for natural conflict.

It is not surprising that, next to sex, the favorite late-at-night topic for women alone is children. After a dinner meeting of some women from Parents Without Partners, I came away with these notes:

MAUREEN, *divorced from an alcoholic husband:* "I never was a model mother or possessive about my children. But after I was alone, I began to put too much stock in them. I can easily see why a lot of women hang on so hard to theirs. I know a widow whose grown son, twenty-three years old, always discusses his dating problems with her. He even takes her to the symphony like a date. I don't expect he'll ever get married and I can't imagine her liking any wife he would pick out."

LUCY, *a divorcee:* "A woman I know had a husband who died of a heart attack suddenly. She has a beautiful eighteen-year-old daughter. She is very bitter about this daughter who she says she is very selfish, and was spoiled by her father. The mother started going out with men, some of them divorced and younger than she is, and the daughter became wildly jealous. She wears very sexy clothes and flirts with her mother's friends. The mother is still very bright and pretty, but her daughter is determined to keep her from remarrying, even dating."

PAT, *a divorcee:* "I know a woman who replaced her divorced husband with the male child. He slept with her until he was five, and after that used to get in bed with her in the morning. One day she noticed he had an erection. She shipped him off to boarding school, which he resented. When he grew up, he was drafted and sent to Vietnam. While he was there, she became engaged. He wrote her, threatening that if she went through with the marriage, he would never come back, he'd get himself killed. She didn't go through with it."

LUCY, *a divorcee:* "I was divorced mainly because he was jealous of the children. We were never around them as babies. We went on long trips right after each one was born. Now I am completely focused on them and I am a good mother. I have more time and patience than married mothers. I take them to Florida each year to visit their father. His wife—he's been married twice since me—won't see them. She stays in her room at the club and he takes me and the boys to dinner every night. The boys carry it off very well. One said afterward, 'Poor dad, he has had three wives, two kids, four dogs and really nothing at all. While we're not rich, the three of us, we have such fun together.' "

MAUREEN, *a divorcee:* "One day, about a year after the divorce, I was baking brownies with the children. I often did something like this when I felt low, it helped me feel we were sharing. A man called up and asked me for a date. I said no, I was busy baking brownies. The kids listened and when I hung up, my little boy said, 'Is that the first time somebody wanted you to have a date?' I said yes, and he said, seriously, after a few minutes, 'Mom, why don't you go? You can't sit around and bake brownies the rest of your life.' "

JANE, *a young widow:* "I feel I am taking a lot out on my children. My patience wears thin and I snap at them. My doctor says, 'I don't think you can help it. When you are more relaxed and adjusted, the children will be, too.' "

MAUREEN, *a divorcee:* "I noticed how jittery my children were soon after Harry and I were separated. I talked to a psychiatrist. He said, 'When you see no tension in them, you will know you are all right. They are reflecting your distress and tensions.' I suggested sending them away to my mother for a while and he said no, they are still better off with you than their grandmother. Now they know what is going on, instead of worrying."

IRMA, *a widow:* "When my husband died, it was a question right away of whether I was going to work and keep my eldest boy in college or stay home with my youngest. We had a family conference and decided it was better for me to go to work, but it would almost break my heart when I'd come home and find the little guy on the front steps waiting for me. One time he said, 'Mom, why don't you get married and stay home again?' I said to him, 'Jimmy, you pick someone nice for me and I'll marry him.' The next night when I came home he had a whole list of men in the neighborhood: Debbie's father, Ralph's father, and so on. After I explained I couldn't take another woman's husband, he was quite depressed. The widow across the street married a widower and I overheard Jimmy saying to the widow's son, 'Billy, you're lucky. Your dad hasn't been dead a year and you have a new dad. My mom isn't even trying.' "

Young children, after losing one parent, usually want the re maining one to remarry. An eight-year-old, despite the fact that she adored her father who died of cancer, almost immediately began talking about her mother finding her another father. One night at dinner she said, "Look at Sally Brown. She has a new daddy, a new sister, a new cat, and two dogs. And here we sit, you and me alone. Mommy, it can't go on this way."

A Westchester widow told me that when her twelve-year-old daughter discovered that a blonde divorcee in the building had remarried, she suggested that her mother try bleaching her hair. A Nebraska divorcee told me, "My seven-year-old son is happy as a lark when I come home and say I have a date. He helps me decide what I will wear and selects the perfume. His older brother used to enter into the game, but I notice now he is rather withdrawn. I think he is getting a little jealous of me."

Keith Smith, an Australian whose television and radio interview programs with young children are enormously popular there, says that one of the few lies ever told by children on shows is their insistence that they have fathers, when they do not. "Children," he says, "like their parents to be normal, average stock-characters."

A widow in Honolulu said that, shortly after she moved there, her little daughter stood up in front of the class and said, "My mommy goes out every night with different men." The widow was not dating at all at that time, but her daughter wanted her to find a new father, so she imagined the dating. A divorcee, who had moved her family to California so her mother could stay with the children while she worked, overheard her son tell a neighbor, "Mommy is out here looking for a new daddy for us. When she gets one, we're going back east and get our cat back to live with us."

Few children like change, even change for the better. When a child bumps up against the cold reality of losing a parent, and having another grieving or short-tempered, or both, he tries fantasy to bring back the past. Adolescent girls, in angry frustration with fate, often blame the mother for still being alive while the adored father is gone. I heard of one case where a girl accused her mother of killing her father. Children, especially in the younger years, are filled with fright and guilt. Sometimes, because they feel they have been responsible for a divorce, or for a parent dying (deserting them because they had not been kind or loving), they are terrified for fear they will lose the other, too.

A young widow in Chicago told me that her little girl used to come and push open her eyes when she was napping in the afternoon. "When I got over my anger, I realized she was afraid I was dead, too." A New York widow said that several years after her husband died, her daughter began to urge her to wear miniskirts and Mary Jane pumps. "I couldn't understand why until one day she confessed to me that she thought if I kept looking young, I would never have to die." Psychiatrists suggest that the eagerness with which young children push their single mothers out to date is not entirely desire for father replacements. They want their mothers to be happy, so they will not go away, too.

A Connecticut divorcee with three young children told me, "Since their daddy has remarried, they are all the more eager for me to find a husband. The two boys are hungry for a father; they hang around a man who comes to the house, and my little Brigid flirts with him. They feel their own father turned them down and when one of the men I've been dating disappears, they feel rejected all over again.

"When I broke up with Gene, whom they had liked the best so far, they were upset. I think they worried, too, because they saw me as not being able to cope with men, to handle them right. I had a date shortly after that with a new man and my eldest said, 'I hope you're not going to start yelling at him the way you did at Gene.' Believe me, that gave Mommy pause. The main reason I gave up Gene was that he got bored with the children, he kept saying, 'Let's go someplace where the door isn't always opening with somebody screaming for something.' Am I going to deprive my kids of a father because I want too much for them? I wouldn't have their father back if I could now. Yet I know no other man will ever be as interested in them as he is."

On the North Shore of Chicago, I talked with a widow, now just thirty-one, who has three children, aged five, ten, and twelve. She was married at seventeen and has been a widow for four years. She said, "At first I was very much interested in remarriage. Fortunately, I had enough money so that I didn't rush off with the first man who asked me, a bad mistake some young widows and divorcees make. My children were also eager to have me remarry four years ago. But now the two older ones are pretty much against it and I must say, when men call for me and are met by these two tall young men, they are rather put off. The only men who are serious now are older. The younger ones want to have their own babies, not take on a half-grown family, and I really can't blame them."

A New York divorcee, whose daughter is eleven, said, "Janie loves to see me go to parties, and she supervises my dressing. She is actually better at putting on eye makeup than I am. She still talks about my remarrying and seems pleased when we have a Sunday outing with one of my beaus. But I notice she is beginning to go off a man if he seems too interested in me, or too affectionate. Recently, she refused to go sailing with one of my more ardent beaus, and ducked when he tried to get her to kiss him goodnight. Later when he made a pretty serious pass and I ducked, he said, 'You're getting just like Janie.' I wonder if I am . . . because I know that if I should remarry, Janie might be very jealous and possessive of me."

Adjustment is easier with young children. Even a stepmother has less difficulty with her own acceptance and the child's (he needs her more) if he is still a toddler. But as early as ages five or six, young children will remember their own parents and have more resistance. And, with each year, possessiveness increases, particularly toward a parent of the opposite sex.

In Philadelphia, a widower married a divorced woman with ten-year-old twins, a boy and a girl. They took their new father's name and regarded him, not the weak alcoholic whom their mother had divorced, as the real parent. But in adolescence, the attitude of the boy changed toward his adoptive parent. At nineteen, he left school and went to San Francisco to join the hippies. His mother persuaded him to come home last Christmas, but the visit was a dismal failure. He was bearded, wearing beads, and talked openly about smoking marijuana. The battle between him and his adoptive father was so savage he left after five days and has not been back. On the other hand, the girl is closer to her adoptive father these days than she is to her mother.

The man's lot is easier, even as a stepparent. He controls the money, or most of it; he is not home all day; and he is used to speaking with the authority of the ruling male in the household. But no matter how hard a stepmother tries, the old legend still persists and many an alert young child milks it for everything it is worth. Stepmothers fight back, under provocation, and sometimes they hit below the belt. But I doubt if there is a stepmother alive who is sly or tricky enough to defeat a young girl who knows all the ways to win over her father, and is not shy about using them. The only way here for an older woman to triumph is by sheer sweet reasonableness, and by not resorting to the kind of bitchery practiced by her stepdaughter.

Among my friends is a woman I shall call Harriet, who was utterly self-contained and happy alone, with many admiring friends and her own successful public relations business. She had no desire to remarry, which may be why a visiting English author was so determined to make her change her mind. They had a wedding that was one of the gayest parties of the year, and went "home" to England on the *Queen Mary*. Harriet moved into his charming house in Surrey—with his longtime housekeeper and indignant fourteen-year-old daughter.

The two incumbent females, daughter Ginny and the housekeeper, resented everything about Harriet, including her American ways. She paid no attention. She found a job in London and rented a small flat there, going down to Surrey only on weekends. She was glad to entertain her husband in London if he wished to come up, but there was no spare bed for Ginny. On weekends, she made no effort to win Ginny over, or to interfere with the running of the household, acting the role of a polite guest.

Ginny one day announced she was going to live with her mother—the mother who had deserted her as a baby and was now living in London with her fifth husband and two of Ginny's half-brothers. Her father raged. But Harriet persuaded him to let the child go away for the summer, and gave the old housekeeper two months' holiday. Meanwhile, she managed to find an efficient replacement. Harriet spent more time in Surrey, gradually the house took on some of her warmth, and she and her husband began entertaining . . . at which she was immensely skilled. One night Ginny dropped in while a large party was at dinner. She said she was leaving and demanded her father drive her to London right away.

Harriet excused herself and took the girl upstairs. There she said, in effect, "I love your father and I want to do what is best for you because he loves you. But I'm not involved with you emotionally and I give you consideration only so long as you deserve it. I don't care whether you live with your mother or not—in fact, if it didn't bother your father, I would prefer it. I can make him happy without you. As for his taking you back to her, you have no right to ask. You weren't invited here, so you can either leave and wait for a train at the station—I don't care how you get there—or you can spend the night. You bed isn't made up but there are sheets in the linen closet. Take it or leave it."

At midnight, when the dinner was over, they found the girl asleep in her own bed. The next day she asked permission to come back and live. The battle was not yet won. The housekeeper had to be retired gracefully. The girl still had temper tantrums and escaped to her "real mother." When she came home, as she did inevitably, because her own mother tired of her, Harriet accepted her calmly, and expected her to take care of her room and get her own meals if she did not eat with the family. One night, when she did not return in time for the evening meal, Harriet put everything away, leaving an uncooked duck in the refrigerator for Ginny to cope with or not, as she preferred. Harriet and her husband returned from a rather prolonged call and found Ginny happily cooking the duck. They sat down at the kitchen table and shared it near midnight.

Today Ginny is married and the mother of two babies. She sees her own mother not at all—the idea of being a grandmother revolted her. But Harriet, at last, has allowed herself the luxury of being fatuous about Ginny's boy and girl, and is the only grandmother they know. On her fiftieth birthday, she had a card from Ginny which she treasures. It said, "I think you're the only pebble on the beach."

12 TRAPS AND SOLACES

I've had women keep me on the telephone for forty-five minutes but I let them go on because I know how important it is for us to make contact at times.

HONOLULU DIVORCEE

Religion is literally my salvation now that I am alone. When people snarl at me, I say a prayer for them. It may not help them, but it is good for me.

MINNEAPOLIS DIVORCEE

I don't read, but I envy people who do. I know a widow who met her second husband at a Great Books course. He is a foot shorter than she is but she doesn't seem to care. All they have in common is brains.

NEBRASKA WIDOW

I tried going to church but all I could see was the casket with red roses on it where the minister was standing.

MINNESOTA WIDOW

Of course I've considered suicide. The first three months after my husband died, I checked the medicine cabinet every night before I went to bed to be sure my secret cache of sleeping pills was still there, just in case.

CONNECTICUT WIDOW

BEING alone, in the words of a divorcee, means, "You are left to your own devices, and some of us devise the damnedest traps." That of course is true. Some women retire to their beds like wombs; others escape in sex or alcohol. When sleep is impossible, television or reading can help; prolonged, these can be very bad habits. But, as a Honolulu widow wrote me, "No habit is really bad if you recognize what you are doing, and why."

One woman's solace may be another's trap. Bridge, for example. Or a dog. But a solace like religion may change your life for the better. And even something little, like keeping a diary, can be a tremendous help because, looking back, you can see tangible evidence of progress, and be proud.

Everyone must choose her own path. But it is surprising how many women, independently, hit on the same things. Looking over this alphabet, compiled after hundreds of interviews, you may discover some familiar ideas, but also some new angles.

ALCOHOL

At a time when you need a cushion between you and reality, alcohol can be a boon. But the woman who lets the cushion become a prop pushes herself into a limbo where nobody wants to help, even if it were possible.

Example 1: A California divorcee with one daughter made an excellent living as an artist in an advertising agency. She was a social drinker only. Then her married daughter was deserted by her husband, leaving five little children behind. The girl's reaction was complete hopelessness; she went into a mental decline and had to be hospitalized. Faced with the fact that her daughter might never recover and the care of five little children, Mrs. X. began to drink more and more heavily . . . never at work, never in public, but at home after the children were in bed. Her work deteriorated. Knowing the problems, the office kept her on long after her shaking hands made delicate work impossible. She finally quit in humiliation and is doing posters. But she cannot stop drinking and, as she cannot eat, either, her health is very bad.

Example 2: A Chicago woman, whose husband had been dying painfully for ten years, went to work after his death in the silver department of a large store. She did very well, but after a while, she became tired and discouraged. She and her husband had always had cocktails before dinner. Now she began to drink herself to sleep every night. Solicitous neighbors tired of having her telephone them, half-drunk, babbling nonsense. Her married sons finally persuaded her to go into a sanitarium. She is not drinking now but she is nearly broke and is finding it hard to get a job, for she is over sixty. Her sons send her what money they can, but she refuses to go and live with them and their wives. And her friends hold their breath—for they fear it is just a matter of time until she starts drinking again.

The real problem drinker, the woman who has always been potentially unstable, will always use a crisis for an excuse to escape into alcoholism. But any woman who has been through a divorce or the death of a husband is in a state where her nervous system may trigger off heavy drinking. Sometimes she stops by herself; one woman told me, "I tried to become an alcoholic, I just couldn't make it." Other women catch themselves before it is too late; warned by a bad experience, their self-respect comes to the rescue. Still others, having seen what has happened to their friends, make a point of watching their drinking far more carefully than they did when they had husbands.

A Detroit divorcee said, "First you drink with people. Then they don't drink up fast enough so you'd rather drink alone. I got so I was afraid to answer the telephone at night, for fear people would know how drunk I was." A Minneapolis widow told me, "My husband and I had always been in the habit of drinking quite a bit, all our friends did. After he died, my house turned into one continuous wake. I got so I couldn't eat breakfast until I'd had a drink, a bit of the 'hair of the dog.' My fourteen-year-old son caught me at it one morning and started to cry. That brought me to my senses. I haven't had a drink for two years."

A doctor told me, "If a woman is used to drinking socially, I

hink one or two drinks, at the end of the day, improve her spirits
ind her appetite—even if she is alone. The danger lies in pro-
onging the cocktail hour until she loses her appetite. She passes
)ut instead of going to bed. She can't sleep unless she is drunk,
ind she begins drinking in the morning, at noon, as well as in the
evening. I have patients who spend their lives in clouds of alcohol. The dreadful part is that it no longer comforts them, gives
them a lift. It drags them down and makes it impossible for
friends to put up with them."

One sophisticated New York widow who has seen this happen
to some of her friends never drinks alone. If she is not having
guests for cocktails, or going out, she drops by her club for the
two martinis she enjoys before dinner. If someone invites her to
have a third, she joins him or her—but she never has a third
alone. A California widow who lives in a small community told
me, "I play golf all day, so I'm pleasantly tired at night and look
forward to a drink and dinner. I make it a point to cook myself a
complete dinner—a good serving of meat, vegetable, salad, and
dessert. I get everything ready, and the table set, before I fix myself a drink and read the newspaper. During the second drink, I
cook my chop or put the finishing touches on whatever I am going to eat. I go without dessert at noon, when I eat with my
women friends at the club, so I can have something sweet at night
—that removes any desire I might have for a nightcap."

Women today are more ashamed when they let their drinking
get out of control than men are. Psychologically, this is bad; it
leads to secret drinking, and reluctance to seek help. But sometimes all that is necessary is one conversation with the family doctor, an airing of problems. In other cases, psychiatric treatment is
needed. Alcoholics Anonymous is also good and supplies companionship with therapy.

BRIDGE

Many country clubs have a bridge membership for women
alone—and in some areas the bridge tables are filled from early
morning until late at night. In other towns, there are "bridge
days," twice a week where married and single women play to-

gether; and the women alone also play bridge at their all-female dinner parties three or four times a week.

Bridge is a fine mental exercise. If you are good enough to take it seriously, and play in tournaments, it is a way to meet people. But it can become a monster that occupies so much of your time you can think of nothing else. You become, in the terms of a Florida divorcee, a "bridge-aholic." She told me she enjoys bridge, but refuses to let the women in her small town know she can play, or she would be swamped with invitations.

A Nebraska woman said, "You have to play, in my town. Otherwise you're not invited out. You see, we all know each other so well we have exhausted all topics of conversation over dinner. If we didn't play bridge, we'd just sit and yawn in each other's faces. Sure, it's a solace for a woman alone; she doesn't have time to think of her own problems when she is playing a tough hand. But she gets into the habit of going out to play bridge so much that she never thinks of doing anything else, like going to a movie, or reading a book."

CLOTHES

A woman whose husband was hospitalized over a year in his terminal illness told me that she made a point of never wearing black during that time. After his death, friends who were used to seeing her in light and bright colors complained when she put on black or gray, so now, "Looking cheerful is a way of life for me." In my opinion, colors do help morale. So does a pretty nightgown or negligee, even if no one sees it.

Most husbands tend to be conservative about fashion—on their wives. Alone, you are free to experiment. I am not at all sure that the dress matters very much when you are going out, because few people really notice it. But I am certain that a new dress that she likes, that she thinks is becoming, can make any woman more attractive.

Changing your style, making yourself over, does not quite fall into the same category. You can become a blonde or redhead, lose twenty pounds, and pay hundreds of dollars for a sensational new coat, and the man you are trying to impress will say, "You've had your hair done differently, haven't you?" But a basic going-over never did anybody any harm, even if you shock old friends. (Wearing a bikini may not endear you to those wives whose figures aren't up to it, or whose husbands don't approve, but what have you to lose? The same wives may also criticize you for spending too much on clothes; just smile sweetly and next time don't mention what you paid.)

The woman who wrote the famous advertising slogan, "Is it true blondes have more fun?" is Shirley Polykoff, a widow. She says, "It's not much fun to live to be seventy-five if you spend the last forty years looking like an old lady."

I agree. Whether you remarry or not—and I have heard of cases where women found husbands after doing a remodeling job on themselves, just like the stories—clothes help your mental attitude. And going shopping for a new dress is a good antidote for a depression day.

DRUGS

Tranquilizers are a great crutch when you are going through a bad emotional time and need to function. So are sleeping pills. But they can become bad habits, traps for the woman alone. Feeling unsure, inadequate, frustrated, and sometimes guilty, she longs for forgetfulness. Often she feels additional guilt afterward because she is not trying harder to solve her problems, to face life squarely. So she resorts to drugs again. Quite accidentally, she can become an addict.

I heard of one woman who has been divorced two years and still has to take a tranquilizer each morning before she goes to work. Another said, "I went through three men and twenty bottles of nembutal the first year I was divorced."

Don't borrow pills from friends. Your doctor is the one to advise you about drugs. Be honest, because he is compassionate and understands what you are suffering, he has helped other women. But also be a little brave on your own: I have had many women alone tell me that the earlier you break your dependence on drugs, the better.

EXHAUSTION

The quick answer all the old hands have for the woman newly alone is: Keep busy. To a certain extent they are right. It is a comfort to be surrounded by friends who want you to come to dinner and lunch, to have the telephone ringing, to have letters to answer. It also helps to have work to do. A young Illinois widow told me that the week after her husband was killed in an automobile accident, while she herself was still in the hospital, she joined five organizations.

Doctors encourage newly alone women to return to their jobs immediately, with the shrewd observation that the longer one delays, the more difficult decisions will be. Women who have not worked for years, or have never worked, are urged to go back to school and brush up, or to do volunteer work. There is hardly a woman alone who, if she can afford it—and sometimes if she cannot—has not tried another form of activity, travel.

What most of us do not realize is that we are not in a stable condition, and that everything always seems worse when we are tired. A brilliant woman wanted a divorce but, in the process of getting free, she went through two months of agonizing discussions and self-doubt. On a Sunday, her first alone, she found herself in hysterics. She was unable to reach her own doctor but after many frantic telephone calls, a friend located a famous analyst who listened to her over long-distance telephone for an expensive hour. Finally he said, "What you need, my dear, isn't a doctor. Just a good night's sleep."

After the first shock is over, a woman alone must watch herself, keep from getting too tired. Invitations still come thick and fast, and she has no desire to sit home alone, without a husband. Often she is out every night: something that never happened when she was married. Unless she sleeps all day—another trap— she becomes exhausted. It is hard to space engagements because, like a teenager coping with dating, you are so afraid to turn down any invitation for fear you will never be asked again. But as an attractive New York widow said, "What is the good of dragging yourself from one place to another when you are so exhausted you hate everybody?"

Food

A Chicago widow wrote, "I find food has a tranquilizing effect. It was hard to eat at first, so I made myself eat small quantities more frequently. Now when my panic comes, I stop for tea or coffee. If I'm not at home I sit someplace quietly. A waitress serves me and smiles . . . the bad moment passes."

Another said, "I weighed one hundred twenty-seven pounds when I was married, but I gradually kept gaining. Then, the year before Chuck died, I went on a crash diet and got down to one hundred thirty. After he died, I wondered what mattered. All I had left was food; it was easier to cut out alcohol and tranquilizers than to stop eating. I now weigh about one hundred fifty, maybe more. Perhaps it makes me look older. I can't help it. I live to eat and that's not kidding."

A divorcee in California, desperately unhappy, keeps "eating and eating. Once in a while, I get hold of myself and lose a lot, but afterward I hide food so even the kids won't know I am grabbing snacks all the time. Or when I feel lousy, I just can't bring myself to get up and heat soup. I'll go to market, but when I get home, I'll find I have nothing except cake and candy and maybe a couple of bottles of champagne. I'll nibble at this, and give the kids money to go out and buy pizzas. The neighbors see them, and they come and bring us food. I suppose they mean well but when I'm miserable, I have to eat for comfort, and when I get fat, I can't bear for anyone to see me. It's a vicious circle. And I can't make myself stop."

More often, really, unhappy women cannot eat. One widow told me: "It was eight months before I could touch a decent meal. My own cooking tasted horrible, of course. But I couldn't even eat what my friends fixed. I got so I hated to be invited out. I'd look at the big portions they'd put on my plate to fatten me up and I'd get sick."

The proper woman alone plans a balanced meal, prepares it carefully and eats under pleasant conditions, watching TV, reading a book, or sitting at a window with a pleasant view. (I heard of one woman who loves fiction but reads only at mealtime . . . so she looks forward to meals.) But, unless a woman is really disciplined, she tends to slip into the trap of eating standing up in the kitchen, or making a meal entirely of sweets, or gorging ravenously one day and not bothering to have anything in the house the next. Women have told me that they did not prepare a single full-course meal for themselves for a year after they were alone. Even with children to feed, they would exist on odds and ends. I know of one woman who has been a widow for five years who fixes dinner for her son (potatoes, meat, vegetables, salad, dessert) and drinks Metrecal herself. ("But I eat a decent lunch with clients, as a rule. My boy just wants to gobble and dash out and I'm not hungry enough at five thirty to sit down with him.")

Some women alone form the habit of eating out, at lunch counters, in tearooms. Even eating regularly in modest places can be expensive, and the quality of the food is seldom as good as when it is prepared at home. Other women eat well at noon, and make themselves sandwiches in the evening. Still others eat a rather adequate breakfast and no lunch, so they are hungry for an early dinner. A divorcee told me that one of the tricks for attracting men is to cook for them and to have a well-stocked refrigerator. A widow who overheard her said, "A woman has to fall in love again before her nesting instinct sends her back into the kitchen to prepare food with inspiration."

I'm inclined to agree. The best cook in my neighborhood is a widow who remarried. When she was living alone, she used to dine regularly on hero sandwiches she bought on her way home from work. Even when she made herself fix dinner for friends, "I really wasn't interested. It wasn't until I met Arthur that I really had fun preparing meals again."

A movie actress, now retired, is still so much in the habit of dieting that she has a hard time eating as much as her doctor recommends. She is no cook either, for in her gala days she always had several servants. While her husband was alive, he did whatever cooking was necessary in the small kitchen of their New York apartment. For a long time after she was alone, she did not know how to light the oven, so when she entertained at home, she bought a barbequed chicken from a delicatessen, potato salad, and ice cream. A friend reported that one night when she arrived at

B.'s apartment, B. said proudly, "I have a big surprise for you, I've learned to light the oven." That night they had TV dinners.

GRIEF

A friend wrote me, "Is there a phase during which one refuses to be comforted? We finally got Lucy J. to dinner. She still is wed to her grief and even looks as if an artist had smudged a gray blur over her features, sponging out all vitality, thickening every line."

Grief cannot be rationalized. Divorce and death are similar in their effect upon a woman; the feeling of loss mixed with anger and guilt, and the search for replacement (or the hope of "patching it up" or meeting the loved one again in "another world") is the same. A single woman can find the loss of a parent, particularly a male parent, similarly devastating. One woman told me that, four years afterward, she still cried for her father. Even the death of someone who has gone through a long terminal illness and was a burden can cause terrible grief—you miss the burden as well as feeling guilt because you sometimes resented it.

The early stages are not the worst. Women I talked with referred to "those blessed zombie days" when nothing seemed real. A young mother who lost her husband at thirty, leaving her with two babies, told me that the entire week after his sudden death is blacked out in her memory; she has no recollection of the funeral service or of moving with her children to her mother's house. Another woman who nursed her husband during a year of horrible stress until he died of a brain tumor was "marvelous" for six months immediately after his death—then she went into the hospital with internal bleeding and came close to dying herself. A newly divorced woman, whom I interviewed early in my research, was so frantically active in creating a new life for herself that it took my breath away: she was dating; she boasted of an active sex life; she had moved to a glamorous new apartment that she was decorating; and, whenever she had a free night, she entertained people like myself, whom she hardly knew. (This in addition to a full-time executive job.) I was not surprised to learn of her hospitalization with pneumonia last spring. What did sadden and shock me was to learn of her death. The doctor said she had lost her will to live.

Most of us survive. Recovery from our various forms of malaise takes time, and cheery friends who try to buck us up are often impatient. Little things spark off big depressions, and only gradually do you realize that, as times goes on, the depressions are not so deep or so hard to control. (One new widow said to me, "I try all the remedies, keeping busy, seeing friends, helping people. I find feeling low is like a bad cold—if you don't do anything about it, it lasts a week; if you try everything, it takes seven days to cure.") Healing any wound is a slow process; Tolstoy says that it has to heal from within.

An older woman I know, who has had more than her share of tragedy, said of a woman who was weeping hysterically at her husband's services, "That kind gets over it fast."

I have the feeling that the stiff upper lip we feel is proper these days—how we long to hear, "She's being wonderful"—tends to prolong our suffering and divert it into other channels, such as illness. A doctor who is a close friend, who has had his own grief, said, "The only way to treat sorrow is to accept it, take it by the hand."

A Chicago woman who has survived two painful divorces put it this way: "Being alone is like having read a book and finished it. You never quite forget what has happened." A California widow, whose husband died young in a tragic air crash, said, "Gradually, the pain subsides. You have memories, but they are tender, good."

Every deeply shaking experience has hidden in it the opportunity for growth and understanding or the germs of defeat. A psychiatrist told me that for anyone to recover quickly, he must be able to cry it out, to go to the full extent of his grief. For grief repressed, and thus prolonged, can become resentment, and that lowest of all human emotions, self-pity.

HAPPENINGS

A Chicago widow told me: "When I'd come home from work I wouldn't put the car in the garage. After the children were in bed I'd go for long rides—sometimes I'd find myself twenty-five miles away from home at three in the morning and I'd stop in for coffee with the truck drivers. After a while, I'd make myself put the car away and put on pajamas and a robe thinking that would stop me. But then I'd suddenly find myself on Michigan Avenue at midnight; I put thirty-one thousand miles on the car the first year my husband died."

An Illinois divorcee: "I slept practically for six months. Every morning I'd wake up, send my oldest to school, put the baby in the playpen, and go back to bed, saying I'd take care of things tomorrow. One day my little girl came home from school and said, 'Mama, you're in bed again and not even wearing pajamas.' That stopped me, because I was afraid she would run around and tell the neighbors."

A Minneapolis widow: "I couldn't keep track of keys. One minute the car keys were in my hand, the next they were missing. I locked myself out of the house until I started keeping one key at a neighbor's. Then I lost that. It got to be a joke at the locksmith's; once I had six door keys made and distributed them among the neighborhood."

A Honolulu widow: "I'd always been a careful driver. But suddenly, I found myself racing. The police all knew me in my neighborhood, and were kind. But I got picked up time after time other places. One night when I walked into the traffic court, the dear old sergeant behind the desk looked up and said, 'What, you here again, Polly?' "

Nebraska divorcee: "You think you're all right, functioning, long before you really are. I have a good friend who went through a divorce a few months before I did. She could almost predict the things that would happen. Once when my car broke down in the middle of the evening traffic rush, she said, 'Oh, no, this will happen to me next week.' And do you know—it did."

Iowa widow: "I took up parachute jumping. My mother-in-law said I was crazy, with three little children. Maybe it was a death wish, but I told myself it was better than alcohol and sex. I know one widow who went crazy and for about a year slept with every man who asked her. One night she said she woke up, like from a bad dream. I stopped jumping, too, after a while. Maybe I'll start again, but I knew I wasn't coordinating and so did the instructor. He was glad when I quit."

INDEPENDENCE

A young man wrote to a newspaper advice column, "My mother is a widow. For the last year and a half she has come to me for everything. Lately she's been asking me to take her shopping. I have no time for my family any more. She has her own home in the suburbs, she works, yet she moans of loneliness and neglect all the time."

A divorcee on the North side of Chicago said to me, "I do everything I can for my son and his wife. I take care of my grandchildren and take them traveling and buy them presents their parents can't afford. In spite of everything I try to do, I know my daughter-in-law loathes me. What should I do—ignore the wife or move far away? It is terrible to move, I feel so helpless. I have no women friends and I'm afraid of seeing men, for fear they will marry me for my money."

A widow in California: "I moved out here to be near my son and his family. I decorated the house for them this Christmas. But they didn't seem to notice. The day after Christmas I took everything down. It's that way all the time. When I go over there I always take presents. Now they no longer even say thank you. And I never can see my son alone, unless I go to his office."

Independence can be a wonderful thing in a woman alone. (Some females are so feisty and independent they carry things to extremes. A brave widow I know had plans to spend Christmas alone—"I'm not religious, it doesn't mean that much to me"— until I practically carried her over to the gathering at my house. Another divorcee in Detroit with six children got together with another divorcee who had five and had a joint celebration. It worked so well—"We couldn't ask anybody else to take our large broods"—that they plan to make it a regular thing.) But most of us need to restrain ourselves, especially when it comes to leaning on married children. There may—and probably will—come a time when you will need their care and support. Until then, as a wise and experienced longtime widow said to me, "Control yourself. Don't try to buy your grandchildren or your in-laws with gifts or attention. Live your own life and don't lean on them. They will respect you a lot more. You may even become a friend instead of an obligation."

JEALOUSY

Next to self-pity, the bitterest trap of all is jealousy. A Massachusetts widow said, "I found myself looking at all the wives I knew, thinking what jerks they were, what did they do to deserve their nice husbands. Sometimes at dinner I'd listen to them complaining how they never had any fun, how they slaved all the time, and I'd come close to saying, 'You don't know what I'd give to be in your shoes.'" Divorcees can suffer even more, because they feel the lost husband is not lost permanently, and no matter how undesirable he seemed at the time of the divorce, time and distance lend enchantment, and his current girls—or wife—drive them wild with jealousy. A Washington divorcee who has done everything in her power to make her ex-husband's current wife miserable still feels "he'll get over this infatuation. She's nothing but a common tramp, she's had affairs with dozens of men, some of them old friends of his. I know Hank. He always was proud of his sexual prowess but he was afraid it was declining, that's why he went for her. One of these days he'll come home and then I'll watch her crying her eyes out."

Thinking like this gets you nowhere. Nor does it help to go ringing his doorbell, dragging the man into court, or, in the case of one woman I read about, tar-and-feathering his car. As for widows, just thinking this way about wives may be destructive to friendship, and to you. For you may unconsciously be making invitations to the husband, all the while you are thinking his wife does not deserve him. Unless a man is divorce prone, he has to be mightily uncomfortable before he will make a step toward breaking up the present arrangement. Bedding down is one thing —but you can build up your expectations and then be badly let down. Or you can just embarrass yourself and him, and leave the wife holding higher cards than ever.

KEEPING THE PAST ALIVE

A Chicago widow said, "I gave away Bill's clothes. Then I suddenly came on a suit he had worn to our wedding twenty-five years ago. I wasn't able to throw that out, although he'd been dead two years. It's kind of spooky."

A Cleveland widow: "Yes, we do keep things. I found myself hanging onto Fred's golf clubs—goodness knows why—because I gave everything else away in two weeks. I certainly can't use them and the boys have their own."

A New York widow: "You have to pull away from his family a bit. The relatives will try to cling to you, and the children. I think even your own family will try to talk about your husband too much, bring him up on every occasion. In my case, I was terribly withdrawn and I pulled away from both families. I didn't want to see them at all. Maybe this was a mistake, but I felt better with new friends who weren't always talking about how Mark did things."

Another New York widow: "Don't ever say, when you do something, 'Jim would have liked me to behave like this.' He's gone. You're on your own."

A Minneapolis widow: "I feel a spiritual presence around me always. It is a great comfort to me. About six months after Fred died, I had a dream. We met in the lobby of his office building and he said, 'You're doing a wonderful job, everything is the way it should be. I'm proud of you.' I don't feel he has gone at all. I feel his presence around me always."

Some women cling stubbornly to the past, making sacred rites of anniversaries, customs. By keeping things as they were, and continuing to live life much as it was when the husband was alive, a woman keeps hoping irrationally for the bad times to go away, and for the good times to come back. Relatives should not be rejected entirely, especially where they help children preserve a sense of continuity. But neither should they be allowed to try to preserve the status quo, blindly.

In the words of a Chicago divorcee whose husband later died, "Take each day at a time, using the AA approach to living. Don't worry about tomorrow, or dwell in the past. Life has changed and you have changed, too. Try to be sure it's for the better.

LITERATURE

Books are to me the greatest comfort and escape possible. Perhaps there is a danger in becoming so involved in reading that you retreat from life. But—like all habits—nothing is too bad if you are aware of what is happening.

MUSIC

I know women who keep music going all the time in their homes, to fill the emptiness. A California widow told me that she has the radio on all night, that it is better than any sleeping pill. But a recent widow who used to be a musician told me that she still is unable to listen to music, it tears her so emotionally.

This is an individual problem. Personally, so-called popular music, with its mawkish lyrics, could break me down worse than anything in the early days. On the other hand, for a while, television was a blessing. Particularly if you have a few favorite shows, you can develop a beginning pattern to your life.

Of course TV can become a monster. But, for a while, it is the best baby-sitter you can hire for yourself. A New York widow wrote me, "I shall always be grateful to Johnny Carson, with whom I spent many nights when I couldn't sleep. I shall also be grateful to the people who put movies on at 4:30 in the afternoon, for they got me through the period of the day when I saw all the other husbands in the neighborhood coming home from work. The noise in my apartment, the sight of people on the screen, occupied my eyes and my mind. Now that I am over the worst, there are weeks at a time I don't turn on the set, then only for a special show."

NO SYNDROME

A divorcee from Montana told me, "It's quite human to go through periods when you feel depressed and wonder what you are doing running around like a chicken with its head cut off. We all see horrid examples around us of people who feel that way—but didn't fight it. There are times, week after week, night after night, when I dread keeping the engagements I've made, when I would give anything to call up and cancel a bridge lesson or a committee meeting which I know will not amount to a row of beans. But I won't let myself. And sometimes when I go out with the greatest reluctance, something nice happens and I find myself enjoying everything very much."

Women who have never married tell me that this *"no syndrome"* never subsides, that in fact it may become a way of life as you get older. This is when a change of scene sometimes benefits. I met a woman who was almost a complete loner when she lived in a New York apartment; for weeks on end she would paint alone in her apartment and see no one except the cleaning woman. She moved to the country, a step her remaining friends deplored, and suddenly was caught up in the whirl of rural living.

Fear of failure, fear of trying, is behind many refusals to participate. No one likes to be a wallflower at a party. Yet what is wrong with being a mouse in the corner, observing? Sometimes a party will be boring; but actually, the most boring parties of all are the ones where other people are having a good time and you are outside, ignored. The too easy way out is to retire, and to say no next time. It is also easy to sit back and make fun of the woman who pushes, who moves into groups, who builds herself up as having a good time.

I have a friend whom other women often criticize because she is always on the run, joining groups that are too young for her, going on tours organized by dancing schools, organizing excursions. But I have discovered something about this woman: men think she is great. There is something about her courage that appeals to them.

OWNERSHIP

One of the great problems of the woman alone is that she lacks the very real discipline she had as a wife. Dr. George Christakis,

Associate Professor of Community Medicine (Nutrition) and Assistant Dean of the Mount Sinai School of Medicine, New York, said, "Married women do better at losing pounds and keeping them off than single women." This is true of a great many other things connected with the life of a single woman . . . like making beds, washing dishes, and (in the extreme) caring about her appearance.

Ownership of property can give a woman alone a feeling of responsibility, of being needed by something, if not somebody. A woman who has never married and has been utterly alone since the death of her parents and a beloved sister, told me, "I bought my house in the country when my sister was ill. We were fond of it. After she died, it became a refuge. When my agency folded, and I was out of a job, I think I would have given up and become a beachcomber if it hadn't been for my house. But I had a mortgage, and I had to keep up payments. Losing it would have meant losing part of myself."

A divorcee in New York has a beach cottage that means so much to her that she even goes out to it during the winter. One Christmas when her father came to New York to visit, he refused to drive out in bad weather to see it. She wept, saying, "You went to see my sister's children way out in New Jersey in the snow, yet you won't come and see my house."

Sometimes ownership of property makes a woman feel trapped. A young divorcee said that, whenever she was persuaded to buy a house, she immediately hated it; but that when she rented, she felt flexible so she usually stayed longer. Age makes a difference; sometimes all a career woman has to show for her years of hard work is her "dream house." And widows frequently said to me, of their homes, "I want to die here."

PETS

It has been said that dogs are best suited to gregarious people, and cats to loners. This seems rather silly. I am for pets of all shapes and sizes for women alone. You are not alone if you have a dog or a cat—or a bird. You can talk to him, instead of yourself.

There is something in the house when you come home. You have responsibility—more in the case of a dog, for you have to take him out at certain hours and give him exercise.

A talented divorcee I know insists pets are nonsense. She loves them (she says) but complains that they utterly complicate your life. You cannot go away for weekends without putting the animal in a kennel or (in the case of a cat or bird) bribing the doorman to feed it. Your friends, or prospective friends, may be allergic to animals. She illustrates this with a story about a fascinating lady who was entertaining the most charming man she had met in years—only to send him out into the night sneezing because he was allergic to cats.

I counter this with the story of a woman I interviewed who has a standard poodle to act as chaperone. Whenever a date gets too fervid, the poodle (a male, given to her by her ex-husband for protection) jumps on the couch and gets between them. Exactly what my friend does when and if she doesn't want such good chaperonage, I don't know. Being a discreet gal, she doesn't give away trade secrets.

Of course, I do not think anyone should have a pet of any kind unless she likes animals and is in a position to take care of one properly. But in this case, I am thinking of the animal, not of the woman.

QUACKS

Women often hesitate to take their intimate problems to a family doctor—or a strange doctor who seems too busy to discuss anything less serious than cancer. Hence, quacks. And quacks can get a vigorous hold on the woman alone.

In searching for someone professionally trained to listen and help you, it is best to ask your own physician for help, or call a hospital that has a medical school attached to it. Meanwhile, here are three definitions which may be of help. *A psychologist* does not necessarily have any medical training but has studied psychology, and many have a doctor of philosophy degree (Ph.D.). Beware, however, of the psychologist who advertises; many of these have no more than a smattering of knowledge and little or no university training. *A psychiatrist* has a medical degree and has specialized in psychiatric work. The difference between a psychiatrist and *an analyst* lies mainly in training. The analyst has to have many more years of study. Every accredited analyst has been analyzed himself as part of his schooling.

The results of any successful analysis are cumulative; the patient afterward is left with an ability to apply what he has learned about himself to new situations and deal with them without help from his doctor. No reputable analyst attempts to attach a patient to him forever. Those who have chosen this field are not strange maladjusted figures, nor are they cashing in on mysteries too deep for people to understand. With any reputable psychologist, psychiatrist, or analyst, a patient has the right to stop treatment if he or she does not like the doctor or his "style." On the other hand, quacks often demand that you sign contracts and make large payments in advance of treatment.

The refusal to seek medical treatment often is a symptom of fear, an emotional refusal to face truth, or what you fear is the truth. Thrift is given as an excuse; often a woman will duck around the corner to a quack and pay more, in the long run, than if she went to the best-trained doctor in her area. Any reputable doctor will gladly discuss fees in advance, and, if you cannot pay what he asks, will direct you to another physician or a clinic.

RELIGION

Religion can be a great solace and comfort. One woman said to me, "It gives meaning to my days. You can't lean on people or things without being let down, but I'm not afraid when the Lord is running the show. I do the best I can and I hope to be able to cope. But He is the one who is in charge."

Faith is a gift, and those who have true religious faith are blessed. But a minister said to me, "Some widows and divorcees in great sorrow make the mistake of thinking you can't ask for help from religion in a crisis if you haven't been active in the church before. That is far from the truth. Religion is for all who are troubled, and the solace is there for the asking."

Sometimes a woman who has drifted away from the church goes

back to it during a time of crisis and finds comfort. A Jewish woman told me, "My husband was not religious and we seldom went to Temple. But after he died, I went every Friday night to services. In the beginning it was just someplace where I could go alone, and be welcome. But gradually I found comfort and made new friends who were good to me. The bereaved are allowed to mourn, but not too long, and remarriage is encouraged. The rabbi and his wife sent me an invitation to a singles musical."

But a Michigan widow told me, "I went back to church in the beginning, and it seemed to ease my pain. After a while, I got tired of seeing the same people and listening to the same old petty troubles. It seems to me that people who go to church are very narrow and set in their ways. The truly religious people are above these things. I take my religion by myself."

Another widow added, "After Tom died, I had the service in my church, which was Episcopal, although he was a Quaker. I tried to continue to go regularly, but all I could see was the casket with red roses on it where the minister was standing. It was too much for me. I finally quit."

And a divorcee in New York told me, "I left my church when I married Arnold. After the divorce I went back and I cried all the way through the service. I tried another church the next Sunday, and the next, trying to find one which seemed right to me. Then I got the horrors because I thought of my mother-in-law, who was a demanding widow and really the cause of our divorce. She used to shop around for churches the way some girls shop around for beaus, staying with one until she got everything she could out of it, then flirting with another. The whole idea repelled me."

SUICIDE

A divorcee in Nebraska, a woman of thirty-eight with three children, was found one morning hanging from the rafters in her barn. She and her husband had both been popular in the neighborhood; they were very athletic and belonged to a group of sports-minded young marrieds. But after the divorce, she seldom went out at night. She worked in the supermarket at the checkout desk for a few hours during the day, when the children were at school. Sometimes, she would stop in and have coffee at a neighbor's house on the way to pick up her children before dinner. But mainly, she was alone. She was seen taking long walks at night. Then came the morning when her oldest son, ten, ran to the next-door neighbor to say his mother's bed was empty and hadn't been slept in . . .

A widow told me, "For a year after my husband died, I buried myself in work. People said what a great adjustment I was making when I was elected to a vice-presidency. What they didn't know was that I cried myself to sleep every night. One night, I just decided it wasn't worth it. I had saved some sleeping pills and I gobbled the whole batch down. The reason I'm here is that accidentally, or maybe not so accidentally, I took so many I got sick. The woman in the next apartment heard me—these paper-thin walls—and called an ambulance."

A California divorcee said, "My birthday was on Saturday. But of course my ex-husband didn't remember. He never had, unless I made it a big point. He came for the children, who were too little to realize what day it was, and went away. My mother had died two years ago and my father had remarried, so no hope of any word from there. I thought I would just drag through the day and forget it. But I couldn't. I started drinking, and about three o'clock in the afternoon decided, what the hell? If I died, my husband would take the kids and marry one of his girls. The children wouldn't miss me, really—they were too little. I was just figuring how I was going to drive my car over the cliff when the telephone rang. It was an old school friend who had just come across my address and wanted me to come to a party that night. I drank a lot of hot coffee and got in my car and drove there instead of over the cliff."

One night when I was in the Midwest, a widow whom I had talked with that afternoon turned up at a large party to which I had been taken. During the course of the evening she caught my arm and led me out to the terrace. She said, "I have a question to ask. How many women alone think of killing themselves?"

There are no statistics on this, of course. But I suspect that suicide is in the minds of more women alone than most people would guess—particularly during that first difficult year. And I see no reason to conceal this. In fact, once when I asked an obviously distressed divorcee if she had considered suicide, she suddenly looked relieved and confessed she had, adding, "Does that happen to all of us?"

Suicide is the tenth cause of death in the United States. Nevada, the traditional divorce mill, has the highest rate—22.5 per 100,000. More women than men try to kill themselves, but nearly four times as many men succeed. (The rate among divorced males is 69.4 per 100,000 as opposed to 18.4 among divorced women.) This may be female inefficiency. It may be a way of attracting attention, an appeal for help. (I interviewed one divorcee who confessed that on three different occasions she had taken an overdose of pills and then called her ex-husband. The last time he threatened to let her die if she made an attempt again. She hasn't—as yet.) But it may also be that in woman, the surviving sex, the simple will to live is stronger. Much as a woman thinks she wants to kill herself, something instinctive within her says no.

One of the three main reasons for suicide, according to French sociologist Emile Durkheim whose nineteenth century treatise is still a classic, is depression when an individual's adjustment to society is shattered, as by the sudden death of someone close to him. Particularly during the difficult early months, the thought of suicide, as one widow said to me, "is always with me. During the day, I exist, I write letters, I go through the motions of living. But at night, when I get into bed, I wonder how much longer I can go on living a life which has no meaning. . . ."

Some women give up. Young children are not necessarily a deterrent. In black moods, women kill their children, and then themselves. But, in a curious way, the fact that a woman in distress has a way out is a solace. More than once a woman alone has confessed to me that one of her great solaces is the bottle of sleeping pills which "will give me peace and release if things get too bad." Or, as Nietzche put it, "The thought of suicide gets one successfully through many a bad night."

TELEPHONE

Talking is the best way to relieve tensions, which may be why I found women alone so cooperative when I was interviewing for this book. In fact, other people often find women alone boring. A widow I know is seldom invited out because her tongue never stops wagging. "She was talking so much she didn't even eat my dinner," a hostess complained.

I have a good friend who says, "I won't make an emotional wastebasket of my friends." But she is a rarity. Most women alone, in the guise of asking advice, come to friends just to talk themselves out, for release.

The other night I heard Johnny Carson, the vicarious late date of so many of us women alone, say, when he was asked what he did when he felt depressed, "I pick up the telephone and call my friends."

The telephone is a great invention, and a solace for women alone. The trick is, I am told, to make calls yourself, not to sit, as in the old popular song, all alone, waiting for it to ring. But try not to make a bore of yourself, even with other women alone. And if you call a married woman, inquire first whether her husband is home, or if she is busy.

UNTIDINESS

A divorcee who is closer to forty than fifty said to me, "Why should I bother fixing myself up? For what? Or who?"

A man I met at a Parents Without Partners meeting said, "I was married for eighteen years and have been divorced for eight. In many ways, I'm more comfortable this way. But the other night a woman complained that I had dirty fingernails. When I went to scrub them, I noticed there were spots on my vest. A wife would have told me about these things. Like maybe I should get married again."

Living alone can be casual and relaxed—sometimes a little too relaxed. Personally, I have a theory that men, when they are clean, are more fastidious than women—no matter how many bath towels and socks they drop. Women skip corners. They bathe for fun and relaxation, not for cleanliness. Perhaps the net result is the same. But my theory is that if a woman does not have a man around, she can fall into bad habits of sloppiness.

Two old friends, a widow and a divorcee, spent their holidays together with their children. It was so easy, and so pleasant, to be together with the children out most of the time on excursions that the two women fell into the habit of staying in nightgowns and robes all day. One night the minister and his wife came to call, and asked solicitously if there was illness. After that they made a point of inviting guests at least once a day so that they had to get dressed.

Working With Your Hands

There is solace in working with your hands, doing old-fashioned handicraft like needlework, embroidery. Just the process of producing an attractive finished product is therapy, and when you run out of projects there are always friends to help. A New Hampshire widow told me that all winter she occupies herself knitting socks and sweaters for the people she meets during the summer, either in her own town or on trips or at the home of her married daughter. Because she has a modest income, she asks that they supply the yarn.

A Midwestern widow works six months out of every year for the Village Fair at her church. She is clever with her hands and enjoys using them, and she also enjoys the workshops where several people join forces and socialize while keeping busy.

A divorcee told me: "Soon after I was alone, I found myself in such a state of nerves that I couldn't read or lie down and nap. I started to do petit point. It calmed me, I don't know why. I'd always keep something to work on in the glove compartment of my car, so if I had to wait when I was picking up the children, I would have something to do. People laughed after a while when I had everything in the house covered with petit point, but it was wonderful for my nerves."

Exercise

A young widow with small children said, "I had never tried ice skating. We had always taken our vacations during the winter, in a warm climate. But it was something I could do with the children. At first I started out like I was taking poison but now I find myself enjoying it so much I even organize parties."

A Midwestern divorcee: "I sometimes think we women, as wives and mothers, forget how to use our legs. We drive every place. One of the first things I did when I had to economize was to sell the car. People thought I was crazy when I started to walk, and the children were terribly upset because it was either walk or use the bus. But we all feel better for it. And I find myself more interested in eating regular meals when I have exercise."

YOUNG PEOPLE

A New York widow who is also director of a small art gallery told me, "After Harold died, my children wanted me to move into Manhattan, into a small apartment, instead of the big one in Brooklyn. I temporized—I knew it would be nice to be near them, but they were all married or busy with their careers and their own lives. I'd kept the old place, with its extra bedrooms, for when they came home weekends. Now I offer the use of the bedrooms to young people who are new in New York while they are getting settled. Some are artists from abroad, some are children of friends of mine. I don't treat them as children, and we become friends, for it is easier to be friends with other people's children than your own. In this way, my life is infinitely enriched. Sometimes my own children complain it is hard to get a date with me."

Young people starting out on careers, or marriages, often need the help of older people, which they will accept more gracefully from you than from their own parents. In exchange, they give you a new window on the world.

Grandchildren are also wonderful, because you can enjoy them without the pressure and frustrations of parenthood—and, unlike their mothers and fathers, you can send them home when you get tired. A Michigan widow said, "When I feel low, I invite my grandchildren for a visit. After a few days, when I ship them back, I thank God I am alone." A Florida divorcee said, "I travel with my grandchildren when I want to make friends. They go up and down the aisles of planes introducing themselves. By the time we arrive, I always have half a dozen people making offers to help. And do you know what? I accept. It's part of the fun."

ZEST

Edna Ferber once said that being a single is a little like drowning, not so bad when you stop struggling. It is no disgrace to be alone. There can even be a kind of glory in flying solo, so long as you retain your zest for life. Not long ago a group of women from Honolulu, most of them middle-aged wives or younger, went around the world. The most popular woman on the trip was a widow in her seventies whom they had worried about including.

The cult of youth these days is sometimes a little difficult for us to swallow; I heard a young man who makes underground films say on television the other day that a lot of the old ladies running around New York these days would be better off in their coffins than in movie theaters. It is bad enough to hear remarks like this when you have a husband who needs you to get up and fix breakfast. When you are alone, you feel you are a failure as a woman and should have emulated the Indian wives who committed suttee by throwing themselves on their husbands' funeral pyres.

But don't let it get you down. Nobody can keep youth indefinitely—including the brash young man on television. What you can keep is zest. One of the great surgeons of our time wrote me, "Don't worry too much about whether you should do something or not. If you want to, do it. You never know what lurks around the corner."

THE QUESTIONNAIRE
REVISITED

THERE is a story attributed to Tolstoy, but it might apply to any writer. Someone interrupted his writing to tell him about current events. He listened, then pulled his manuscript back in front of him, took up his pen, and said, "Now to get back to real life . . ."

When I composed the questionnaire, I was just starting to write this book. In the year that has passed, whether I was writing, interviewing, or going about supposedly doing other things, I have been submerged in the problems of women alone and I have hardly read a newspaper, gone to a party, or taken a ride on a bus, that some comment relating to the subject has not caught my eye or ear. Therefore, right or wrong, I have inevitably come to some personal conclusions about the answers to the questions I asked a multitude of other women alone. So here, for what they are worth, are my answers.

1. *Do you think the best place for a woman alone is in a big city, the suburbs, or a small town?*

I think this depends on age. An older woman is happier anyplace where she has put down roots and has friends. A young woman—or a not-so-young woman who has enthusiasm and drive and is not tied down with children—will find opportunities for meeting people and doing interesting things far greater in a city. Kind as friends may be to her in a suburb, they will tend to smother her and prevent her from developing herself, taking up new challenges.

2. *Is it better for her to live by herself or with another woman —a relative, friend, or roommate? Does age make any difference in her decision?*

It is better for her to live alone, no matter what her age. Ill health may make it necessary for her to move in with a sister, a daughter, or to take a relative in to live with her; but the situation is never ideal and should be avoided if humanly possible.

3. Have you any suggestions about living arrangements—a house versus an apartment, a place in the country, etc.?

Some women feel emotional attachment to their houses, where they have lived happily with husbands and raised children. In this case, if they can possibly afford the maintenance, it is best for them not to move into smaller quarters. A move into an apartment may also make a woman feel a loss of self-esteem, in which case she is better off in her old place, even if it means taking in roomers. But many women alone tell me that they prefer apartments because they feel safer and less lonely surrounded by people and—inevitably—there is less responsibility. As to the country versus the city, that is a personal matter. Some women who have lived all their lives in a city have built weekend houses, with retirement in mind. If they have managed to make friends nearby, and become a part of the community and its activities, this arrangement may be very happy. But unless a woman is a real loner, the deep country can be very depressing.

4. When you are left alone, either by divorce or death, is it better to live in the same place or tear up roots and make other arrangements?

The instinct is to tear up roots, to look for a change of scene, another start. This is invariably a mistake. You need all the friends you have around you when you are first alone, and you are in no state of mind to make big decisions. Wait at least a year before you do anything—and this, real estate people tell me, includes selling your house.

5. Would it make a difference in your decision to move if children were involved?

It shouldn't. Sometimes, when children are small, the instinct is to flee back to the comfort and safety of "home," to a locale where they will have grandparents and cousins and aunts and uncles. Eventually, this may be the ideal solution. But it is better to put in that year of waiting before you make the decision.

6. *Do you feel lonely sometimes? What do you do about it?*

No matter how long a woman has been alone, there are always times when she feels lonely. Remedies vary, from entertaining to calling friends and relatives to burying oneself in a book or taking up painting. One woman said to me, "Activity helps. Take a walk. Don't just go to a movie. Walk to a movie that is several miles away, or go to a museum." A divorcee with young children said, "There is always washing to be done. I leave it for low times; it gives me a feeling of accomplishment." Other women find diversion in cooking. A woman who works said, "Baking bread is great therapy. Kneading it, slamming out the air bubbles, is a marvelous release for all your hostilities. And the result is extremely soul-satisfying. Even if you shouldn't eat it yourself because of your figure, a loaf of homemade bread is a wonderful gift for friends who have done things for you—and gives you an excuse to dress up and deliver it."

The total answer here seems to lie in doing something about loneliness instead of merely feeling sorry for yourself. One widow said, "I make myself sit down and plan a party. After I've called a few people, and been accepted, then I have to get to work and start fixing up a menu."

7. *What are your major interests? Have they changed since you have been alone?*

Bertrand Russell says, "Happiness requires a hobby and a crusade." When a woman has many interests and cannot find enough hours in the day to pursue them, living alone may not be a torment. On the other hand, it seems to me that a woman alone must have a feeling of purpose, of compulsion (the crusade) which drives her to get up out of bed and go to work even when she doesn't feel like it. Otherwise, even though she has a plethora of interests she tends to get a feeling of drifting, or purposelessness. Hobbies are fine for diversion, for weekends, for evenings. But a woman who, say, plays golf seven days a week, unless she is planning to go into serious competition, may find herself wondering what it is all about after a while.

8. *Are some times worse than others?*

Of course. Weekends can be grim. Holidays can be hell. A young divorcee in the Midwest told me that the first Christmas, which her children spent with her ex-husband and his new wife, she stayed in bed, trying to forget it was Christmas. Around noon, an old friend, a widow, called from California. Betty started to cry and couldn't stop. But, in a way, the tears were a release because "I was really feeling suicidal, thinking I wouldn't be missed if I turned on the gas and stuck my head in the oven, the way other people were sticking in their turkeys." A divorcee whose child was away at summer camp told me that one Saturday she went to three movies.

Late afternoon and early evening can be depressing, even if you have had a busy and tiring day. This is because the return of the man of the house used to mark a period to the all-woman day and the beginning of you as part of a team, a couple. Sometimes this meant a cocktail hour, time to relax and talk over things with your husband in a congenial atmosphere. Sometimes it meant dressing up the children for their father's arrival—and putting on a clean dress or pair of slacks yourself. A young widow with children said to me, "All day I function. But in the evening, there is no reason for me to clean up the kids or even put on lipstick. I push them in front of the TV set and get a book and go and lie down in my unmade bed. Then after a while I get up and begin fixing dinner and nothing seems so bad."

A divorcee whose husband was an automobile salesman with unpredictable hours told me, "It's those Sunday morning breakfasts that kill me. We used to make a big thing of them, for it was the only time in the week we knew we could be together, undisturbed. Now I sleep as late as I can and wander off to the drugstore where I have orange juice and coffee and fried eggs with all the other miserable women alone."

The only possible answer for filling these painful voids is to make other plans deliberately—to entertain at cocktails, or Sunday breakfast, extend a special invitation for morning coffee (a widow I talked with eventually met a divorcee her age at Parents Without Partners and they made a point of meeting for coffee every morning). Eventually, when the pattern is broken, the worst of the pain passes. There will always, I suspect, be bad times, some of them coming unexpectedly. The salvation lies in knowing that time heals and friends fill gaps.

9. *What do you do about weekends and holidays?*

Keep busy. If you don't have invitations to accept, plan something yourself. Don't wait until the last minute and make one of those pathetic appeals to friends who are already up to their ears in guests. If everything falls through at the last minute, pamper yourself with a present and fall back on a good movie. Try not to feel sorry for yourself. And don't call everybody up the day afterward and complain.

10. *What do you miss most about not being married?*

One woman summed this up by saying simply, "my husband." The pattern of being part of a couple, of having someone to talk things over with, of being "in" not "out" in many social gatherings is hard to forget. There are also times when you would like to bop inconsiderate wives over the head for some of their cracks in your direction. Resist the temptation. Say you are getting a head cold, or have to feed the cat, and get up and go home.

11. *Have you met many new friends since you have been alone? Men or women? How did you meet them?*

Women friends are easy to make in the "alone" category. The trick seems to be not to let any get too intimate until you decide they have something more to give than bitterness or misery. Men friends come harder. Opportunities to meet new people come when you (a) join clubs, especially the singles variety; (b) take lessons in dancing, bridge, flying, etc.; (c) travel; (d) go out socially—the slimmest category.

12. *Do you think being financially secure is a blessing—or is it better to have to earn a living?*

One of the most fascinating women I met was left, a divorcee with a small child, with hardly a cent and has worked a handful of miracles. Her son is now married and she still has three separate careers—a job as secretary to two doctors during the day; baking bread and buns and special jams and jellies for sale in the evening; selling Christmas cards in season. Everybody likes her and vies for what spare time she has—including her new daughter-in-law. She keeps on working because she enjoys it and she has found that the busiest people always have the most time.

Most older women are very certain that financial security is a blessing. Younger women with money worries think everything would be solved, that they would automatically be happy as larks if there were enough money. Frankly, I doubt it. Some women don't need the push of necessity to keep occupied. For those who do, who vegetate in lush surroundings, I don't think money is a blessing. Having to get out and learn the satisfaction of supporting yourself is good for morale.

13. *How about volunteer work versus a paying job?*

Consensus of opinion is that most volunteer work cannot hold a woman's continued interest over a period of time, that a woman will neglect a volunteer job because it interferes with her golf, or because she does not feel like getting up and going out. There are exceptions. But if volunteer work was not the answer before a woman was left alone, it is not apt to be so when she is.

14. *Do you go out with groups of other women who are alone? How often?*

At first every woman alone is invited to all-woman functions. For the most part, the younger woman keeps away from these as much as possible. Older women say they have no choice.

15. *Do you still see people whom you knew when you were married? Who makes the effort to keep up these contacts—you or they?*

Most women alone have close friends among married couples—perhaps not the same ones as when they were married. Both keep up contacts, as a rule—which means that the woman alone must try to entertain as she did when she was married, if not quite so often or quite so lavishly.

16. *Do you feel uncomfortable in a restaurant without a male escort? At the movies or theater?*

Most women said no, but they preferred a male escort.

17. *Would you go to Europe alone? Would you travel in an organized group if you knew no one in advance? Would you go on a cruise alone?*

A surprising number of women refuse to consider the idea of traveling alone under any circumstances. They stay home in preference. More sophisticated travelers go alone, or join a tour, but keep away from cruises, feeling they are overcrowded with single women, divorcees, and widows trying to find men. I tried to discourage a pretty widow from going on a long cruise. But her postcards to me said, "I never had more fun in my life." So you never can tell.

18. *How many unattached men do you know?*

The answer varied from none to about four. One woman said, "Five and a half." The half was a homosexual.

19. *How do you pay back social obligations?*

Some women alone have joined clubs mainly because they can sign tabs and entertain without embarrassment. Others give one of the men guests, usually the husband of a friend, a large bill or their billfold, and ask him to take care of paying and tips. Entertaining at home is difficult for some women, without the support of a man. I agree; but it gets easier as time goes on. And it is important to pay back social obligations in some way. You are not expected to give an eye for an eye—a theater party for a theater party, for example—but unless you make some effort, even dear old friends begin to forget you.

20. *How do you return hospitality when you do not think the couple would enjoy the entertaining which is possible for you to do?*

Some women send flowers, occasional gifts on special occasions. One woman told me quite sensibly, "I invite them and leave it up to them whether they want to come or not."

21. *Would you go to a party alone?*

The answer should be yes. It isn't, always. But I found many women who prefer to go alone; it leaves them freer, it also allows them to go home alone, at a convenient hour, without embarrassment. One woman from Alabama has a sound rule: "Be one of the first to arrive and leave early." By arriving early, you make contacts with other early birds, and are not tossed immediately into a large group of strangers. By leaving early, you avoid putting your hostess on the spot, finding someone to take you home.

22. *Would you go home alone?*

If you have your own car, fine. If not, and you are dressed up, you can ask your host to call a cab, or go out on the street and help you hail one.

23. *Do you think the pressures of holding a job are worse if a woman is alone?*

Once panic subsides, no. If she is responsible and takes a professional attitude toward work, she finds employers prefer her to young single girls.

24. *Is an unattached woman in an office subject to unfair passes? How does she handle this?*

Now I question that word "unfair." A woman can invite a pass or discourage it by her behavior. Nor does she have to go to bed with the boss to hold her job. On the contrary. Once the fun-and-games period is over, he is apt to find excuses for getting rid of an ex-mistress.

25. *Should she quit if her boss falls in love with her?*

That depends. If it is real love, if there is a chance of marriage, a good chance, she may prefer to temporize. But the woman who becomes an office wife also runs the risk of becoming a tired old cliché.

26. *Do you feel that in your daily life, your contacts with tradespeople, plumbers, etc., you are discriminated against because you are alone?*

Some men prefer to work for men, and a male voice at the other end of the telephone commands attention. On the other hand, women alone can, if they are clever, play on the sympathy of service people and reap the benefits. We all should remember that there are fewer and fewer handymen left, most of them are older and set in their ways, and young people regard such occupations as temporary. In any case, anger and insults pay off badly. A sweet disposition and a sense of humor collect rewards.

27. *Have you had any unpleasant experiences with service- or repairmen who work for you?*

This can happen. The best protection is a big dog, or a good neighbor. (One case where you are quite justified in asking help from the husband of a friend.)

28. *Is your job more important to you because you don't have a husband? Are you able to be more satisfactory as an employee?*

The answer is yes in both cases. Young children can be complications but in most cases working widows and divorcees have taken in relatives to care for children and so are left free to work late, if necessity arises, or to be sent on company trips.

29. *Who repairs the little things around the house now?*

You either do it yourself or try to hire help. Most women do the little chores themselves.

30. *Do you feel free to call on the husband of a neighbor—or a friend's husband—when you need things done that require heavy lifting, etc.?*

If there is a janitor or a handyman available, most women prefer to use him. But husbands of friends can be called on occasionally. They don't mind; in fact, most of them feel flattered. Their wives may not care for the idea quite as well; their cry is that there is plenty of work to be done at home. I would say, tread lightly and carry your own hammer. When it comes to lifting, go ahead and ask for help. Don't risk a bad back.

31. *How do you meet unattached men?*

Most women I interviewed said socially, through friends.

32. *Have you become more aggressive about meeting men than you were before?*

As one of the women I interviewed said the aggressive woman alone was probably an aggressive wife and, before that, an aggressive young girl. But often is that a woman sheds her wife-type behavior and is able to mingle more freely with men than she did when her husband was around. Some wives construe this as aggressive; I don't.

33. *Would you date a man you met in a bar?*

I have met women who do, and they say the selection is far better here than at singles parties, or clubs for single parents. This attitude perhaps depends upon age. My attitude—and that of many other women—is that a man whom I would enjoy knowing might be very suspicious of a woman who allowed herself to be picked up in a bar, and expect her to be at least on the make, at worst a whore.

34. *Can you ask friends to look about for eligible men?*

You can. You probably should. Most women don't.

35. *Do you think your chance of remarriage would be improved if you moved to a community where people didn't know your husband?*

Most women said no. Men, nice eligible men, are scarce all over. Meeting them is a matter of luck. Some women don't have much luck. And it's important to stay where you know people.

36. *Would you sign up for a computer program to help you meet men?*

On the whole, no. Answer: "This is for young kids, for kicks. I don't think the kind of man I'd like to meet would be so hard up he'd have to depend on such things to meet women."

37. *Would you remarry? Or do you just want an escort? Would you settle for an escort who is homosexual? Married?*

Very few women are actually opposed to remarriage, in theory. The problem is finding an attractive eligible man, and not settling for "just an escort." Sophisticated women in large cities tell me that they enjoy the company and wit of homosexuals who make no demands, but function as pleasant escorts. In smaller communities, the attitude is not so liberal. As for married escorts, most women said no—except on rare occasions when the wife knows and has arranged the date.

38. *Would you date a married man regularly if he says his wife has no objection?*

Most women said no.

39. *Do you feel safer with a married man who says he loves his wife than with one who indicates there is trouble at home?*

Most women said yes. But that doesn't mean you won't get passes from a contented husband, once in a while. The happily married men usually are less neurotic than the complainers and won't make embarrassing scenes—something to be avoided at all cost.

40. *What would you do if the husband of a neighbor or a good friend made a pass at you?*

When you are taken by surprise, the only possible answer is to remind him that you care too much for his wife's feelings to respond, and that he should think of her, too.

41. *Would you go out with a man who is much younger if he asked you?*

Some women answered, "Why not?" Others were more suspicious of motive. The sophisticated women agreed that if a young man found them attractive and interesting, there was no reason to look for an ulterior motive. But a divorcee who has since re-married told me, "Watch out for those young 'uns. They're devils."

42. *Would you enter into an intimate relation with him?*

Here the usual answer was no. I'm not sure that I got the truth.

43. *In whom do you confide if you have problems? To whom do you go in a crisis?*

A woman alone is lucky if she has relatives nearby. Some friends can also be counted on. But not all, so don't be disap-pointed by the dropouts who are busy with their own problems. And don't wear out your welcome. Remember the story about the boy who kept crying, "Wolf!"

44. *Do your children object to your going out on dates?*

The teenagers are crucial here. Particularly if the loss has been recent. Married children are delighted to see a mother date. So are young children, as a rule.

45. *Is there more jealousy from a boy than a girl?*

Not always. The girl sometimes resents the idea of your replac-ing her real father. Even if he has remarried, she dreams of hav-ing him back on an old full-time basis, and resents anything you do that could interfere with that.

46. *Are you timid about living alone? What precautions do you take?*

Most women aren't timid, in the exact sense of the word. They are glad to have neighbors to call on in case of emergency. They also have learned—some the hard way—that if you live alone you must take more precautions than were necessary when married. For one thing, it is never wise to invite a stranger into your home if you are alone, unless he or she has credentials from a service company. An ounce of precaution often prevents an unpleasant experience.

47. *Do children of divorced or widowed parents suffer more than ordinary children? Do you find discrimination against them by other parents or children?*

Any child who is in the least unusual suffers. A mother told me that her son was teased constantly as a little boy because his father had died in an automobile crash. His playmate, whose mother had divorced an alcoholic husband, was also the butt of many jokes. There seems to be a certain amount of discrimination against single-parent children by parents, too; these youngsters are more apt to be blamed if trouble arises.

48. *Are women alone resented by wives? Do you feel you are deliberately excluded from parties because you are alone?*

A woman alone complicates social situations and can be a nuisance to any hostess—including her best friend—if the party requires matching up the sexes. In another more disquieting way, women alone are resented simply because they are constant reminders to wives of "what might happen if—" Sometimes the slights are imagined. But sometimes they are quite real. And occasionally, let's face it, they are deserved. But a woman without a husband seldom has the same rapport and intimacy with a married woman after she is alone. As one divorcee put it, wonderingly, "It was one thing when I complained about what Rick did when we were married. It's quite another when I talk about him as my divorced husband. I get the feeling that they think I've ducked out on my responsibility—even though they quite encouraged me when I was talking about divorce."

49. *How do you define promiscuity?*

The answer was just as our mothers did—having intimate relations with more than one man at the same time. The double standard still waves. Single men boast about promiscuity, but not women. Even young women.

PROBLEMS

1. An attractive divorcee with young children did everything possible to get her husband to return to them after a trial separa-

tion because of his infidelity—even to agreeing to allow him to have mistresses. He loves the children, and wants to see them, but thinks he must be free. Often he takes them on weekends with his various girls. Should she allow this?

The answer, to a woman, was no. The children should be kept available to him (never hurt them for the sake of your pride), but in your home, not on a weekend basis. Additional advice: Forget him, get a divorce, try to start a new life; this man obviously does not want a permanent relation or cannot maintain one.

2. A divorcee with young children feels her disposition and serenity are suffering because she has no sex life. Her only prospects are two married men whose wives she has not met. One says he is madly in love with her and wants to divorce his wife. The second says he finds his home life and wife satisfactory but is attracted to her physically and would like an affair. Which should she pick?

Most women answered, "Neither one." One divorcee said, "At least the second man is being honest, you could trust him not to make a fuss. It's the neurotics who make a mess of their own lives and will ruin yours, given a chance."

3. A widow with teenage children is courted by a bachelor who resents any mention she makes of her late husband. He is pleasant with the children but does not warm toward them. Should she give him up or try to fit him into the family?

Give him up. He is immature and his spots may be blacker after you get to know him better.

4. While a woman neighbor is away, her husband escorts you to local parties. One night he makes a pass, promising you it will only be this once—he will tell no one. You are secretly a little in love with him. Should you weaken?

I quote two remarks from sophisticated women. One said, "After you start something, you can never draw back, or say no again." The second, "The male ego is such that he can not believe that after one experience, you will be able to resist him." Unless you want a full-fledged affair, with all its complications, it is better not to get started. A woman who made such a decision over two years ago tells me that the gentleman in question still follows her around at parties, whispering in her ear, "I'll get you yet."

5. A woman who has never been married but has achieved success in a job has a client who wants to divorce his wife and marry her, but insists she quit her job. She likes him and wants to get married but fears she is not domestic. What would be your advice?

My cynical friend said, quickly, "Let him divorce his wife first, to prove he is on the up-and-up. Then talk money frankly with him. He may discover both of you will be more comfortable if you hire a competent housekeeper and continue to work. At any rate, wait and see before you break all your business ties." I quite agree . . . but I might add that many women who do not think they are "domestic" enjoy running a household when they come to it late in life, more than the rest of us to whom it is an old story.

6. You meet a man to whom you are immediately attracted and begin an affair with him at his apartment on your second date. Afterward, instead of dressing and taking you home, he gives you $5 for a taxi. Do you see him again when he calls you?

A number of women felt that the original mistake the woman made was by starting an affair without knowing the man longer. A younger divorcee, more used to the pattern of romances in big cities, said, "Men are spoiled, especially the attractive ones. I know a number who don't call for their dates, but expect them to meet them—and often get home on their own. The only way to handle this is to tell the gentleman you were annoyed, and expect him to have better manners if he wants to see you again. Too many women today are either doormats or so coy the gent never gets the message."

7. You meet a man at a cocktail party given by mutual friends. He asks you for your telephone number but does not call you. Do you call him if you are giving a party?

If the party is a big one, you could write him a note asking him to drop in—adding your telephone number so he can let you know if he can make it. If he doesn't call, forget him. And don't put yourself in the embarrassing position of calling him and being refused. Casual does it; he may need just a little push. On the other hand, asking for your telephone number may have been just a way of ending a conversation politely.

8. At the suggestion of a mutual friend, a man escorts you to a party at her house. He also takes you to dinner beforehand. Do you wait for him to call or do you invite him to dinner next?

Extra men are always useful. If you found him pleasant and need a man for a small dinner, ask him. If he is busy, let him make the next move.

9. Your eighteen-year-old daughter is violently opposed to your marrying a nice widower. To show you how unsuitable he is, she makes a pass at him herself (or says she has) and tells you that he was interested. What do you do?

Discuss the situation with him. And believe him, rather than your daughter, if he protests. Her opposition to your marriage is a normal reaction at her age. If you allow her to dictate, both of you will be sorry later.

10. You are a divorcee with a young daughter. You meet an attractive man, also divorced, who has weekend custody of his two boys. You go to his house with your child on Saturday and Sunday and cook for the group and treat them like family. The boys become fond of you, so he goes out sailing and playing golf and leaves you alone with them more and more often. Do you tell him off? Or do you continue, hoping this will become a pattern and he will marry you?

If you don't like the arrangement, tell him to get another baby-sitter. But if you are madly in love, and wouldn't mind taking this on a permanent basis, let him have his fun during the day with the boys. But be sure they are always boys.

11. You are having an affair with a divorced man. He tells you

how much he hates his ex-wife but he is over there a great deal. He explains this is for the sake of his children. But when you try to get him to settle down and pick a date for marriage, he says he is afraid his ex-wife will turn the children against him if he re-marries. Should you give him up?

Yes.

12. You are a recent widow. A woman in the neighborhood, a divorcee, has been very good to you. Gradually you begin to wonder if she is a little too fond of you and might have homosexual tendencies. You are not sure and you dread any direct confrontation. Besides, she can be very amusing. What do you do?

Get rid of her the way you would get rid of a man you are not sure about—gently or firmly, depending upon her reaction. Don't wait until you find yourself in an embarrassing situation.

13. You meet a widower to whom you, a divorcee, are much attracted. He seems to like your teenage son. But you are disturbed by the fact that he lives with his twenty-eight-year-old daughter who is also his assistant in his law office. You have never met her, but the mutual friend who introduced you tells you that his daughter resents any woman in whom he shows any interest. Do you give him up—or do you ask to meet his daughter and try to make friends?

The quick—and probably the right—reaction is to give him up. Some braver women suggest that a compromise might be reached, asking the daughter to find her own apartment, but stay with her father in business. One bright-eyed woman said she'd find a beau for the girl, then marry her father.

14. Your husband left you for another woman after twenty years of marriage. You can't believe it is anything more than a temporary attraction, for the girl is stupid and silly. What do you do? Your children want you to refuse to divorce him. But you resent him so much you don't think you could ever live with him again.

Wait. Temporize. She may seem stupid and silly to you, but gives him something he needs badly—or thinks he does. Try not to be bitchy; in the words of the old wives, don't cut off your nose to spite your face. Agree to a divorce if he *really wants it* (let the children try to argue him out of it, you just be sweet and reasonable), but ask him to be absolutely sure, as you love him very much. Make an effort to be as detached as you would be if you weren't involved. Maybe it won't work. Again, it just might. If there is any screaming to be done, leave it to the other woman.

15. You have been a widow for four years, and have made what your friends call a "good" adjustment, which includes friends, mostly women or married couples, and a pleasant job teaching bridge. One of your pupils, a man slightly younger than you, proposes. He has never married and, up until two years ago when his mother died, lived with her. Your friends say he is looking for another mother, or is marrying you for your money. What do you do?

Don't listen to your friends. If you like him, and feel life with him would be interesting, go ahead. But not too fast. Get better acquainted with him and be sure you know what you are doing.

16. A woman friend with whom you have been playing bridge introduces you to her "beau"—a widower. The next day he calls and asks you to go out to dinner with him. Do you ask her advice about going? Or do you go without telling her? Or say no?

This is a matter of female ethics. The nice woman answers, "I would say no. If he stops going with her and tries again, and you like him, you might accept an invitation." A more practical answer may be, "Go without telling her. Find out if he is really her beau. Time enough to decide what to do if you're really interested." Of course, if the woman is a good friend and you know darned well the man has been sleeping with her, you say no and tell him why. There are times when female solidarity is the best policy.

17. You are a widow. A man some years your senior, a widower, has been taking you to dinner occasionally. On your birthday, he gives you a pair of pretty earrings. You are delighted, thinking

they are costume jewelry. Your daughter tells you they are real and worth quite a sum. What do you do?

One answer is, "It depends upon what kind of a man he is and his intentions." I think it depends upon your intentions. If he is a bore, and you certainly don't want to have your acquaintance deepen, return the jewelry and explain that it is too valuable for him to give you, a casual friend. If you like him, however, and think this might be serious . . . keep them and wear them when you are with him.

18. An old friend-of-the-family, who has never married, suggests that you and he travel together. You will have separate rooms, etc. What do you do?

Go ahead. This might be a very happy arrangement. If you travel together congenially, it might be the answer to your traveling problems.

EPILOGUE:
HAPPINESS IS NOT A GOAL

The first year, you think you can't stand being alone. The second year you begin to think—well, maybe. By the third, you have found a way of life. I'm not saying I wouldn't get married if the right man came along, but if he doesn't, I'll survive.

NEW YORK WIDOW

Loneliness as a situation can be corrected but as a state of mind it is an incurable illness.

VLADIMIR NABOKOV

People think they want intimacy but they avoid it because in order to confront another person with intimacy you have to show your self, to shed the image you want to protect.

ERICH FROMM

IN suburban Chicago I met an attractive widow of forty-five who had just returned from a medical checkup at the Mayo Clinic. She was trying to sell herself on the idea of a retirement village in California because her doctor had said to her, "You may live another thirty years. What are you going to do with them?"

A Los Angeles divorcee who has climbed to vice president of an advertising agency in the ten years since she was alone told me, "It's a strange thing. I was very busy with our annual conference and it was a great success, the highlight of my career thus far. But afterward I felt terribly depressed and let down. My boss suggested I take a vacation. I did, but then I only felt worse. I even went to my doctor. I think I ought to have something in which I'm important and my job isn't enough."

A widow with whom I shared a twilight drink on the New Haven train going to Boston said wistfully, "My children think I should get married. There's a man, yes, an old family friend. He's nice, but rather a bore and terribly set in his ways—as I guess I am. I don't want to have that much intimacy with him. But I keep thinking of those old ladies who sit around in apartment lobbies talking to the doormen because they have nobody else—and sometimes I am tempted to say yes. The idea of a lonely old age bugs me."

A Denver divorcee told me, "My married friends say they envy me because I'm free to make decisions, go where I want to, entertain whom I will. Do you know what is wrong—I'm *too* free. Nobody needs me or gives a hang what I do or when. I'm expendable. In my next reincarnation I'd like to be a dog."

To some degree, all of us who are alone in this couple society have a sense of despair, of not living life completely. For those of us who have lost husbands through divorce or death, there is the additional sense of failure; the association of loss with failure is automatic, and failure is not popular in our materialistic society. Busyness does not help—enough. Nor does the achievement of success in a career. In our male-oriented minds, marriage is still considered the only important career for a woman. Anything else comes in second, a poor second.

Yet, if you stop to think about it, we are the strong ones. We have not compromised in order to conform. And just the process of survival has made us think. We can not be satisfied with the status quo, like our married friends. In the process of living each day, we have to change our ways of life and this influences our inner attitudes. The reason we suffer more is because we are having growing pains.

The essayist Joseph Wood Krutch wrote in *The American Scholar*:

> Security depends not as much upon how much you have, as upon how much you can do without. And that is true for society as well as for the individual. Every technicological advance is also a hostage to fortune. And the more we teach adjustment, group activity, getting along with the group, and so forth, the less any individual is prepared for the time, so likely to come in any man's life, when he cannot or will not call upon group support. Ultimate security for him depends upon the ability to stand alone, or even just to be alone. Belonging is fine. But to belong to anything except oneself is again to give a hostage to fortune.

Standing alone has a close relative called loneliness. But after a crowded life, where demands left us too tired to think, or unwilling to think, loneliness can be healthy, a period of enforced seclusion when you search for values.

A woman who has been a widow for eleven years said to me, "Of course I'm lonely sometimes. Anyone who says she isn't is a liar. But the loneliness always has a hidden core of hope. I keep feeling that some place something good must be waiting for me."

The English actress Dame Edith Evans, seventy-nine, told *The New York Times*, "I have a secluded little flat right near Piccadilly Circus in London, which is very much like living near your own Times Square in New York, and I am alone most of the time.

But there is a difference between loneliness and aloneness. You can be alone like I am and not lonely.

"Thirty years ago I lost my mother and my husband in the same year. I was inconsolable. I think of them often, especially my mother. I took her for granted, simply because she was my mother. I had so little conscious appreciation of the security and warmth they gave me. Now if I could only have them again. I want to say things to them. Share little triumphs with them. We never do enough for the people we love. . . . But I had to press on.

"Now I'm not really lonely. I'm involved with many theatrical activities which fill my life and I'm very fortunate people come to see me . . . I enjoy young people . . . but as Noel Coward said recently, 'If a person over fifty tries too hard to be *with it,* they soon find they are without it.' "

Some women when they are first alone try to fill the gap with the phony intimacy of sex. A divorced singer told me: "I went from a two weeks' affair with a married man to an engagement with another which lasted three days. I hopped in and out of bed, telling myself it was the new morality. What I was really trying to do was get friendship and closeness the easy way. Now I know there's no easy way. In order to get friends, you have to give."

Change makes you think, willy nilly. It forces you to act. A woman from a small town in Nebraska told me: "I'd been bored for years. Yet when my husband died I kept making excuses, why I couldn't move. Then a good friend said to me, 'If you really want to enlarge your horizons, you have to do it now; in five years you will have the good excuse that it's too late, you're too old.' "

Just your change of status brings you into contact with a whole new group of individuals, other women alone. And it gives you sympathy with that other class of rebels, the young people who do not like the old-fashioned prejudices and hypocrisies of society any better than you do. Unless you deliberately choose to get trapped, just the process of adjusting yourself to a life alone broadens your mind, your attitudes, your level of tolerance.

A woman who had just gone through a painful divorce from her husband of twenty years, wrote me, "The whole thing is very sad, because I can't help feeling it will not benefit him a bit. But I have begun to adjust to the situation as I never would have believed possible. And I've begun to see that his disposition the last couple of years has not been so angelic—nor has mine—so there are advantages."

Of course we aren't happy all the time. Who is? I picked up the telephone on the most beautiful weekend of last summer, Labor Day, to hear another woman alone say, "I've hit bottom. This marvelous weather depresses me. I did better in the rain." That is a joke between us because last spring we went through a mutual spell of depression on the beautiful Easter weekend, when the sun was shining and families were spending the day together and there was a love-in in Central Park. I was alone and my friend's young daughter was spending the weekend with her father, so together the pair of us climbed on a bus, missed the location of the off-Broadway show we wanted to see, and went and ate in a dark basement in Chinatown . . . and felt better.

Happiness is not a goal. It is a by-product that comes—and goes—at the most unexpected moments. It can vanish during a pleasant evening with old friends, and send you scuttling home to draw your blinds and shut out the sight of other families together. Yet a chance conversation on the street, an encounter at the bank, a telephone call or a letter from an old friend, will send spirits soaring.

Happiness is not a goal; it is too precarious.

But self-respect is.